Zarina Bhimji

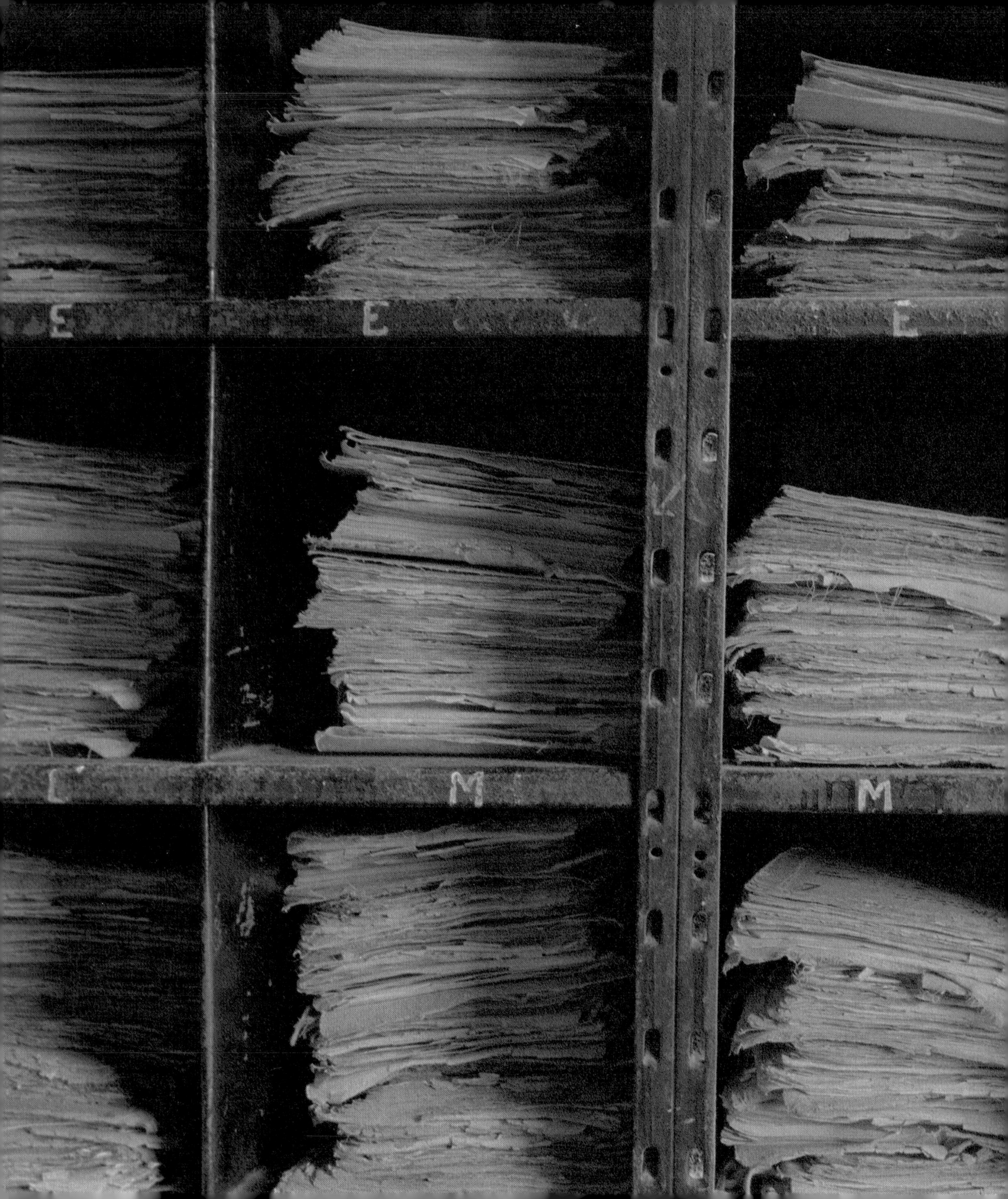
E
E
E
M
M

Zarina Bhimji

Whitechapel Gallery
Kunstmuseum Bern
The New Art Gallery Walsall
Ridinghouse

Contents

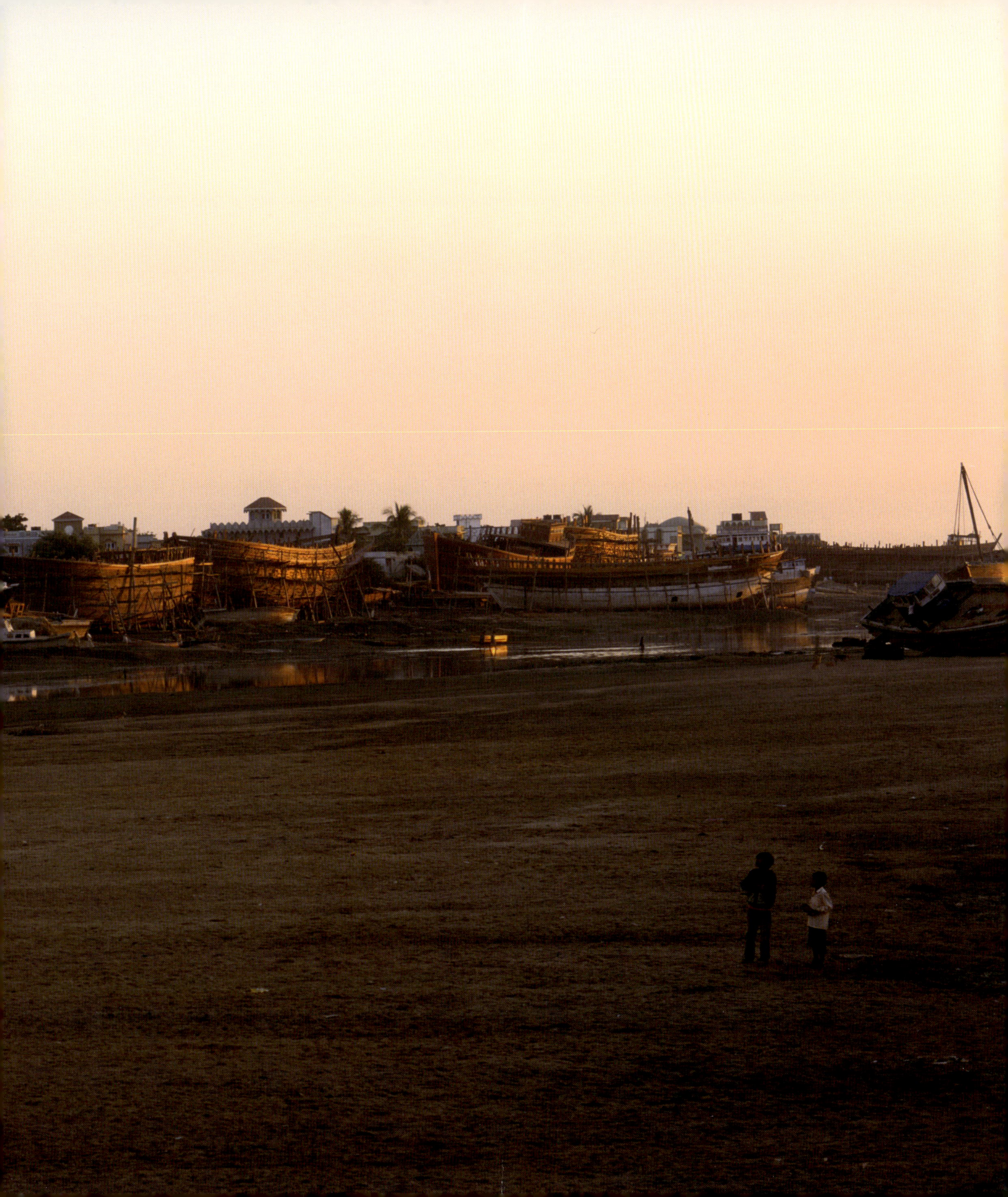

Foreword

Architecture and landscape are the protagonists in the quiet yet profound dramas that unfold through Zarina Bhimji's films and photographs. A building might feature in her work as a historic monument; as a composition of texture and colour; or as an atmospheric play of darkness and light. As our eyes explore the surface of her remarkable images, however, we can also see the unmistakable traces of incarceration, death or exodus, but inflected with deliberate ambiguity and transience.

Like many artists and writers who have experienced exile, Bhimji combines her subjective experience with a detached perspective on the flows and convulsions of history. Born in Uganda into a family of Indian descent, she left Africa for Britain in 1974. As a result, her framework of reference is unusually wide, encompassing three different continents, and reaches back to the British Empire and the migration that followed in its wake as much as to a postcolonial present.

Bhimji's ravishingly beautiful and painterly panoramic shots of different landscapes, and her close-ups of buildings worked over by time, are the result of a process of poetic distillation where place (in this case East Africa and South Asia) becomes the material itself, and new ways of seeing can emerge. She captures the decay of abandoned structures of power as they surrender to the forces of entropy. Bhimji's cinematic vistas are complemented by a soundscape of news broadcasts, ambient sound and music that creates a second layer of narrative. Sound and picture combine to transform image into metaphor, politics into poetry.

This book marks not only the world premiere of Bhimji's latest film installation, *Yellow Patch* (2011) but also presents the first major overview of her 25 year-long career. Aside from *Yellow Patch* and the critically acclaimed *Out of Blue* (2002) it also includes a wide selection of the celebrated photographs which preceded and continue to inform her moving-image works.

Many of these bodies of work arose from commissions in the United Kingdom. We are grateful to those agencies and institutions who supported the artist's vision early in her career.

Yellow Patch was co-produced by Artsadmin in London and made possible by major donations from Arts Council England, de Appel Arts Centre, The New Art Gallery Walsall and Outset Contemporary Art Fund. We pay tribute to the vision and generosity of all these organisations in supporting the creation of an important new work. Simultaneously with Bhimji's Whitechapel Gallery exhibition, *Yellow Patch* is also presented at The New Art Gallery Walsall, creating a new model for institutional collaboration; the entire exhibition is co-organised by Whitechapel Gallery and Kunstmuseum Bern. Early in the genesis of this project, Manick Govinda pledged his role as Executive Producer of *Yellow Patch* and we are grateful to him and to the central role played by Artsadmin in the film's genesis and realisation.

Previous spread: *Breathless Love* (detail), 2007, Ilfochrome Ciba classic print, 127 × 160 cm | 50 × 63 in

We also thank the following organisations and individuals for their generosity in lending important works: De Primi Fine Art SA, Lugano; the Government Art Collection; Haunch of Venison, London; Kadist Art Foundation, Paris; Nottingham City Museums and Galleries; Talwar Gallery, New York; Victoria & Albert Museum; Paul van Esch & Partners; Maysoune Ghobash; Buzzy Moitre; Adam Prideaux; Shamina Talyarkhan and those who wish to remain anonymous.

At the Whitechapel Gallery, Shamita Sharmacharja, supported by Paula Morison and Priyesh Mistry were led by Achim Borchardt-Hume in the conception and organisation of both this publication and the exhibition, with Chris Aldgate and Patrick Lears expertly taking care of its installation. Special thanks are due to Sue MacDiarmid for making sure that *Yellow Patch* and *Out of Blue* are presented to the highest possible standard.

In Bern, we thank Kathleen Bühler and her team for their passionate commitment and tireless dedication to the project from its very inception, while in Walsall the same thanks are due to Deborah Robinson and her colleagues, Hannah Anderson and Kevin Storrar.

We are grateful to TJ Demos for his important new text in this catalogue, a scholarly and incisive analysis of Bhimji's aesthetic strategies and how these sit within a broader context of post-colonial discourse. This is complemented by an illuminating dialogue between the artist and the exhibition's curators, Achim Borchardt-Hume and Kathleen Bühler. The book is co-published by Whitechapel Gallery, Kunstmuseum Bern, The New Art Gallery Walsall and Ridinghouse where we thank Publisher Doro Globus for her invaluable input and Louisa Green for all of her support. Herman Lelie and Stefania Bonelli are responsible for the clear and elegant design.

The ACNE White Art T-Shirt Project provided vital funds for the book, as did Amrita Jhaveri to whom we express our most sincere gratitude. Whitechapel Gallery thanks Karima and Gaurav Burman for their invaluable support of the exhibition in London. In Bern, we thank the generous funding of Stiftung GegenwART and its patron Dr. h.c. Hansjörg Wyss, which made the exhibition and publication possible.

For more than two decades, Zarina Bhimji has been making photographic series and ambitious film installations that are as visually enticing as they are intellectually incisive. We are immensely grateful to her for the tremendous work required in bringing so many pieces together, and for giving our institutions and our audiences the opportunity to become immersed in her unique vision.

Iwona Blazwick OBE, Director, Whitechapel Gallery
Dr. Matthias Frehner, Director, Kunstmuseum Bern
Stephen Snoddy, Director, The New Art Gallery Walsall

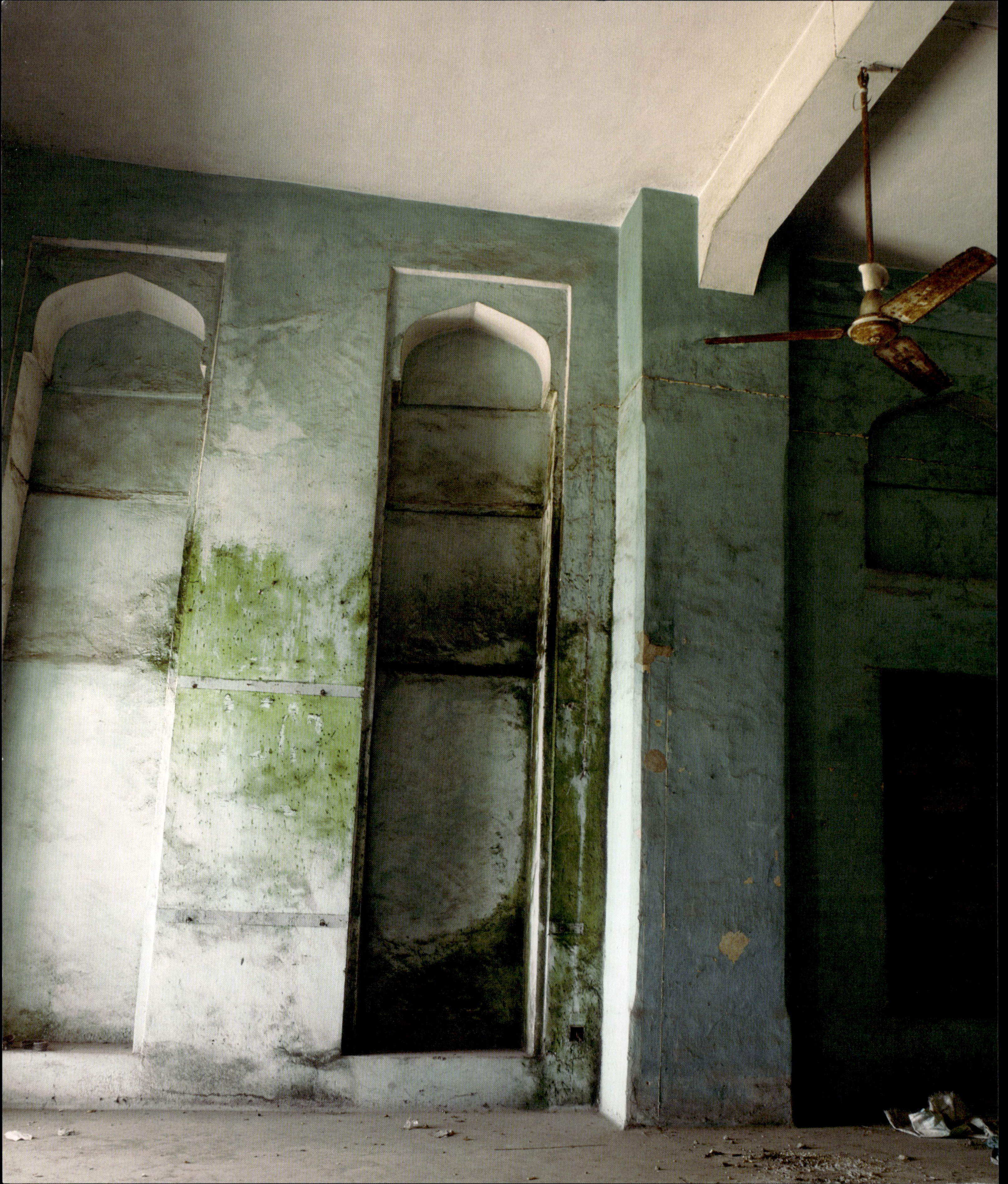

TJ Demos

Zarina Bhimji: Cinema of Affect

Yellow Patch (2011), Zarina Bhimji's most recent film, includes a slow zoom onto the crumbling facade of an old palace in Kutch, India. With its focus on this site seemingly abandoned from a distant time, one filled with untold complexity and depth, the film builds on a signature trope of the artist: her meditative and careful approach to what I will call her cinema of affect. Bhimji's films strike poignantly on an emotional level, mobilising cinema's ability to correlate moving images and carefully selected sounds with subjective sensation. Her films thereby define a postdocumentary approach that relinquishes information and factual presentation in order to probe the poetic and aesthetic elements of colour, texture and rhythm. Yet, they nonetheless connect with postcolonial history and the difficult mobility and displacement of Indians to Africa in the early twentieth century and then to Britain in the early 1970s, which included Bhimji's own family. It is the links between aesthetics and politics, historical consciousness and affective sensation, as developed in Bhimji's films, that I shall explore here.

The three-story palace in *Yellow Patch* (p.105), a *Haveli* house – Persian for 'enclosed space', and designating the beautifully crafted wooden mansions found in India and Pakistan – first appears at an oblique angle. Its state of disrepair is immediately evident, as are the unkempt grounds that surround it. Dating from the late eighteenth century, it is exemplary of an eclectic colonial-Indian architecture, which slowly reveals itself to the camera. The steady advance and smooth pan produce a disembodied viewing experience, even as the attentiveness to the physicality of the building and the world around it is also stressed.[1] Bhimji focuses acutely on the environment's material sensuousness and interaction with the subtle effects of light and wind. This sensitivity is characteristic of her aesthetic, which is also demonstrated in several of her earlier works including *Out of Blue* (2002; p.77), and *Waiting* (2007; p.99). The artist is drawn to old abandoned buildings, frayed textiles, spider webs, which assemble a repertoire of recurring visual tropes. Here, the buildings perform as characters, thematising Bhimji's relationship to her parents' homeland; as such, their cinematic exploration is deeply personal, even if the film is not immediately concerned with the artist's biography.

Throughout the film's 29 minutes, viewers gradually come to witness several such resonant sites in Gujarat and Bombay, which speak to the many attachments and desertions of the past, connecting to Bhimji's own family history. Having grown up in a small town near Jamnagar in the Indian state of Gujarat, her father moved to East Africa at the age of 11 in the early twentieth century, travelling to the frontiers of Britain's

Ambivalence (detail), 2007, Ilfochrome Ciba classic print, 127 × 160 cm | 50 × 63 in

expanding colonial empire. The film loosely retraces that journey, which includes several locations: it begins with shots of the Princess Dock in Bombay, constructed by the British in 1885, where Bhimji focuses on an old administrative building full of ancient files redolent of British colonial bureaucracy and containing the tantalising traces of stories now forgotten. It moves on to shots of the decaying ornate buildings and desolate windswept desert area of the Rann of Kutch, once a princely state, now a remote and culturally unique region of Gujarat that borders Pakistan. It closes with footage from the Mandvi port in Gujarat, where many Indians embarked for Africa in the wooden boats called *dhows*, still being built today. Overall, the film is cast in moving colours and warm sunlight. Steel grey skies arc over the rippling mirror of the sea, and abstract blue-green compositions emerge on decaying walls. These subtle details endow the film with captivating visual allusions and an associative metaphorics.

Adding to this visual array of geographical sites is a soundtrack of disparate sources which helps the film build on its resonant panoply of visual sensations, generating a wide range of affects, including ominous dread and painful loss, as well as the excitement of rediscovery and loving intimacy. There are oceanic sounds of symphonic strings; chattering typewriters and the shuffling of workers; recordings of the natural elements such as waves, thunder and birdsong; and ghostly voices making confessions and proclamations, as well as the lyrical and poetic Sufi songs sung in melismatic and haunting ornament. Short sound clips of what appear as political speeches echo in a chamber of distant remembrance. Phrases such as 'the soul of a nation, long suppressed...' emerge from the background, as another man's voice explains how he was 'made by the British'. The fact that these and other voices include those of the independence-era leaders Mohandas Gandhi, Muhammad Ali Jinnah, Jawaharlal Nehru and Louis Mountbatten – recorded both at the time of India's and Pakistan's postcolonial emergence and after – is, however, never clear in the experience of the film; rather, the voices hover in ambiguity and perceptual estrangement.[2] The result is that while the content brings to mind the historical experiences of burgeoning national freedom and colonial repression, the uncertainty of the references places viewers in the role of figuring out how to relate to these experiences in the present, as if that history continues to resonate with our own contemporary events. These off-screen sounds and voices poignantly spatialise the image, casting its presence into an expanse of present and past, so that the visual presentation of present-day India takes on momentous significance and temporal breadth, even while the meaning is never clear or univocal. Indeed, Bhimji's film shows itself to be redolent of the formidable complexity and depth of history, but where meaning inevitably overflows the grasp of documentation and information, and remains open-ended.

The first instalment of a two-part series of films that explore the history of Indian migration to East Africa, as well as the contemporary aftermath of that passage, *Yellow Patch* was 'inspired by my father's journey from India to East Africa', the artist explains. Rather than an autobiography, however, the film opens on to a more expansive story about migration. 'This story is the lived experience of many East African Asians', Bhimji adds.[3] The second film will continue that journey by revisiting places connected to the later part of that migration, focusing on sites in Zanzibar, Kenya and Uganda, various destinations for some 32,000 Indians in the late nineteenth and early twentieth centuries. Many of them came to work on the construction of the Uganda Railway (now known as the Kenya Railway), which stretches over some 582 miles from Mombasa to Lake Victoria, and to pursue related employment opportunities. Built between 1885 and 1905, the railway was part of the colonial conquest of East Africa, the imperial history of which came to an end in Uganda with independence in 1962.

As such, *Yellow Patch* explores a history prior to the one that concerns Bhimji's past films, such as *Out of Blue*, which investigates what some have termed the 'psychogeography' of postcolonial Africa and Europe, and particularly the artist's relation to the mass-traumatic experience of Asians being expelled from Uganda by Idi Amin in 1972[4]; and *Waiting*, which portrays old textile factories in Mombasa and Voi, Kenya, and reflects on the production of sisal (used to make sacking and ropes) during the colonial period. The sites used for these films – the architectural ruins of workhouses, factories, military barracks and police prisons – provide symbolically rich locations for Bhimji's metaphors of painful loss, brutality and abandonment, as well as mystery and beauty, which significantly complicates the meanings of her works. Similarly characterised by their dreamlike sensibility – owing to the camera's steady drifting around depopulated sites that are the material and architectural remainders of the colonial project and its immediate post-colonial transition – these films, like *Yellow Patch*, offer no clear voice-over narration, contextual inter-titles or speaking figures that would otherwise explain the history that informs them (although *Out of Blue* includes glimpses of fleeting figures that appear silently like living shadows in the background).

In *Yellow Patch*, the focus on the materiality of specific locations (for example, the focus on architectural details, atmospheric conditions and interior spaces) comes without information that might otherwise tell us what we're looking at. Similarly disjunctive is the aforementioned soundtrack to Bhimji's films, which characteristically offers a montage of ambient sounds, such as whispering voices, the buzzing of insects, peacock calls and distant human cries, all suggestively metaphorical and emotionally provocative, but without interpretive direction or specific contextualisation. Slow-paced and meditative, the camera glides through the locations, as if making a ghostly visitation

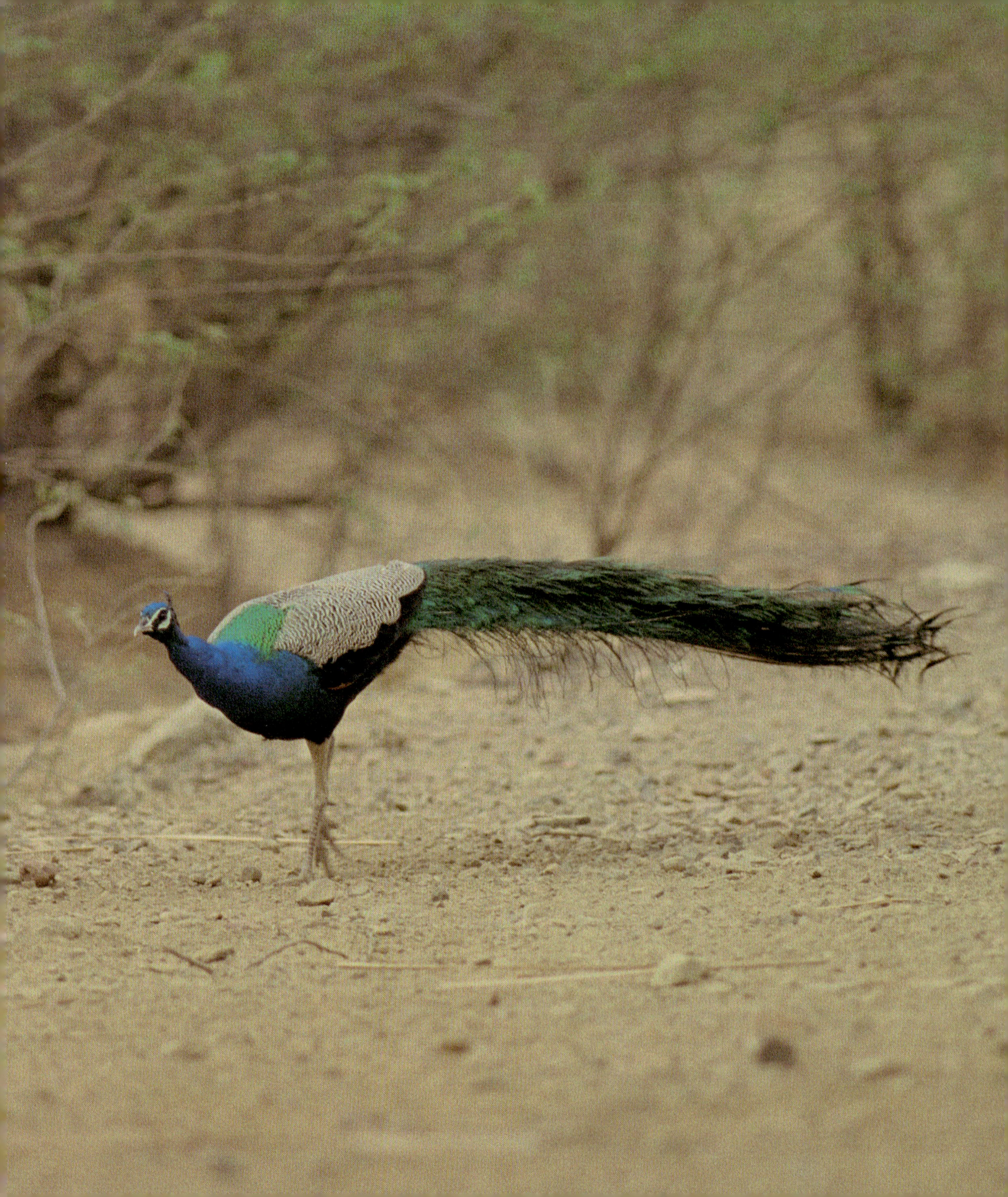

to places haunted by past unresolved experiences. Unlike the use of a hand-held camera that might indicate the filmmaker's subjective viewpoint, Bhimji's sense of visuality is disembodied and decontextualised from her own specific personhood, floating over its objects, as if haunted by them. These elements define Bhimji's aesthetics of opacity, a poetics of the image disconnected from background information, which is striking for an artist who confronts such complex postcolonial histories in her work.

As Gilane Tawadros observes, we know that 'the echoes of "something that is not there any more" haunt the works of Zarina Bhimji',[5] but the identification of this 'something' is withheld from her films. It is true that with her participation in the 2008 Guangzhou Triennial (p. 34), and the *Who Knows Tomorrow* exhibition in Berlin in 2010, the artist began presenting some of her research materials alongside the display of her films, including her storyboards and initial conceptualisations – she calls them 'treatments' – which emerge out of intense historical and geographical investigations (and for this exhibition, she will present her storyboards for *Yellow Patch* (p. 32) and select historical quotations in vitrines in the gallery). Her research is extensive, typically involving significant time spent in libraries reviewing historical documents and scholarship regarding the periods and places that her projects explore, as well as site visits, which then lead to her construction of treatments and storyboards (including storyboards for the audio track), and finally to the production of her films. For this reason, it is all the more noteworthy that she withholds this historical research from the actual films. If anything, her work is informed by the blockage of information, as much as it results from the collection of historical research. 'I am interested in the tension between lyrical, intense beauty and sociopolitical language', she explained recently in relation to *Waiting*, 'through the visual it is important for me to remain allegorical even if I touch the subject of politics.'[6]

Wrapped up in this tension and this allegorical quality is Bhimji's relation to her own experience of living in East Africa as a child, and her family's embroilment in the traumatic episode when Asians were given 90 days to leave Uganda by Amin. From early on in her career – for instance, at the time of her participation in Rasheed Araeen's *The Essential Black Art* show at London's Chisenhale Gallery in 1988 – she made it clear that her work, which has included photographs, mixed media collages, sculptural installations and films, concerned this history:

> I want to create [and] communicate new meanings by bringing Indian languages, objects, memory, dreams, conversations from East Africa and Indian backgrounds, as well as my experience of Western culture, to play in between two realities.[7]

Film still (detail), *Yellow Patch*, 2011, single screen installation, 35 mm colour film, HD transfer with Dolby 5.1 surround sound, 29 min 43 sec

And this desire to trace her and her family's history (but not only that history) marks her most recent film *Yellow Patch*, which goes back further, to her father's migration from India to East Africa, before her family was forced to leave Uganda for the UK. This leaves us with the following questions: *why* does her work reject the historical account, the discursive treatment, the contextualisation and what is gained by her formal decisions regarding her filmmaking projects?[8] What is behind Bhimji's negation of information and her desire to place 'beauty and sociopolitical language' in 'tension' in order to make 'allegorical' films, and what is achieved by this approach? Alternately, *how* does her work reflect on that historical narrative, make it relevant and compelling, in ways that circumvent the direct testimonial or documentary account? By answering these questions, my hope is that we will gain a new perspective on the singular character and workings of Bhimji's art.

In 1998 Bhimji made the first of two research trips to Uganda, the country she was forced to leave as an 11-year-old girl. The experience of visiting her lost homeland led to a series of photographs entitled *Love* (1998–2007; p.87), which portrays various emotionally charged sites in Uganda, and which relates to her first film, *Out of Blue*, commissioned by Okwui Enwezor for Documenta 11. As she explained:

> During my first visit back to Uganda in 1998, I listened to the land, to the sounds in the air, to the smell of guns, and I realised that it had to be a film. So I started doing research, looking through the African and international press from 1972 to 1974 – newspaper cuttings on Ugandan Asians leaving Uganda – and from that I put a film narrative together.[9]

That period of the early 1970s is key, for the turbulent postcolonial context in Uganda that Bhimji lived through has strongly marked her life and art, and for her, to return to Uganda nearly 25 years later was to revisit the primal scene of postcolonial violence as well as the source of positive childhood memories of a place suddenly taken away from her.

On 5 August 1972, General Idi Amin announced his decision on national radio that henceforth all Asians with British passports (approximately 60,000 people) would have to leave the country and would have to do so within 90 days. It was one year after he assumed power by military coup – a coup largely welcomed by the West, including Britain, as it put an end to Milton Obote's left-leaning government, allied with Julius

Nyerere's socialist Tanzania. A few days later, Amin amended his statement to include all Asians – Ugandan citizens as well – applying to some 80,000 people in total who would be expelled within three months. The move was part of the dictator's 'Africanisation' of Uganda, which included the declaration of an 'economic war' on those 'outsiders' – even though many had lived in Uganda for several generations – who were perceived as owning the majority of the country's resources and businesses. As an act of ethnic cleansing, it formed part of Amin's strategy of achieving full economic independence justified as part of the country's process of decolonisation. It followed on the heels of other recently emancipated African states, namely Libya, to which Amin turned, on behalf of Uganda, to replace Britain and Israel as financial donors and suppliers of arms. Indeed, Libya's Colonel Gaddafi had expelled Italians as soon as he assumed power in 1969, and Amin followed suit by expelling Israelis in 1972 (in order to court the support of Arab governments) before turning to the Asians later that year.[10] With his unpredictable shifting policies, Amin's politics exemplify what Achille Mbembe terms the 'socialisation of arbitrariness', which, joined with the 'violence of economics', characterise the extreme authoritarian regimes in postcolonial Africa of the 1970s.[11]

Why had Asians come to Uganda? As historians point out, the African territories that Britain conquered in the late-nineteenth century had pre-capitalist economies – people in East Africa typically lived and worked on the land[12] – and so an external labour source was required. Following the Berlin Congo conference in 1885 that divided up African colonies, Britain turned to its developed colony, India, to provide the resources for its African colonies and encouraged Indian migration to East Africa, Mauritius, South Africa, the West Indies and Guinea. Indians served variously as soldiers in the imperial army, as labourers to build the railways and as artisans, machine operators, plantation workers, administrative clerks and small traders in the expanding market.[13] It was this context that Bhimji's father entered when he moved to Uganda in the 1910s, returning to India only to marry before bringing back his wife, Zarina's mother, to his new home.

If in 1972, Amin acted against this 'foreign' labour population, then part of his reasoning was that Asians had discriminated against Africans (what Amin called 'Asian business malpractices'). Yet, as Mahmood Mamdani points out in *From Citizen to Refugee*, his harrowing firsthand account of the expulsion, 'It was not the era of independence, but that of dependence – of colonialism – that politicised race, tribe and religion in Uganda. This was the kernel of truth in the theory that colonialism rested on the basis of *divide and rule*.'[14] According to Mamdani, Amin extended that colonial logic, which began with the practice of separating tribes and using them against one another, formalising divisions between races and ethnic classes into legal, political and economic groupings. As Mamdani explains 'there was rigid compartmentalisation in the newly colonial political economy', such that laws prohibited Africans from entering trade and Asians from owning land. In the hierarchical economy that emerged – which Bhimji's family had to negotiate – 'Africans were primarily peasants and workers; Asians primarily shopkeepers, artisans and petty bureaucrats; and Europeans bankers, wholesalers and the administrative and political elite.'[15] Indeed, the postcolonial government of Obote, the first prime minister of independent Uganda, followed suit. In 1968, a committee was charged with 'Africanisation in Commerce and Industry' and made far-reaching Indophobic proposals, implementing a system of work permits and trade licenses in 1969 to restrict the role of Indians in economic and professional activities. By the time Amin assumed power, there was an established tendency to segregate and discriminate against Asians, which Amin exploited further with a new intensity.[16] In 1972–73, he continued with his economic war by nationalising British and other foreign-owned businesses and properties.[17]

Amin's eight-year rule left a wake of brutality and destruction that was announced early on by his treatment of Asians. Given the order to leave, they could depart with only 50 pounds in cash and minimal baggage. This meant that those living in Uganda – many for several generations – were forced to give up their life savings, houses, property and much of their personal possessions, and were then denationalised and thrown into an uncertain refugee status, all within the space of three months.[18] After Amin's announcement, his forces secured the borders of the country to prevent unregulated flight and banks were ordered to stop illegal transfers of assets. Many were robbed by troops on their way to the airport, where they endured invasive baggage searches and despite Amin's promises to the contrary there was no compensation for lost property (although some businesses and properties were returned by the subsequent Ugandan government in the 1980s). Because of the strategic lack of clarity about who must go – Asians with British passports versus those with Ugandan citizenship – all were rendered uncertain and anxious, resulting in internal discrimination within the Asian community and between Africans and Asians. It is difficult to appreciate fully the dire consequences of Amin's order to leave.

To its credit, Britain accepted the transfer of expelled Asians, including some non-British. About 27,200 came to the UK, while others went to Canada, India, Kenya, Pakistan, West Germany and the United States.[19] Yet the reception was far from smooth – interminable queues, bureaucratic difficulties, discrimination and the indignities of emergency refugee housing awaited those who came to Britain.[20] Moreover, right-wing MPs argued against letting Ugandan Asians into the country, claiming that even though they were British citizens, they had no links to the home country and that their immigration would only lead to racial tension. Those who did not leave Uganda faced potential arrest, torture, even death (exile organisations with the help of Amnesty International have estimated that up to 500,000 died over the course of Amin's reign, which came to an end in 1979 when he was overthrown and sent into exile).[21] Still, Bhimji's family managed to stay safely on for two years, illegally, until 1974, when they left Uganda for the UK. Ultimately, Uganda's Africanisation policy represented a massive theft by Amin's regime and his country's willing businessmen, who nearly unanimously congratulated Amin on his decision to expel the Asians.[22] But more, Amin's extreme act of social engineering, stripping Asians of their African identity and Ugandan nationality, constituted a form of ethnicide, resonating with what Mbembe calls post-colonial 'necropolitics' – the governance over life and death – which was realised through the horrific forced evictions of whole ethnic and racial populations, who were summarily stripped of an integral part of their identities.[23] That Britain didn't intervene on behalf of its citizens – allowing Amin's expulsion decree – meant that Amin achieved his short-term goals.

As indicated earlier, once Bhimji completes her initial research for a film, she moves away from the informational address of her subject in order to centre on an emotional response to the material, one built out of rhythmic, aural and imagistic affects. As she explains in relation to *Out of Blue*:

> originally the research started with wanting to understand the basic history of what happened in Uganda, but then I wanted to understand what the word 'asylum' means, or the word 'stateless,' from a political and personal perspective. From that, I put an idea together about how I could communicate this feeling. And how I could enlarge it through sound and create a rhythm out of it.[24]

Take the beginning of *Out of Blue*, which commences with a panoramic shot of an African countryside, rendered in a meditative tempo. Gorgeous rolling hills appear in the distance, with lush green flora in the middle ground shrouded by a sea of mist. Bhimji's camera then pans left, moving from the cool blue of the early morning to the warm tones infusing the land below the rising sun. We hear the buzzing of insects, as well as the low foreboding murmur of a mysterious string instrument with a distant female voice singing ominously, while the camera cuts to a stunning shot of the glaring red sun. Returning to an overview of the misty land, the film introduces a British voice on the soundtrack, heard as if on a radio with an interrupted signal and speaking in largely inaudible tones. In the foreground, smoke begins to rise from the brush beside a tree. Gunshots ring out, as the burning savannah comes into view in a series of close-ups. An ululating female voice adds to the sense of emergency and to the complex layering of images and sounds, as the fire builds in intensity. Throughout this passage, the fact that the soundtrack was sourced from Ugandan radio is never identified; that the landscape is Uganda remains unexplained and the meaning of the fire is left a mystery. (Although in her 'treatment' for *Out of Blue*, Bhimji reveals her own associations: 'A deep fire would start at 3:45 pm when Amin announced on Radio Uganda that all Asians were to leave.')[25]

Such withholding of details characterises the film's other passages as well. Later, we see several buildings that look like old military barracks. In the interior, fabrics hang from the ceiling beams, mats lie on the floor, as if a large group of people were staying there but are no longer present. Other rooms seem to be one-time prison cells, the walls divulging palimpsests of graffiti, blood stains and burn marks from untold violence and captivity. There is a shot of a bunch of rifles standing on end and lined up against a wall; shadows of figures appear unexpectedly in doorways. Toward the end of the film an old airport can be seen, its decrepit tower showing the sign 'Entebbe, 3789 feet'. The building is decaying with broken windows and corroded surfaces, but no indication is given that it was from this airport that many Asians (and later Bhimji's family) flew out of Uganda during the expulsion.

However, the fact that no, or few if any, people appear in Bhimji's films does not mean that they are devoid of subjective content. Indeed, Bhimji speaks of how the filming of architecture leads to an 'architecture of the internal', by opening up 'imagining' in a way that is 'instinctive',[26] which is clear in these passages. 'I am interested in the traces of war, its unspeakable horrors and rites of passage and rebuilding',[27] she explains. In this regard, her cinema of affect is partly achieved by negating factual information, motivated in part by the artist's questioning of the presumption that the fullness of the past, including the complexity of its meanings and subjective effects, *could* be adequately captured. Her scepticism has led commentators, such as Deepali Dewan, to observe that her films are built out of 'anti-documentary images'[28] – in the sense that they reject the documentary image's association with objectivity, neutrality, factual truthfulness and evidence, as in conventional understandings of that representational mode.[29] As Bhimji explains: 'My work is not an idea of fact or scraps of evidence to support the assertion of history. The process is something about traces as symptoms of strange structural links between history, memory and fantasy.'[30]

In this sense, Bhimji's abstraction constitutes a critical, postdocumentary act. This quality distinguishes her filmmaking from that of other like-minded artists who

Film still (detail), *Yellow Patch*, 2011, single screen installation, 35 mm colour film, HD transfer with Dolby 5.1 surround sound, 29 min 43 sec

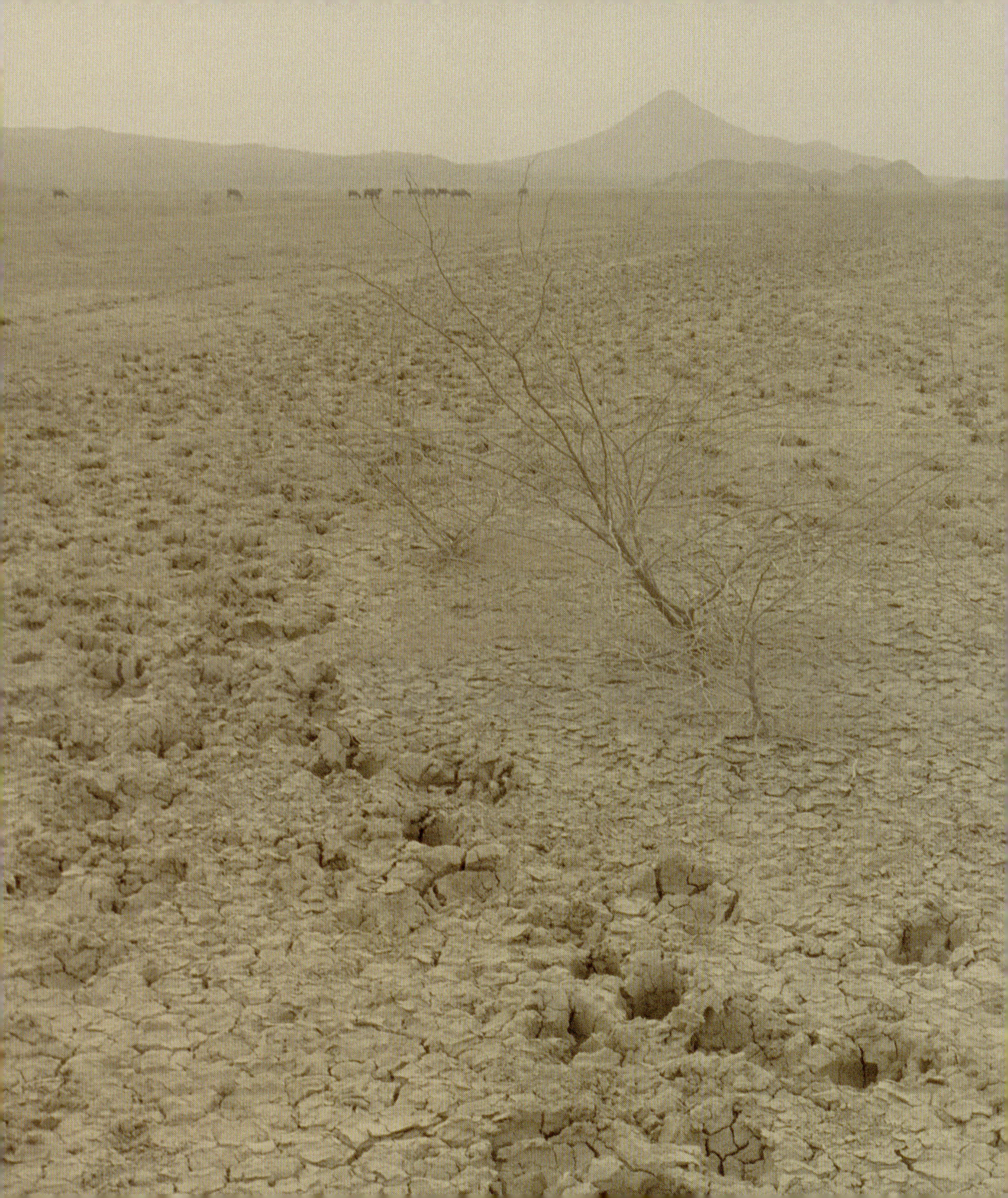

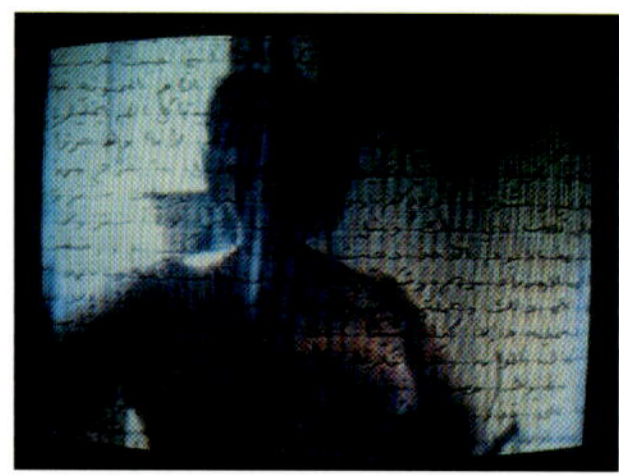

Mona Hatoum, film still from *Measures of Distance*, 1988, colour video with sound, 15 min

emerged during the 1980s context of postcolonial British art and who were also redefining the parameters of documentary at the time. Consider Black Audio Film Collective's *Handsworth Songs* (1986), or Isaac Julien's *Territories* (1984), or Mona Hatoum's *Measures of Distance* (1988): each of these investigates Black British diasporic identity and multicultural politics via a reinvented poetic documentary approach. *Handsworth Songs* investigates the history of the riots against the perceived police repression and racist policies during Margaret Thatcher's regime in the mid-1980s, weaving together in a lyrical montage a series of stories of Afro-Caribbean British people in the area of Birmingham that disputed the official government's claims (mimicked by the mainstream news media) that the uprising's violence was mindless and without legitimate cause. *Measures of Distance* explores the subjective effects of Hatoum's displacement in London during Lebanon's civil war, through a video montage that mediates her distanced relation to her mother in Beirut. In contrast, Julien's *Territories* examines London's Notting Hill carnival as a place of cultural hybridity and an allegory for the diasporic conditions of video's carnivalesque blurrings and transformations of representational codes. Each achieves its ends by using a form of voice-over narration marked by a theoretically informed sophistication in the analysis of race, politics and postcolonial subjectivity. Bhimji's films clearly possess an affinity to these various modellings of the aesthetics of the diasporic, especially in their ambition to reinvent the creative possibilities of documentary practice beyond the merely informational, and to endow the image with a lyrical quality opening on to a space of agency beyond the potentially victimising representations of the conventional media reportage of sociopolitical crises.[31] Yet, unlike these precedents, Bhimji's films are marked by their rejection of such discourse-heavy presentations and specifically by the absence of the voice-over.

Still, Bhimji's films are not simply abstract, for they do carry reference and signification, as well as a visual-aural relation to researched historical conditions. There are, as the artist puts it, 'traces as symptoms of strange structural links between history, memory and fantasy', which rupture the serenity and abstraction of the white cube environment, bringing her postcolonial history into view, even if she negates that history on another level. In this translation of historical research into aestheticised imagery, her filmmaking bears comparison to other artists of her generation, such as Steve McQueen, insofar as his films also offer a powerful range of cinematic affects in relation to postcolonial histories, and do so without narrative contextualisation (differing again, for instance, from the essayistic kind of discourse – intense filmmaking that is creatively developed in the work of the Otolith Group).[32] If things cannot be 'fixed' through documentary in relation to 'facts', and 'it is impossible to get to the truth – ever', as Bhimji states, then the goal is: 'How to express the emotional, warmly and deeply.'[33]

Steve McQueen, film still from *Gravesend*, 2007, 2 parts: HD with sound, 18 min 4 sec, looped; silent 8 mm, 54 sec 6 frames

Bhimji's desire for emotional expression and her negation of informational content are no doubt connected. One explanation for their intertwinement is the artist's sensitivity to the fact that strong emotional events often resist linguistic expression. Particularly with the case of traumatic experience – as is well established in Freudian psychoanalysis and in the poststructuralist philosophy of history[34] – shocking events tend to overflow the language of comprehension, interrupting its ability to communicate, which has been frequently observed in the reception of Bhimji's work from early on. As one interviewer picked up on the fact that the artist had read Elaine Scarry's book *The Body in Pain: The Making and Unmaking of the World* (1985), and had underlined the point that 'physical pain does not simply resist language but actively destroys it.'[35] Clearly the sensitivity to the way in which painful experiences resist language informs Bhimji's approach to the expressive image and offers insight into her films, which access and activate the emotional through a cinema of colours and sounds, movements and rhythms, rather than through verbal or written language and description. Indeed, part of the emotional affect of her work is also the anxious, estranging and saddening transgression of language by psychologically challenging historical events. Her films 'speak', in other words, with a telling silence.

How can we further specify what I have been calling Bhimji's affective cinema? 'Affect' designates emotional feeling stimulated by an outside source, such as a filmic image, in contrast to what originates internally; and it is usefully further distinguished as pre-structured bodily sensation prior to its formalisation as 'emotion'.[36] As such, affect designates a flowing and transformative quality that makes it difficult to analyse, structure or organise via interpretation, and in this sense affect exhibits a similar resistance to language as does physical pain. For Steven Shaviro, affective cinema is both 'symptomatic' – in that it provides indices of complex social processes, which it transcodes and rearticulates – and 'productive' – in that it does not simply *represent* social processes and historical meanings, but also participates actively in those processes and meanings, which it partially constitutes.[37] We might relate the affective image to the 'crystal-image', as described by Deleuze in his writings on cinema – that is, the one that multiplies distinct temporalities, mixing past and present, as well as joining virtual and actual aspects of the image's historical, mnemonic, subjective and imaginative values.[38] This offers a helpful way to describe Bhimji's allusive aesthetic and its associative metaphorics. Building further in this direction, the anthropologist Christopher Pinney, writing about Bhimji's use of photography, points out how the artist's imagery is uncontainable. It always goes beyond its representational significance, which resonates again with Deleuze's theory of the crystallised time-image: 'Photography, because of its ineradicable *more-than*, intrinsically constitutes a kind of xeno-epistemics', Pinney notes. 'It will always capture more of the world – its surplus or *xenos* – than the photographer expects or desires. Photography becomes a *xenography* that might take its place at the centre of this new form of knowledge production, and action.'[39] In this sense, Bhimji's is not just a diasporic aesthetic of the postcolonial subject; it is also one that cannot be easily circumscribed or pinned down. *Xenography* is a snapshot and a generator of mobility.

Part of the implication of this 'ineradicable *more-than*' that characterises Bhimji's aesthetic is that her metaphorical charging of images will always result in a certain multiplicity of meanings. As Stuart Hall observes:

> ...look at Zarina Bhimji's lightboxes, which, like the eerily evacuated Ugandan landscapes of her recent film *Out of Blue*, speak volumes through absence, summoning up the profound sense of emptiness and loss which forced exile produces, and the silent devastation left behind by those who wreak a brutal revenge on difference.[40]

While Hall's observation is insightful, the point I want to stress is that such metaphors – for instance, Bhimji's landscape of emptiness and loss that Hall describes – are never limited or final in their interpretive possibilities; indeed, the image 'speaks volumes'. It remains full of virtual potential, ever capable of further crystallisations. The artist's description of the beginning of *Out of Blue* makes this clear:

> The film starts with a panning shot of a misty romantic landscape. The mist, however, turns out to be smoke from the burning ground. Should that be read as a political statement on a country like Uganda, which has suffered so much destruction, or as poetic evocation of landscape as a metaphor for personal feelings of nostalgia and grief?[41]

It is this relation to surplus and unknowability, as well as indeterminacy and infinitude, that marks Bhimji's cinema of affect.

Perhaps at a fundamental level, this stress on the postinformational affective image, one that is complexly charged and endlessly multivalent, is also related to Bhimji's desire to relocate and reexamine her powerful childhood experiences, defined by the traumatic relation between intense feeling and youthful incomprehension. As she stated in the early 1990s:

> What I am doing is trying to make sense of my own history. To do this I need to project back into the feelings I had as a child, when I was eight, when I first came to England, the clothes I wore, the food I ate with my parents. These things are so relevant to what I do now. The tiniest memory can evoke all kinds of feelings. One strong sensation is that of a sense of loss – almost like death. I remember a line by TS Eliot, 'We had the experience but missed the meaning.' You can never return to what you didn't have but I need to make sense of those moments.[42]

In a certain sense, Bhimji's work re-opens extremely emotionally disturbing experiences to regain meaning retrospectively. In so doing, Bhimji defines a way to work through past traumas: 'It is important for me to take charge of my childhood myself, in order to control my adulthood. I need to make light of my childhood experience, to release the pain.'[43] In this regard, the affective joins with the psychoanalytic working of the image, rendering it subjectively functional in relation to the traumatic past. The films are thereby defined by a certain 'belatedness', a term Bhimji has used more recently, which describes the experience of visiting places resonant with her parents' history. Specifically, the history of Indians who made their way to East Africa, including the sites where Ugandan Asians lived, were arrested and deported. Bhimji's cinema offers a belated reckoning with the past, with filmic gestures made a generation later, this time apprehending and feeling the meaning that comes after researching and analysing the historical events in question – a belated affective response informed by retrospective comprehension.

Yellow Patch, as we have seen, adds a new thematic dimension to Bhimji's project by extending back to a migration that connects to an earlier point in her family's history, as it is not directly about her childhood experience, in the way that *Out of Blue* was. Rather, the film concerns the distant history of her parents' generation, a distance that is perhaps translated into the allegorical dimension of the film, which does not carry the same pathos or sense of ominous fear and traumatised experience that marks her earlier work. The distance also appears between image and reference, a poetic and lyrical disjunction that again invites the multiplication of meanings. It is a film of diverse sensations without defined meanings: the pinkish glow of the old stone houses set against the blue sky; the blurred yellow streaks of sunlight stretching over an ochre plaster wall; the dusty bone grey of a set of antlers lying strangely on a concrete floor; a spider's web appearing against the warm wooden colour of an old wooden *dhow*.

Pointing to this aesthetically captivating quality of her films, Bhimji has frequently used the term 'beauty', which I take as offering a way to describe the complex aspect of her sound and imagery that verges on the transcendental, insofar as its significance moves beyond our own immediate factual and material experience of the world. Her films draw together visual pleasure and affective depth, historical and psychoanalytic insight, and as such they are beautiful. For instance, consider the *Haveli* houses in *Yellow Patch*, spaces of 'safety and tenderness' that Bhimji has described as 'architecturally beautiful'; for her, they figure as 'parents' or 'lovers', indicating an affective investment in their imagery.[44] For the artist, beauty is more than the visually pleasurable: it designates the act of presenting the unconventional and unexpected in a way that challenges social and political hierarchies. As well, to present blackness – that of races other than white – in an unforeseen light, for Bhimji, constitutes a beautiful act. The term takes on an emancipatory capacity, which relates to the freedom of becoming something beyond what cultural norms allow or otherwise control. As such, the beautiful designates a space of liminality, of potentiality, one that avoids the characteristic stereotypes of identity, or what Okwui Enwezor terms the 'Afro-pessimism' according to which Africans are frequently represented.[45] Not that Bhimji's film portrays black people; rather, it is the poetic ambience of such figures, their historical spaces and environments that offer a complex representation that deepens our understanding of the history of Indians and Ugandan Asians.

Given this transcendental aspect of Bhimji's films, it seems appropriate that she uses the music of Abida Parveen, beginning with *Out of Blue* and continuing with *Yellow Patch*. A Pakistani singer of the Sufi faith, Parveen draws on seventeenth-century Urdu poetry about love and tenderness in her moving songs. It is not that Bhimji's films are spiritual in the way that Parveen's music is; rather, the connection is that Bhimji's poetic images also take us beyond the simple facticity of things. Her work defines a poetic ambience, which opens up an allegorical realm of resonant sensations with multiple affects. Bhimji's images crystallise historical significances and mediate between particularity (the architecture, say, in *Yellow Patch*) and what the artist calls her desire for her films to gain 'universal' significance, where images, sounds and affects can be diversely interpreted and will find distinct and specific resonances with distinct and specific viewers. As she has explained: 'It is essential to find a universal language, to go beyond personal references, yet it can only come out of personal experience. The language I use is related to vulnerability.'[46] At the same time, her films express the paradox of representing what resists representation: in relation to *Yellow Patch*, she mentions that 'the individual details' of her films 'are essential in trying to speak of the unspeakable that wants to be spoken. It is not about capturing an existing thing, it is about creating a new one.'[47] This too might be said to be a universal experience. Between representation of the past and production of new meanings lies the transformative capacity of Bhimji's affective cinema. By picturing the beauty of India, we can combat the victimising images of Asian refugees, and thereby open up new ways of relating to the world.

Consider in this regard the sense of desertion and emptiness as expressed in *Yellow Patch*: the buildings are depopulated, sites appear evacuated, only wild dogs roam the desert. These images might literally designate the history of Indians abandoning their homeland for East Africa in the early twentieth century, and beyond that, the specific history of the journey Bhimji's parents made. Historical and psychological meanings intertwine, as the evacuated spaces take on a sense of loneliness and subjective loss that also opens on to what we know of the desolate and tragic future that was to await those who stayed in Uganda after they left India, resulting in the postcolonial expulsion and the second loss of home – an exiling of exiles. Yet for the artist, Kutch is also a place associated with her mother (who was born in Bhadreswar), a connection further mediated in the film by a mysterious passage of a female figure wearing a white sari who is seen from behind rocking back and forth, and by the use of Parveen's music, some of which is sung in Bhimji's familial language of Kutchi, creating sounds 'that absorb the viewer at a primal level'.[48] In other words, *Yellow Patch* generates a crystallisation of the image, unleashing both melancholy and joyful sensations, such that trans-generational homesickness and memories of passionate desire for one's homeland collide. The image crystallises because Bhimji incites desire and imagination, and at the same time withholds information that might otherwise direct interpretation, or render it too particular and personal.

Consider one last particularly striking scene midway through *Yellow Patch*, which for me exemplifies this complex aesthetic. It occurs when the camera slowly reveals an old marble statue by slowly panning upward from the figure's white feet and pausing to focus on the rendering of a richly brocaded gown. The shot depicts one of the hands that holds an orb in its lap, one finger broken off, then ascends past its floral neckline to the face, which, save one eye, is badly disfigured and appears monstrous. The camera eventually zooms out to show what we already suspect: it is a sculpture of Queen Victoria, the first 'Empress of India', whose reign lasted until 1901 and who oversaw the British Empire's construction of the Princess Dock in what was then called Bombay and the initial building of the Uganda railway. Now the sculpture sits in disrepair against a dirty old brick wall in some untold location. Multiple meanings converge in this scene that characterises the steady and meditative rhythm of Bhimji's films. We encounter a regal official portrait of the Queen, as well as a personification of the British Empire holding the world symbolically in its grip, connecting us to the history of the colonial enterprise and its political-aristocratic image regime. But more: the statue's crumbling intimates the ultimate failure of that otherwise timeless imperial vision, of the desire to set British rule in stone. The ruination of the statue speaks to the disintegration of the once glorious colonial project. Moreover, its decomposition reveals the betrayal of its promise to secure modernisation, civilisation and progress for Britain's colonial territories. By extension, we have an allusion to the failure of the empire to protect its Asian citizens when they were persecuted by Amin some 70 years later.

Soon after this sequence, the film includes a shot of wild dogs resting in a trash-filled street running alongside a crumbling old colonnade. Is it an image of nature's inevitable victory over culture, showing how the erstwhile grandeur of empire turns inevitably into forgotten ruins? Juxtaposed against the image of Queen Victoria, this passage signifies the hubris of erstwhile imperial ambitions, or perhaps an allegorical picture of the wild dogs as the empire's anonymous and pitiful subjects, who will nonetheless eventually outlive their subjection and triumphantly have their revenge on their one-time imperial masters. There is no way to finalise the meaning – such potentiality is the truth of Bhimji's generative cinema. What becomes ultimately clear is that *Yellow Patch* is not a fatalistic condemnation of colonial tragedy, a pitiful expression of multi-generational grief, or a film of victimised personal trauma; rather it is a celebration of the overcoming of difficult historical circumstances, a focusing on the beauty of becoming and survival, of movement forward. This conclusion is also established by the juxtaposition of the Indian-built Mandvi port – a living harbour that still sees the construction of wooden *dhows* – and the British port in Mumbai, which, with its filing cabinets and heaps of papers, appears as a decaying but still intimidating image of the bureaucracy of control (a premonition of the contemporary state of surveillance and data collection that we confront today?). By beginning the film with shots of those files, one wonders what amazing stories lie within those cakes of papers now seemingly turning back into pulp – it is this curiosity and desire for remembrance that Bhimji cultivates and explores throughout the rest of the film. With the Mandvi port – by far the more alluring one – we are left with a symbol of the beauty of indigenous knowledge, skill and creative survival, expressed via a critical and experimental cinematic intervention. It is one that goes beyond facts and enters into affective imagery of poetic constructions, which lets us feel the emotional complexity of this lived history and leaves us with a revitalised relation to the present.

1 My understanding of the film, based on viewing early cuts, is informed by conversations with the artist during September, 2011, and by the artist's 'treatment' – or, pre-production conceptualisation – for *Yellow Patch*. Here, she writes further about her use of architecture: 'It's not about describing a house or making it picturesque. It is to go beyond the description. It is to reveal attachment, to explore subtle shadings of our attachment. To build up emotional intensity, empty/full, communal/solitary, rational/irrational with sound.'

2 The artist explained to me that she collected some of these materials in the British Sound Archive. (Conversation with the author, 12 November 2011).

3 Zarina Bhimji, Press Release for *Yellow Patch*.

4 Chika Okeke-Agulu, 'Conversation with Zarina Bhimji', *Art Journal*, Winter 2010, p.66.

5 Gilane Tawadros, 'The Revolution Stripped Bare', in *Fault Lines: Contemporary African Art and Shifting Landscapes*, Gilane Tawadros and Sarah Campbell (eds), Iniva, London, 2003, p.20.

6 *op cit*, Okeke-Agulu, p.68.

7 Quoted in Mark Haworth-Booth, 'Introduction', *Zarina Bhimji: I will always be here*, Ikon, Birmingham, 1991, n.p.

8 As the entry for her Turner Prize reads: 'Bhimji's inquiries into the past and present of her chosen sites become intensely personal: historical fact can only be abandoned, allowing her image-making to begin, once this level of knowledge and intimacy has been achieved'; *Turner Prize '07: Zarina Bhimji, Nathan Coley, Mike Nelson, Mark Wallinger*, Tate Liverpool, Liverpool, 2007, n.p.

9 Maite Lorés, 'Interview with Zarina Bhimji', *Contemporary*, no.49, 2003, p.60.

10 See Phares Mukasa Mutibwa, 'Expulsion of the Asians', *Uganda Since Independence: A Story of Unfulfilled Hopes*, C. Hurst & Co., London, 1992, pp.92–97.

11 Achille Mbembe, *On the Postcolony*, University of California Press, Berkeley, 2001, p.32 and p.67.

12 See *op cit*, Mutibwa, *passim*.

13 For an extensive account of the passage to East Africa from India, see the historical and contemporary testimonials collected in the three-volume series, *We Came in Dhows*, Cynthia Salvadori (ed), Paperchase Kenya, Nairobi, 1996, which Bhimji also consulted during her research for *Yellow Patch*. Also, in her 'treatment' for *Yellow Patch*, Bhimji mentions MF Hill's *Permanent Way: The Story of the Kenya and Uganda Railway*, East African Railways and Harbours, Nairobi, 1949, as a further historical source.

14 Mahmood Mamdani, *From Citizen to Refugee: Uganda Asians Come to Britain*, London, Frances Pinter, 1972, p.15. Also see Mahmood Mamdani, *Citizen and Subject: Contemporary Africa and the Legacy of Late Colonialism*, Princeton University Press, Princeton, 1996; and Bhimji's 'treatment' for *Out of Blue*, part of which is published in *Art Journal*, Winter 2010 and includes excerpts from newspaper reports of the expulsion from the early 1970s.

15 Mamdani, *From Citizen to Refugee*, p.15.

16 See Hasu H. Patel, 'General Amin and the Indian Exodus from Uganda', *Issue: A Journal of Opinion* 2/4, 1972, pp.12–22. On the fragmenting results of Africanisation policies under postcolonial regimes, see Mamdani, *Citizen and Subject*, p.20.

17 According to Mamdani, Amin created a 'semi-fascist state' – 'fascist' because the object of his policies [was] to organise all of society's resources, human and material, and put them at the service of capital; '" semi" because Uganda's productive resources [were] not sufficiently advanced to permit him the sort of organisation and control that was possible for fascist Japan', p.61. For a film portrait of Idi Amin, see Barbet Schroeder, *General Idi Amin Dada: An Autoportrait*, 1974.

18 In his book *From Citizen to Refugee*, Mamdani recounts how many Asians nonetheless refused to become refugees: 'A refugee is not just a person who has been displaced and has lost all or most of his possessions. A refugee is in fact more akin to a chid: helpless, devoid of initiative, somebody on whom any kind of charity can be practised; in short, a totally malleable creature. A part of this book is the story of those who *refused* to become refugees', p.8.

19 The fact that Ugandan Asians had British passports was part of the legacy of the colonial agreement made decades earlier, when Britain offered citizenship to Indians for indentured labour in East Africa, a deal Britain never thought would end up with Indians ending up in the home country.

20 See Mamdani, *From Citizen to Refugee*, *op cit*.

21 See Patrick Keatley, 'Obituary for Idi Amin', *The Guardian*, 18 August 2003, at: http://www.guardian.co.uk/news/2003/aug/18/guardianobituaries.

22 See Mutibwa, pp.92–97 and pp.115–20; and Jan Jelmert Jørgensen, *Uganda: A Modern History*, Taylor & Francis, 1981. As reported in Jørgensen, some 5,655 firms, ranches, farms and agricultural estates were expropriated, including cars, homes and household goods, most of which was reallocated to individuals, government bodies, and semi-state organisations (including the state-owned Uganda Development Corporation) (pp.288–90).

23 Achille Mbembe, 'Necropolitics', *Public Culture*, vol.15/1, Winter 2003, pp.34–40.

24 Maite Lorés, Interview with Zarina Bhimji, *Contemporary* no.49, 2003, p.60.

25 See Zarina Bhimji, 'Outline of a Film', *Art Journal*, p.74.

26 *Op cit*, Okeke-Agulu, p.70.

27 Bhimji, unpublished 'treatment' for *Out of Blue*.

28 Deepali Dewan, 'Tender Metaphor: The Art of Zarina Bhimji', in *Fault Lines: Contemporary African Art and Shifting Landscapes*, *op cit*, p.136.

29 See, for instance, Frits Gierstberg et al., (eds), *Documentary Now!: Contemporary Strategies in Photography, Film and the Visual Arts*, NAi Publishers, Rotterdam, 2005.

30 *Op cit*, Okeke-Agulu, p.69.

31 Moreover, her early work is indebted to the conceptual context of the politics of representation, such as her mixed-media project, *She Loved to Breathe – Pure Silence* (1987; p.47), which investigates the history of the Home Office's 'virginity inspections' of immigrants from India during 1970s, and recalls the work of conceptual artist Mary Kelly (who was Bhimji's tutor at Goldsmiths in the early 1980s).

32 See my essay on the Otolith Group: '"Sabotaging the Future": The Essay-Films of the Otolith Group', in *Migrations: The Politics of Documentary During Global Crisis*, Durham, North Carolina, Duke University Press, forthcoming.

33 Interview with the author, 22 August 2011.

34 For example, see Sigmund Freud, 'Beyond the Pleasure Principle', *Standard Edition*, James Strachey (trans), vol.18, Hogarth Press, London, 1953–1974, pp.31–32; and Maurice Blanchot, *The Writing of Disaster*, Ann Smock (trans), University of Nebraska Press, Lincoln and London, 1986. In his book *The Step Not Beyond*, Lycette Nelson (trans), State University of New York Press, Albany, 1992, p.50; Blanchot explains that 'Writing is not destined to leave traces, but to erase, by traces, all traces, to disappear in the fragmentary space of writing more definitively than one disappears in the tomb, or again, to destroy, to destroy invisibly, without the uproar of destruction.'

35 *Zarina Bhimji: I will always be here*, Ikon, Birmingham, 1991, n.p.

36 See Brian Massumi, 'The Autonomy of Affect', *Parables for the Virtual: Movement, Affect, Sensation*, Duke University Press, Durham, 2002; and Steven Shaviro, *Post-Cinematic Affect*, o Books, Winchester, 2010, who explains that 'affect is primary, non-conscious, asubjective or presubjective, asignifying, unqualified and intensive; while emotion is derivative, conscious, qualified and meaningful, a content that can be attributed to an already-constituted subject', p.3.

37 Shaviro, *Post-Cinematic Affect*, p.2.

38 See Gilles Deleuze, *Cinema 2: The Time-Image*, Hugh Tomlinson and Robert Galeta (trans), University of Minnesota Press, Minneapolis, 1989.

39 Christopher Pinney, 'What is to be done?', *Source* 48, Autumn 2006, p.17. Pinney draws on the concept of 'xeno-epistemics' as developed by Sarat Maharaj, 'Xeno-epistemics: Makeshift Kit for Sounding Visual Art as Knowledge Production and the Retinal Regimes', in *Documenta 11: The Catalogue*, Okwui Enwezor et al., (eds), Hatje Cantz, London, 2002.

40 Stuart Hall, 'Maps of Emergency: Fault Lines and Tectonic Plates', in *Fault Lines: Contemporary African Art and Shifting Landscapes*, Gilane Tawadros and Sarah Campbell (eds), Iniva, London, 2003, p.33.

41 Maite Lorés, 'Interview with Zarina Bhimji', *Contemporary*, no.49, 2003, p.61.

42 'Interview with Sonia Boyce', in *Zarina Bhimji: I will always be here*, Ikon, Birmingham, 1991, n.p.

43 *Ibid*.

44 Conversation with the author in September 2011.

45 See Okwui Enwezor's title essay in *Snap Judgments: New Positions in Contemporary African Photography*, International Center of Photography, New York, 2006.

46 'Interview with Sonia Boyce' in *Zarina Bhimji*, *op cit*.

47 From the artist's unpublished 'treatment' for *Yellow Patch*, p.6.

48 *Ibid*, p.7.

Overleaf: *Shadows and Disturbances* (detail), 2007, Ilfochrome Ciba classic print, 127 × 160 cm | 50 × 63 in

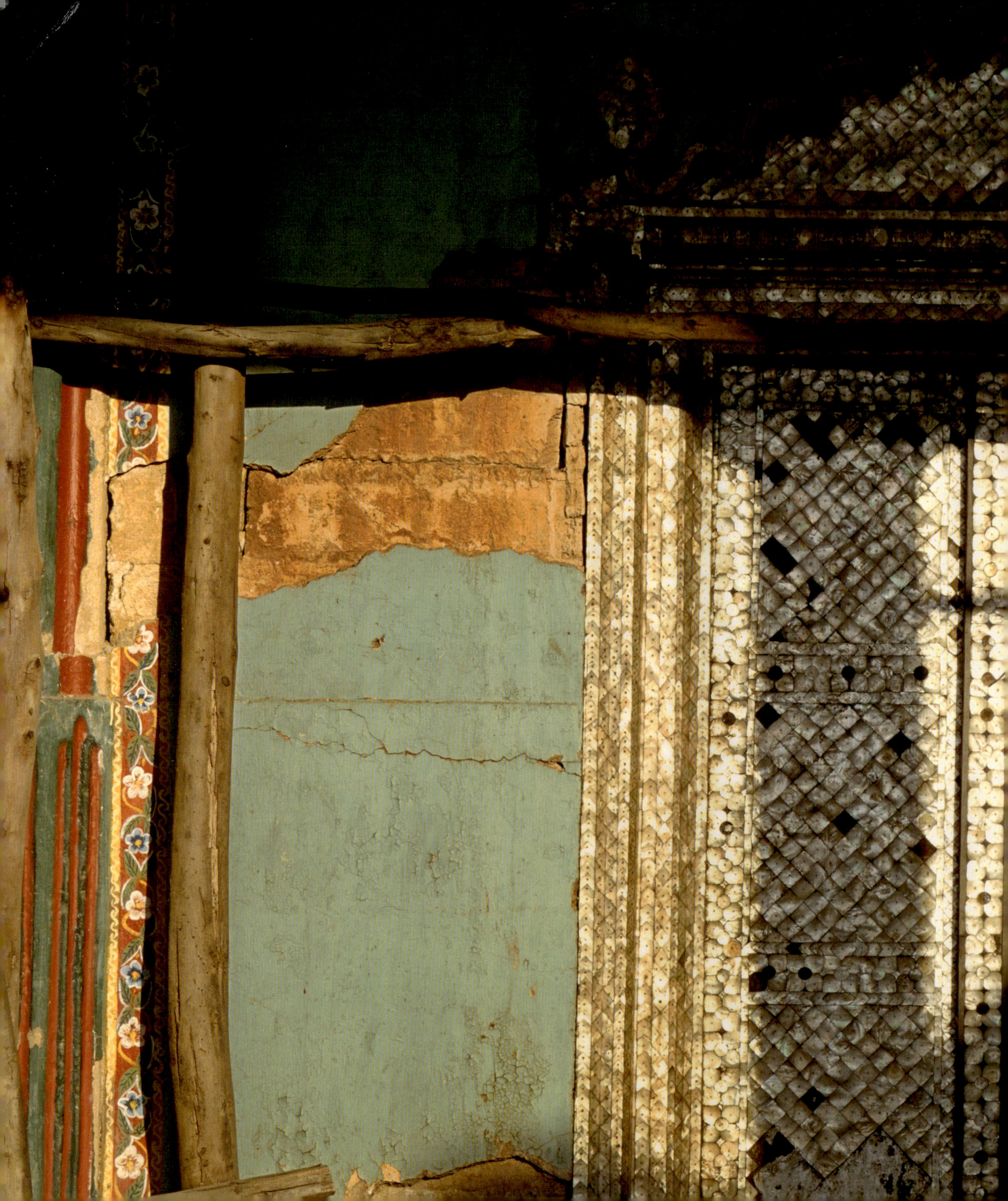

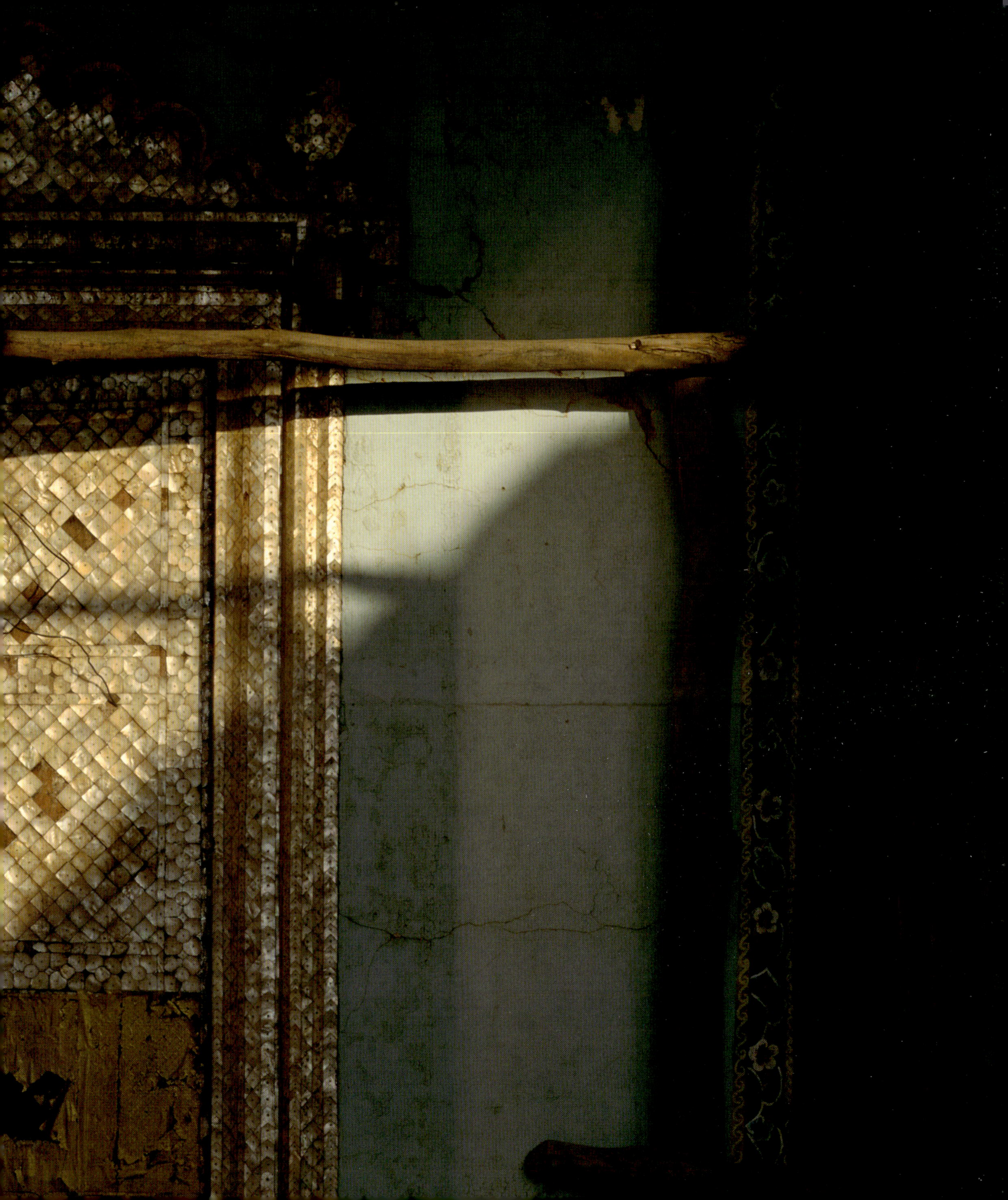

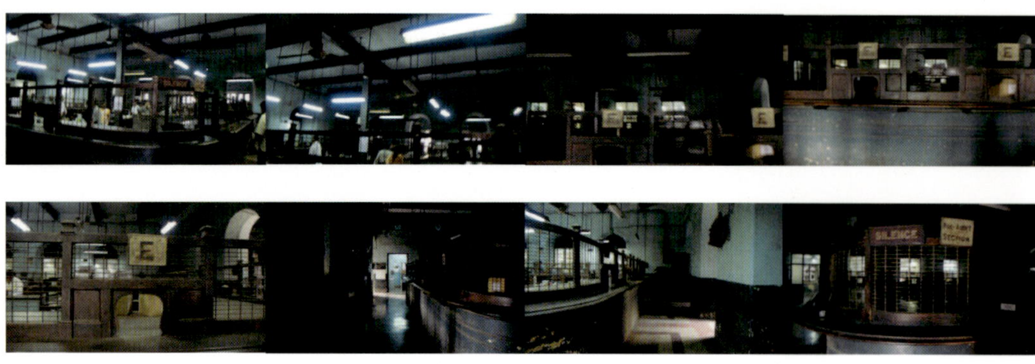

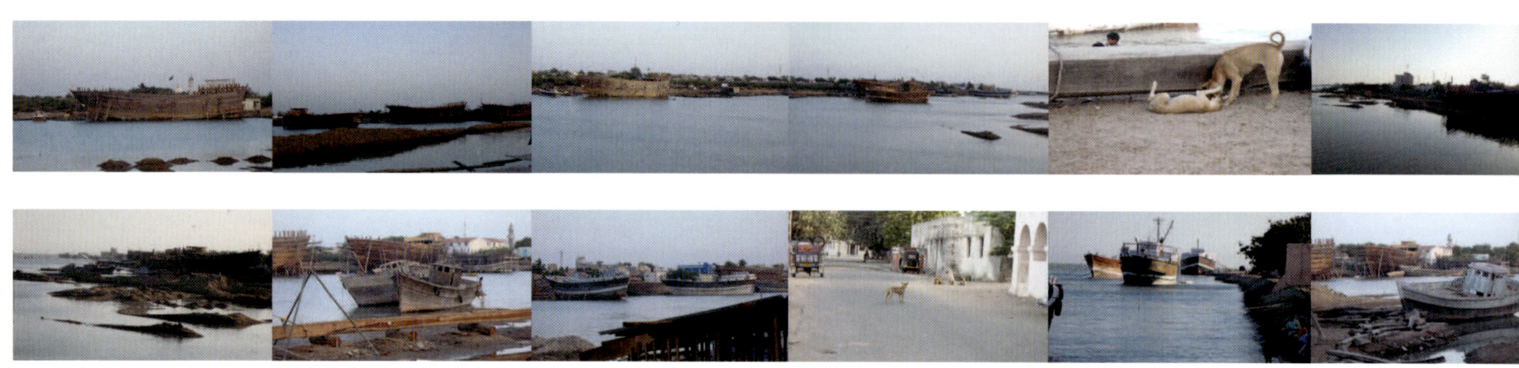

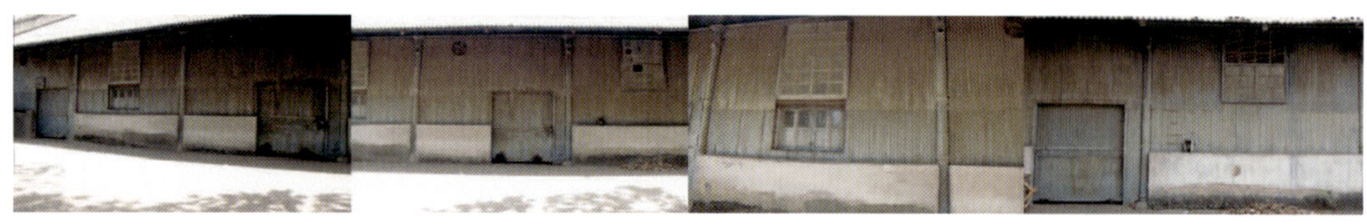

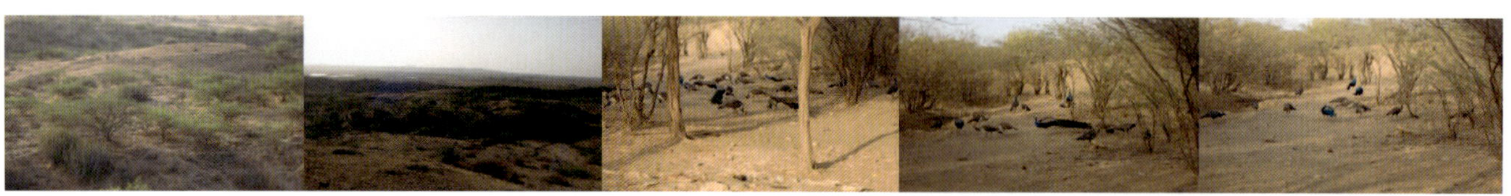

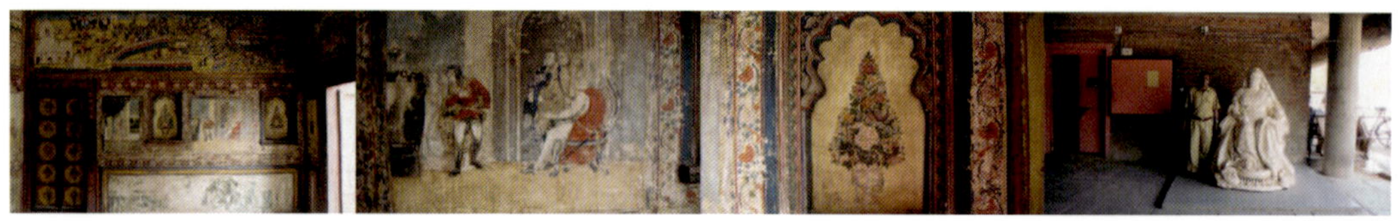

Selected preparatory storyboards, 2008, for *Yellow Patch*, 2011, 4 × 6 in photographic prints joined together with tape

From Politics to Poetry
Zarina Bhimji in Conversation with Achim Borchardt-Hume and Kathleen Bühler

Achim Borchardt-Hume What drives you to make the work you make and what drives you to give it the form that it takes; what is that relationship?

Zarina Bhimji I don't know fully. Working as an artist, I am interested in lots of different things: anthropology, sociology, painting, poetry, history and so many other subjects. Part of the drive is being able to delve into all these different ways of thinking and to respond to them through my own forms. I do so by way of a set of constellations. Research gives me time to think about ideas of gestures, shapes and light. After this process, a structure for the work develops. I search instinctively for how to form a narrative through aesthetics. The process is like having a toolbox to carefully examine sounds, light, texture, fictional possibilities and what I think of as 'camera presence'.

Kathleen Bühler What made you decide to become an artist?

ZB The idea of making art formed at school through my interests and experiences as I was growing up. I subscribed to the feminist magazine *Spare Rib* and a few years later I joined the Labour Party. Then I went to Greenham Common Women's Peace Camp where women were protesting in a peaceful manner. They hung children's clothes on barbed wire fences, which to me appeared like installations. Looking back, it was this mix of ethical and intellectual reflections that stayed with me throughout my career as an artist. We were new immigrants in early 1970s Leicester, where the National Front, for instance, would violently disrupt festivals. They randomly attacked people with batons. There was a lot of aggression from schoolteachers, there were Enoch Powell's speeches against immigration; it was a very different time. As the next generation, we decided that there had been enough 'Paki bashing'. We took the law into our own hands: in our defence we threw red chilli powder at the National Front.

ABH How did this type of experience inform your time at art school and your early work?

ZB When I entered art school I discovered new research modes and forms of knowledge production, something I found very exciting. How could I translate this approach to my own interests? The idea of the spatial, the installation, has always been a central concern of mine. When I was making *She Loved to Breathe – Pure Silence* (1987; p.47) I had direct questions about the nature of institutions. It was important to me not to make work that could just be stuck to the wall. I wanted the work to have that gesture of standing independently. Unconsciously I was thinking of this as 'Paki bashing' too. That's how I developed the idea of using chilli and turmeric on the floor. By making a performance piece that reactivates itself every time it is shown, it acts as a metaphor for changing culture.

ABH You start each new project with extensive research – both in libraries and through site visits. Some of the research for your latest project, *Yellow Patch* (2011; p.105), is part of this exhibition, including storyboards. It is only recently that you made this research public for the first time, what prompted that decision?

ZB I have copious books with my own notes and collect maps, portraits and historical documents. When I finished *Out of Blue* (2002; p.77) almost ten years ago I wanted to continue some of the conversations I had started in that film. I was wondering how so many Indians had ended up in Africa. It was a simple question, perhaps even somewhat naive, but I needed to research it for myself in order to arrive at something else. This research is separate from the final form of *Yellow Patch*. In 2007 I was invited to participate in the Guangzhou Triennial. As I was in the middle of an intense research phase, my intention was to use the gallery space as a laboratory. Since then I have grown more comfortable with exhibiting the research.

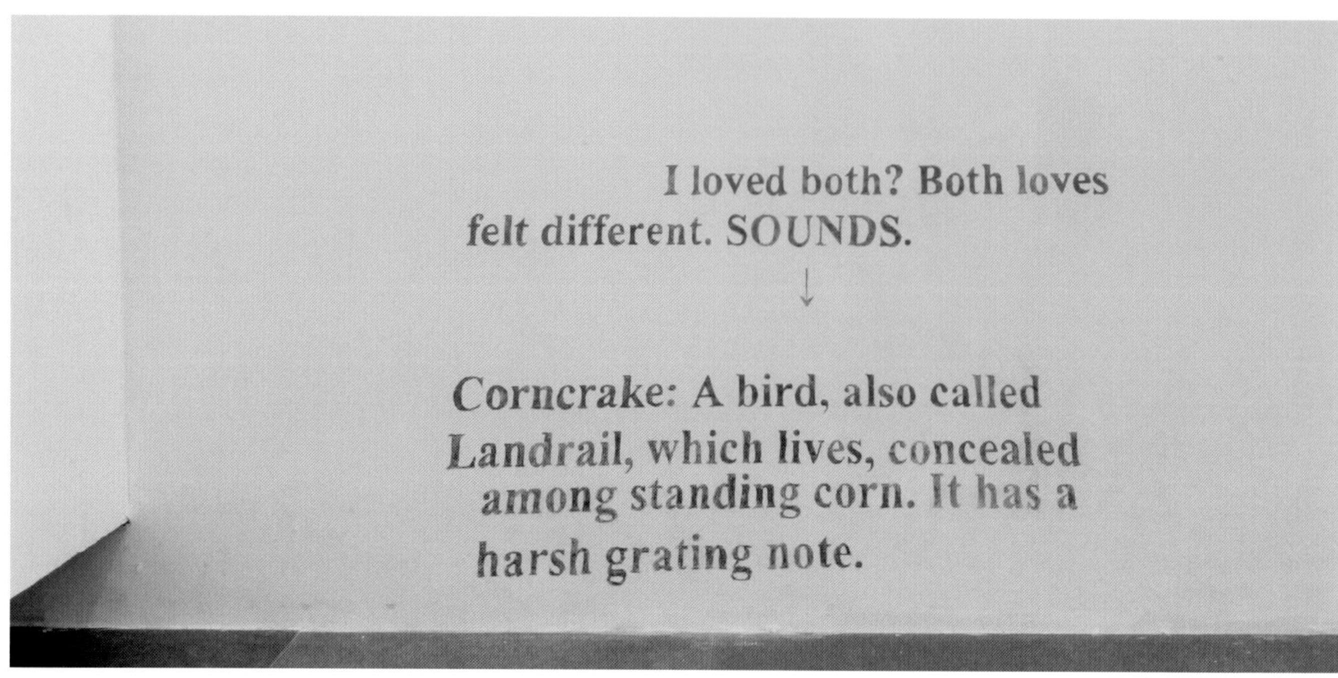

Notes, installation view, The Third Guangzhou Triennial, Guangzhou, China, 2008

ABH What did you present on that occasion?

ZB I exhibited a series of unframed photographs and texts as a way of showing my thinking while still in progress – the notion that many years later you get a sense that finally you might be able to inhabit a situation that occurred in the past. For example, I was thinking what it may have been like for an Indian man, or African man, such as my father, to be barred from lots of places by the British on the basis of his skin colour. I pictured myself as a little girl standing next to him. This episode, by the way, is fictional, not personal; I fictionalise to make sense of things, this is part of my research. I like to create characters like my father, or my son, or my daughter. In my work the personal and public connect. What was it like for him, in front of me, to be told by a British man that coloured people are not allowed to enter? I imagine what these situations might have felt or looked like. In the end I wrote a text about this feeling which I displayed in the exhibition.

KB What does the research process for one of your large film installations typically look like?

ZB I take photographs, make recordings, meet people and talk with them. A very informative part of the process is getting to know the people at the sites I have been interested in from afar. I speak various local languages, so this also really helps me to think about sound. I like to play with multifaceted cultures. I am a product of three diverse cultures myself, the languages become like poetry with simultaneous translation. The English title, *Yellow Patch*, for instance, is in fact a subtitle for the Gujarati ઝંગબાર. Research is always a crucial part of my process. I work in the British Library, the London Library, SOAS Library, the Maharashtra State Archives, the Zanzibar National Archives, to name but some. History is recorded differently in each of these places. In the Zanzibar National Archives I found legal accounts in Gujarati and Arabic from the time when Sir John Kirk was British Administrator of Zanzibar. How did the Montagu-Chelmsford Reforms get negotiated? I followed this discussion through all these different perspectives.

During the research for *Yellow Patch* I gathered a lot of material and wrote countless notes that act as thinking spaces. They open up a space that I can only describe as 'in between'. My work is not about the actual facts but about the echo it creates, the marks, the gestures and the sound. This is what excites me. It is not carefully planned but gets stitched together as I go along.

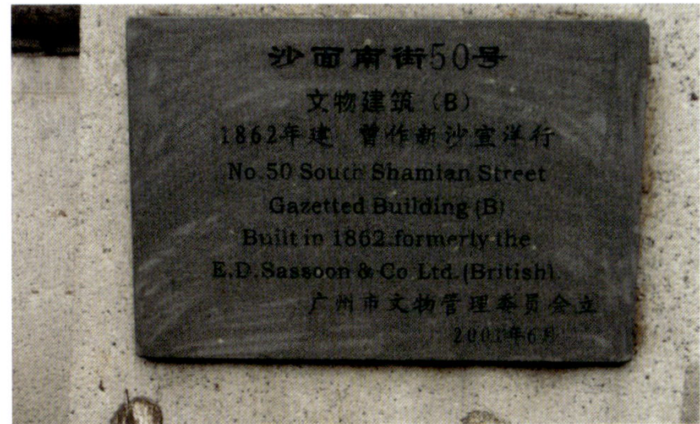

Research photograph taken by Bhimji, Guangzhou, China, 2008

ABH Can you give us an example?

ZB There is a quote by Lord Curzon from a speech he gave in Oxford in 1915 which is a very good example. He said: 'The sacredness of India haunts me like a passion. It is only when you get to see what India really is, that she is the strength and the greatness of England; it is only then that you realise that every nerve, every sinew, a man may bring should be used to draw even tighter cords that bind us to India.'

ABH What do you like about this quote?

ZB To be honest, it came as a surprise to me because of how emotional Curzon appears, yet it made me also wonder about economics and politics. It helped me to shift my thinking. What was interesting to me was the temperature of what he said. It seems very urgent and deeply felt. I was very moved and disturbed by it. It is discoveries like this that make academic research become real for me.

I am not quite sure how, but somehow this helped me to work out the structure of *Yellow Patch*. For instance, one shot in *Yellow Patch* shows cupboards that were left behind by the British in the offices of the port authority in Mumbai, or what was then known as Bombay. I was amazed to find that they were still there. I drink in all these details, I take photographs of every turn in the staircase, the corridors, the rooms, outer and inner elements, knowing I may never be able to return. I ask myself, if the effects of Partition were ever forgiven? Many people died in the name of independence, hundreds of thousands of screams have been uttered and much has been lost. We have spoken before about the idea of belatedness: is the loss mine as well as theirs? These are the types of questions I ask myself during the making of the work.

KB On the one hand, you appear to be proud that India can inspire such passion in a man like Lord Curzon, who was part of a society and a culture that exploited the country. On the other hand, he seems more like a stranger.

ZB In the end I don't think through the histories in a factual way; for me they all exist together in my work in a purposefully ambiguous way.

ABH You mentioned this idea of belatedness – to me this is very curious given that so much of our collective experience of the world now seems to be geared towards a continuous present. In this context, the concept of belatedness is especially interesting since it is always experienced on a personal level. Most people, at some stage, reach a point in their lives at which they become aware that it is no longer possible to return to a place from the past. There is this sense of irrevocably coming too late to something. How does this relate to your interest in India, especially given that you were born in Uganda and brought up in Britain?

ZB In Leicester, Indian men used to gather in the park to play cards in the early 1970s and a lot of them didn't speak English. They used to say that the Queen had taken their children away. This interested me a lot as a metaphor. When I was in India and I came across the statue of Queen Victoria, I understood much better what they meant. Suddenly, I felt the weight of power. I mentioned earlier the Partition of India and my feeling of belatedness. I felt it again here. My father is no longer with us, but the old world grips me. When I was in China, to give another example, I was gripped by how the very old and the very new coexist.

ABH Is that the atmosphere you seek to evoke in your films?

ZB Yes, it is a bit like the feeling that follows making love, when you make pictures that are full of tenderness. I am interested in the spaces, micro details and the light of these distant interiors. Light is a key element in my composition and becomes just as intricate and important as human presence or its lack thereof. The stillness creates a suspension of everyday life, and yet there is a narrative inferred by way of mood and a sense of mystery and incompleteness. So that atmosphere is tactile, moist light. But as I worked further I kept coming back to ideas of disconnection and belatedness, and that nothing is ever complete.

KB So, rather than describe a real-life journey, do you seek to portray an emotional journey by putting the viewer into the mindset of somebody who may have experienced such a voyage?

ZB I thought about this for a while when I made *Out of Blue*. I thought that there are legal documents, which people depend on, documents such as marriage certificates. During a war these often get destroyed; so, how do you know who you are? We have newspapers and documentaries, but in order not to fix things, maybe the fictional is more interesting to me as an artist, because I am able to scrutinise it with my camera.

ABH Is this split between fact and emotion not a fiction all along?

ZB I would like to think so.

KB In your project synopsis or 'film treatment' for *Yellow Patch*, you state your interest in the archaeology of spaces and the ways in which history may manifest itself in physical structures such as houses.

ZB For me, this is best explained through part of the research I did for *Yellow Patch*. In January 2001 at about 9 o'clock in the morning there was a big earthquake, 7.7 on the Richter scale, in the seismically-active area of Kutch in the Indian state of Gujarat. It is known as the Bhuj earthquake and damaged or destroyed over 800,000 houses – a quarter of the housing in the area. When something like that happens you do feel a large-scale betrayal by the earth. I just wanted to understand what happened. In Bombay I went to the *Times of India* offices to read about how they had reported the earthquake. I felt connected to it; I wanted to know every element of it. I became very excited about this as a metaphor for migration. It inspired me to come up with the title for my photograph *Elastic Waves* (2007).

ABH How does this relate to your depictions of the desert and especially the sound you use in those sequences?

ZB I became very excited about the origin of the desert, these zones of scarcity and hardship, the very low rainfall and the intense silence. The beauty is overwhelming. The myriads of unfamiliar plants, mostly leafless and spiny – a thorny jungle stunted and populated with half-nibbled shrubs and trees – where people are few and far between, giving a desolate and barren appearance. India borders with Pakistan in the desert, the Rann of Kutch. This space helped me to think of the Partition of the sub-continent in 1947 which separated Kutch from its close neighbour Sindh, severing age-old ties between hitherto closely connected regions.

A lot of people migrated away from the hardship of this desert, and did so via the Mandvi port on the periphery of India on the shore of the Indian Ocean. When I started reading about the Indian Ocean I was amazed by how complex it was, the sea had for centuries been their main road to the world outside. In the 1760s, a ship that was built, equipped and manned in Kutch made the voyage to England. I discovered a little seafarer's manual, *Pothi*, written in 1664 in Gujarati in the Kutchi dialect. This port became a focus for me.

ABH Do these locations become your characters? And do these characters indirectly tell a story, a story which closely connects to the history of the place?

ZB They do not necessarily connect to the history of the place, but the nature of film language is that you need to have a character plot. I do have 'characters' in my head, but they are just my way of creating a pace, rhythm and structure for the film. The characters I create are temporary and in my mind; and they disappear as the film gets developed.

KB I wanted to ask you about the way you use landscape. When I first saw the opening shots of *Out of Blue*, I did not immediately realise that this was a landscape in Africa. Thinking back, this makes me wonder to what degree your understanding of landscape is informed by the tradition of British landscape painting. Did this ever cross your mind at the time?

ZB I constantly keep coming back to the idea of landscape like in *Yellow Patch*. As a young artist, I often went to the then Tate Gallery to look at paintings by historic British landscape, artists such as Turner or Constable. I like their scale, their sense of stillness and silence. I am drawn to the misty landscapes and seascapes of Caspar David Friedrich, the light, the blurriness, the muted colours all intrigue me. The natural landscape, on the other hand, is the raw material of the human psyche. It is

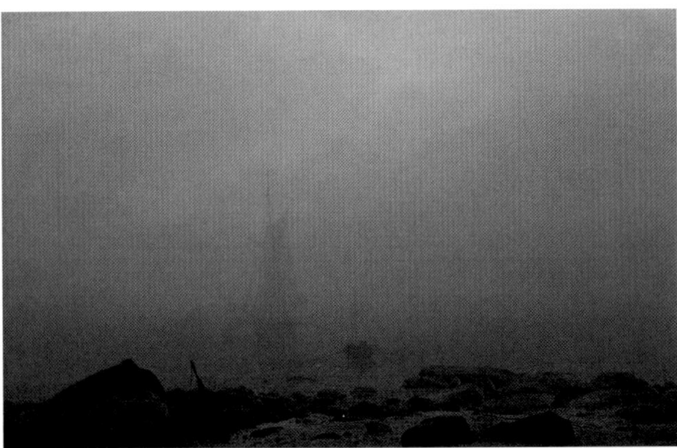

Caspar David Friedrich, *Seashore in the Mist*, c.1807, oil on canvas, 24.2 × 50.2 cm | 9½ × 20 in

where my heart belongs. It was where I first felt passion and since leaving that landscape the passion has been withheld.

KB The fire in *Out of Blue*, for me is menacing because I associate it with war and the hurting or killing of people, an association the soundtrack reinforces; but for you it is connected to fertility?

ZB When I was travelling through Uganda, I noticed that burning the land to make it more fertile is a common agricultural practice. I thought the fires looked beautiful as I was driving by, and that they could be interesting as a metaphor for Africa in *Out of Blue*. The reinvention of the country was what was also happening to the soil, which gets renewed so that new things can grow there. At the same time, the landscape has this intense beauty, which is all the more poignant if one bears in mind what happened there. That's the starting point, but of course I do other things with the sound. I take recordings from the radio where people are celebrating with their voices sounding passionate. Then I bring in the vocals of Abida Parveen. It is a dramatic way to start the film, to enter into the next scenes.

It was to do with my passion. When I was a child in Uganda, it was in these remote, lush forests that I discovered what passion is. I got in touch with my own personal passions there. I like taking personal details such as this idea of passion and making them into larger, more public statements, so that they operate between the political and the poetic while at the same time remaining open-ended and universal.

KB So in a way it is not violent at all?

ZB No, it is meant to be beautiful, tender. You can never return to that moment of change and that evokes all kinds of feelings. *Out of Blue* actually started off with me making three map dresses – one of India, one of East Africa and one of Britain (p.39). I made the dresses in response to my father passing away and being buried in England. Maps never feel personal, they always feel accurate, and I wanted to make them human. I wanted to talk about cartography and being connected. When I made these dresses I hung them on my ceiling, I took pictures of myself naked, and they became a sketch, and I decided to make a film. I have never shown them outside my studio before.

KB In your research file for *Yellow Patch*, you compare the South Asian peninsular to the body of your mother.

ZB Not the whole peninsular, but specifically the Rann of Kutch, a large expanse of salty marshland in Gujarat, which I mentioned before.

KB In your proposal you write: 'Kutch is a place I associate with my mother. In the desert I look for ways to connect. I ask her about the way she was before I knew her.'

ZB I would not take this too literally, though not all that long ago the Rann was a very remote region.

KB There is an obvious resonance here in how your mother envisions herself and how you envision the landscape.

ZB The question that preoccupied me was how does a young woman at the peak of her beauty, stepping out into life, getting married and so on, experience colonialism. The piece I made called *Shadows and Disturbances* (2007; p.30) is about the kind of beauty I mean. Ever since I first went to the Rann of Kutch as a student I felt there was something very special about it. However, it was particularly this question of youth and beauty that preoccupied me. I took some black and white photographs. If I had used colour, it would look like a holiday brochure. It is for the same reason that I took the black and white pictures of the seascapes in Zanzibar which is how *Yellow Patch* ultimately started. I felt that I had to look at the sea, '*bhar*', the Arabic word for sea which I like. I was intrigued to learn that the Indian Ocean is made of six separate seas, each one linked to a regional economy. This revealed to me the connection between people, history and politics. The crossings were quite dangerous as people had to face extreme storms and gales. I was intrigued to learn that the Portuguese sailor Vasco da Gama had employed an Indian pilot from Gujarat to navigate. I became fascinated by the movement across the Indian Ocean.

ABH How did you manage to get the port authority in Mumbai to allow you access to their premises which generally tends to be highly restricted?

ZB As I was reading I came up with the Port of Bombay scene. The British had acquired Bombay from the Portuguese in the early 1660s. Before that the port of Surat had been the principal point of call for the East India Company. Suddenly, Bombay became very important. Riding on the back of a motorbike around Bombay and having read the history of the city, I saw glimpses of the cotton mills that are falling apart. The relationship to England in the seventeenth century when these mills were a major part of industrialisation is echoed in the disbanded factories around Manchester today, which is very moving to me. Feeling English and Indian and an artist all at the same time, I like that there are these overlaps and connections.

At the port, I focused the camera on the traces of migration: a high, colourless room lined with shelves, stacked with boxes filled with an undefined watery light. Capturing the architecture, light, texture, atmosphere, details and colours of walls and floor, I focused on their physical experience and to make this as intense as possible.

ABH Briefly going back to Africa, Lord Delamere was determined to introduce European modes of agriculture and is often quoted as saying that Kenya was a 'white man's country'. He was especially attracted to the Kenyan highland which suggests that European settlers were especially drawn to landscapes that evoked a certain familiarity. To some degree, our experience of landscape is always constructed. Landscape painting plays a key role in this context. An idyllic landscape is recognised as such not necessarily because it is particularly idyllic but because it looks like what we have learned to identify as an idyllic landscape.

ZB Lord Delamere was leased thousands of hectares of land which to do so had to be taken away from the Africans. This is beautiful land which creates a curious paradox when we look at it from today's vantage point in relation to its history. For me this creates a particular conundrum: how can we talk about landscape and Africa without it becoming clichéd?

ABH Does this mean that for *Out of Blue* and for your next film to be shot in Zanzibar you are looking at the history of how the African landscape had been portrayed and described by the first generation of colonial occupants?

ZB As part of my research in East Africa I want to spend some time in a place where the British historically had to grant permission to visit. This restricted access to Africans left the land almost untouched. I want to visit these places and make sense of how to film there. I want to test the feelings and emotions I have from the painterly quality of the landscape. That said, I am just as interested in understanding what 'Englishness' is through the role of the missionaries and the history of the 500 km-long Kenyan railway.

ABH One of your earlier works in the exhibition, *Cleaning the Garden* (1998; p.61) specifically references the English obsession with gardening. The preoccupation with creating ideal landscapes by great eighteenth-century gardeners such as Capability Brown is a particular English expression of Enlightenment culture. Their gardens pretend to look natural but are in fact carefully manufactured.

ZB The idea for *Cleaning the Garden* developed when I was commissioned by Photo 98 to make a work for Harewood House, a stately home near Leeds. I decided to look at the traditions and histories of both Islamic and English gardens. While working at the house I began to feel like a servant and I decided to inhabit the role. The final work combines eighteenth-century adverts from English newspapers offering a reward for the return of escaped servant boys engraved onto mirrors with photographs and lightboxes, which in turn show the gardens of Harewood House and the Islamic gardens of the Alhambra in Granada, Spain. Text, typeface and texture are as carefully considered as the images. I started to use pomegranate, pubic hair, saffron and chiffon fabric to explore desire and pleasure.

KB *1822–Now* (1993; p.71) also functions as an installation though it tackles a very different set of ideas. Like *Cleaning the*

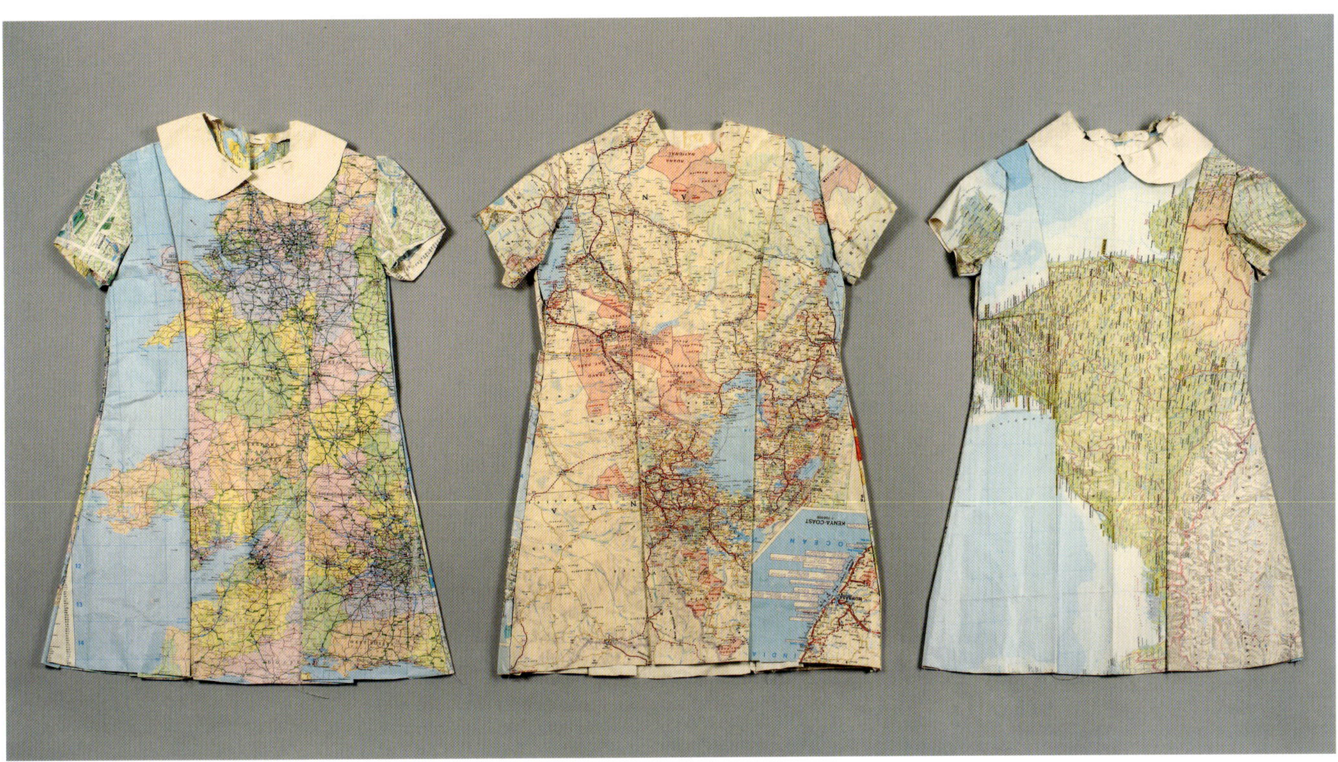

Untitled (A Sketch), 1999, dresses made out of maps of the United Kingdom, East Africa and India, 93.5 × 182 cm | 36 ⅘ × 71 ⅗ in (framed)

Garden and much of your earlier work, it was the result of a residency. Can you tell us a little more about this project?

ZB This installation resulted from my residency at Kettle's Yard in Cambridge in 1993. I looked at the theories of eugenics from a combination of personal experiences and observations such as hostility towards mixed-race relationships, schooling and schoolchildren in Antwerp, where the work was eventually shown. I asked people to sit for me for half an hour to create long exposure photographs using a 5 × 4 camera. I hoped the dissolved and blurred image would attempt to erase any generalised preconception about genetic predictability. I wanted the photographs to look like paintings. In my early work, with regard to the medium of photography, I used various toning techniques, copper, selenium, lightboxes.

KB *1822 – Now* creates a type of interior. In many of your other works such as *Out of Blue* there is a certain polarity between the landscape and all these enclosed spaces through which the camera is moving. *Waiting* (2007; p.99) also focuses on a building and something that is happening inside it, as do many of the photographs from the *Love* series (1998–2007; p.87).

ABH It is a very symbiotic relationship though because exterior and interior are filmed in the same register. How would you describe the dynamic between landscape and architecture in your work?

ZB It is difficult to categorise these spaces, I do not have a precise order, more a chaotic order, if such a thing is possible. I move in and out of spaces quite fluidly which is probably why exterior and interior can be read similarly. The composition, selecting what lens might be used, how much to show or not to show, is very instinctive for me both in architecture and landscape. The play between the lenses to make particular things more monumental versus making an everyday view excites me. All of these spaces have to come together and feel part of the same overall structure. For example, when we were filming the water scenes, a lot of the boats felt very object-like and

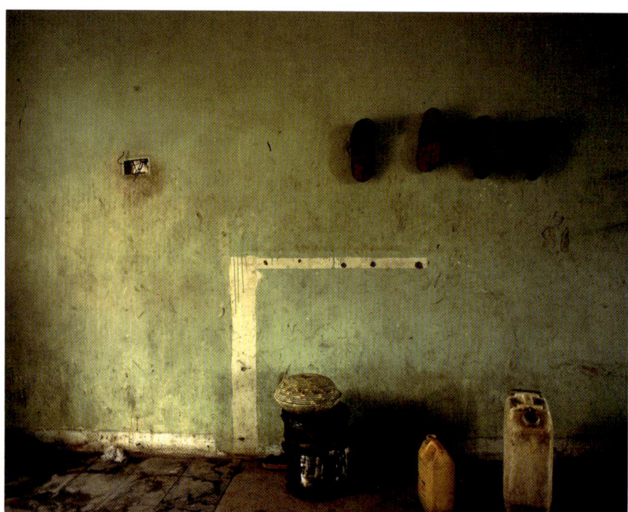

Memories Were Trapped Inside the Asphalt, 1998–2003, transparency lightbox, 130 × 170 × 12.5 cm | 51⅕ × 67 × 5 in

sculptural. Sculpture can often be about inside and outside space at the same time, and I felt that at the point where the boats were becoming almost sculptural. At the same time, I of course also differentiate between interior and exterior spaces, but it is hard to separate them out. I will think about this question next time I film and maybe I will understand it more!

ABH Do you experience both the landscape and the buildings as something that inevitably will have to be left behind? *Out of Blue*, for instance, ends with the image of a plane taking off from Entebbe airport which is from where most of the Indians displaced from Uganda departed in the 1970s.

ZB No, I don't. The airport scene was motivated by my response to a certain set of tonal values. When we were filming at the airport I saw some swallows flying against the blue sky and somehow they made me think of Mark Rothko's colour field paintings. This had not been part of the original script but I thought to myself, let's film this. For me, it is very exciting to bring this idea of Africa and of painting together in one moment.

ABH In *Yellow Patch*, the panoramic shots of deserted landscapes and abandoned houses create a strong sense of absence, the rear view of the elderly woman on a swing being a rare exception.

ZB I am very wary of including people in my films. I don't actual see her as a person, for me the focus is largely on the shape of her hair.

KB Is this because including people might divert the viewer? The dynamic is different if the spaces are empty. There is nobody there who can bar the viewer's access to the space you show.

ZB I could give you theories about it, however, that is not really what it is about. It is about these particular spaces, rather than about individuals, about form and sculpture, about making the work in one place and then projecting it somewhere completely different in a very different spatial situation. I purposefully show my films as installations in gallery spaces and not in cinemas, because of the possibilities this dislocation opens up. A large picture projection is a necessity as the work is about physical sensations. It is not about capturing an existing thing or moment; it is about creating something new. I play back sound at normal speed and at slower speeds to reveal sound echo, the reverberation of voice and the human body. Sound is part of the narrative.

KB On the one hand, your camera work is very formal: beautiful, balanced and highly aestheticised; on the other hand, it feels like a subjective camera, like a first-person view. How do you experience the process of filming?

ZB The way I work is that I like to get to know a place quite well before I go to film it. In 2008, for instance, on a two month-long reconnaissance trip in India I spent a lot of time getting to know the people related to particular places, as well as the quality of light and other details of specific spaces. Both the people and the spaces have become my friends by the time I get to the actual filming, I have lived with them in my studio for years. I am moved by their knowledge and the generosity with which they share this with me. These people and places become my open-air studio. On these trips, I spend a lot of time taking Polaroids that I use as sketches. I have to live with these images, listening to them, feeling them before I film.

KB Listening to them?

ZB Listening to them, yes; to test what a picture feels like the moment you have taken it. It is like when you walk into a room, you can listen to a room, can you not? I like to be on my own with the Polaroids, which is why I do not take an assistant with me. So, the film gets built as I go along: doing the research is a way of finding the right places. I search through books and photocopy images, and think to myself: 'Oh, I would love to find a place like this'; but then I take the picture and see if there is something else that might come out of it.

ABH These places you describe could be called 'found places' in the sense of the 'found object' as described by the Surrealists, this object you accidentally chance upon and which then triggers a series of memories and associations, Proust's famous Madeleine being the prime example. You seem to recognise something in these places which not even you can identify exactly. These found places are then being reworked into this carefully choreographed narrative. There is a curious dynamic between what is within and what is outside your control.

ZB I agree. For example, there is a temple we filmed which is over 1,000 years old. The Director of Photography was advising that I shot some of the things that were very typical of the temple, but I did not want them. I was very insistent on what type of light I wanted throughout the film. I wanted a lot of it in the water scenes. However, anything exterior I wanted to be filmed at dusk or dawn. I wanted soft buttery light with pinky glows. I wanted it to look not like the India you know because it is not about India. The light is a metaphor for grief.

ABH What motivates this grief?

ZB Although I have relatives in India, because of the long migration period, it takes time to relate. That is what is sad; you can never really go back. Migration is about having to abandon family and friends. I wonder whether it is both, the one who leaves and the one who is left behind, who die? Separation causes rupture and cultural inheritance is being questioned. The loss of this attachment may awaken anxiety; the new environment may be hostile and therefore assimilation not straightforward. Refugees are forced by circumstance to leave their country with returning home often out of question due to political reasons. This brings isolation and loneliness, and results in a complex process of mourning. Culture, language, place and experience become mixed up or superimposed onto one another.

KB When does a location feel right? Is this to do with the atmosphere and the sound which you listen to?

ZB I will give you an example from *Waiting*. I take a list of ideas with me when I travel. In a café in Nairobi, I started talking to a man who knew the manager of a nearby sisal factory. The moment I walked into the factory I knew that this was one of the locations for filming. I still have the photographs.

KB It looks like a sketch for the whole film.

ZB I like it because it feels like a cradle, hair in a cradle and lots of cradles, a bit like the aftermath of a snow fight. In a way, it is a very instinctive language. I find it beautiful, the way it is just blown in the air like cotton.

KB First, it is the pure pleasure of the image and its textural quality?

ZB Yes, which is not to say that I am not interested in the politics behind the image. Months later when I returned back to my studio I discovered that I needed to understand the colonial economy better. I wanted to engage with what it could be like to be a young African boy in a colonial situation. The sisal looks like a European man's hair cut up. I found this place very atmospheric.

KB I am interested in the politics of perception, and the way perception opens up a road to knowledge and to understanding the world. Politics and visual sensuality are often falsely portrayed as polar opposites whereas I would like to rephrase this dynamic. For me, it is not about everyday politics but about what we present in a gallery to create an aesthetic experience which reflects on a life experience. This, for me, is what makes political art.

ZB I agree. This is why I am resistant to *Yellow Patch* being described as a film about migration, because there are many facets to it.

ABH I was fascinated to learn that the visual element of the film develops independently from the sound. It is, of course, an integral part of the cinematic experience for eye and ear to register autonomous experiences. Do the sounds you use have anything to do with the sounds you mentioned before in the context of the Polaroids, to your experience of 'listening' to these images?

ZB They can do. I record different types of sound when I travel, either with my HD camera or my iPhone. In the case of *Yellow Patch*, I recorded specific sounds that it might be hard to find here: peacocks, particular pigeons, the sound of boats, markets.

The sound evolves independently though. For instance, I cannot think about the soundtrack while editing the visual footage for *Yellow Patch*. I love working with a mute picture first.

ABH ...which means that the final film consists of two independent, yet closely related narratives.

ZB Yes. Once I am happy with the full edit of the images, I will sit down and write the sound script.

KB Sound recordings by Abida Parveen appear both in *Yellow Patch* and *Out of Blue*.

ZB Yes, Abida Parveen sings love songs written in a poetic form called *ghazal*, which consist of rhyming couplets and a refrain. She sings in Urdu, Sindhi, Saraiki, Punjabi and Persian. Her music is very tender and beautiful, describing surrender in love. It is unusual for Sufi poems to be recited by a woman and she has a powerful voice. Her voice is magical, spiritual and beyond words. It is a different place to rest in.

ABH Much of the sound is recorded independently and becomes integrated only at a later stage. This strategy of displacement, of taking something out of one context and putting it into another is a classic twentieth-century aesthetic strategy...

ZB I recorded mosquitoes without knowing why, just because the sound they made struck me as beautiful. When you hear it really loud, it is like a musical score. By removing a particular sound from its context and taking it elsewhere it almost becomes an inverted sculpture.

ABH You first adopted these particular strategies of filmmaking in *Out of Blue* which in terms of its language and ambition marks such a departure from your earlier work. What motivated this dramatic shift? Was it a difficult film to make?

ZB It seemed a natural evolution for me to work in film. That said, working in 35 mm film, away from home, of course, adds a lot of complexity.

KB Did your family or friends ever talk about the events of 1972 and the expulsion of all South Asians from Uganda under Idi Amin? I am asking because sometimes these things become a taboo shrouded in a tacit agreement not to mention them, what Freud described as the thing you cannot grasp yet which continues to haunt you throughout your life.

ZB I don't remember, though I assume that they must have been talked about. I certainly never thought of the subject as a taboo.

ABH Given your own background, what is your vantage point on these events now?

ZB It is really important to me not to give preference to either the Indians or the Africans or the British. I want everybody to be able to participate in the work. No one is privileged.

Also, Africa is always portrayed in this very brutal way in the newspapers. For me it is different. It is where I was brought up and I did not see it like that. I remember running around in forests with African kids and seeing all these colourful insects and butterflies; I love the place. I feel it is where I experienced both tenderness and betrayal.

ABH This is interesting, because this is precisely the problem with most historic narratives that they usually tend to privilege one voice. It is either spoken from the vantage point of the coloniser or the colonised.

KB Which is why I feel it is so important that you used a first-person camera so that the gaze is not positioned; it could be African, Indian or European.

ZB Yes.

ABH You spend much time and effort on securing permissions to film in often rather inaccessible places. This part of the project is only indirectly visible though it seems an important part of the process.

ZB It is a hugely important to my way of making art that I work outside the studio. For *Yellow Patch*, for instance, we gained access to the Port of Bombay even though security at the moment is very tight. Going out and talking to people generates another kind of conversation.

ABH What is the relationship between your film and the still photographs? You mentioned the Polaroids, the storyboards and the many pictures you take on your research trips. Yet it is often only after the film, during the research, for which these images were taken, that a small selection of them is released into the world as autonomous works or parts of a series such as *Love*.

ZB Everything starts as research. I always start with Polaroids, they have this smoky painterly feel to them and I like them as objects. I use them as a way of working out composition and lighting, and also as a record. I take digital pictures which work on a number of levels. I shoot things which I want to know more about as well as things that are more strongly related to film. Digital is far more instant than Polaroid. When I return to my studio some of these images are collated into storyboards. Then I spend time taking out anything that is superfluous to arrive at a precise contained form. At this point, I also record sounds that work like sketches. Some of the Polaroids, which are shot with a medium format camera, eventually become works in their own right. Some images work better as still photographs rather than film, and the other way around. I am interested in both forms.

KB Just as in your earlier photographs you always retain a strong sense of composition. Would you say that in all your work the formal elements are carefully controlled?

ZB Not completely, some are more instinctual and some are found. I respond to what feels right when I look through the lens.

KB So you recreate a memory from the images you first take in the run-up to the films; or maybe not a real memory, but rather a fictionalised memory because this memory never existed in the first instance?

ZB Yes.

ABH Before you started work on *Out of Blue*, did you see other film works which you found particularly inspiring?

ZB When I was trying to work out how to film the landscape shot, somebody suggested that I watch Terrence Malik's film, *The Thin Red Line*. I was also really interested in Iranian cinema like the films by the Makhmalbaf family, all of whom, including a girl of 15, make films. I also love *Pakeezah* and *Mughal-E-Azam* and directors such as Bimal Roy, Andrei Tarkovsky, and Jane Campion.

KB How did you decide on the title which inevitably recalls the idiom 'out of the blue'?

ZB The title was inspired by the Gujarati word *dhamal* which means 'a lot of noise'. In 1972, many people referred to the events in Uganda as *dhamal*. Hence I wanted to use this word. Indians often do not use the definitive article, so 'out of the blue' became 'out of blue'. The Gujarati is the title, the English the subtitle, and not least by way how the titles are visually arranged I wanted to make sure that people look at the work from that position. I used a similar strategy for *Yellow Patch*.

ABH Colours appear again and again in the titles of your works: *Out of Blue*, *Yellow Patch*, *Red & Wet*. In earlier conversations you have often alluded to painting as a reference for your films.

ZB Colour is important at all stages of the process. It is also true that I do love painting, I love the work of Vija Celmins, Caspar David Friedrich, Constable, the list goes on and on. There is a softness to painting that I respond to strongly.

ABH How would you describe the principal driver for your work? Is it an attempt at trying to understand something?

ZB Perhaps less an attempt at understanding, but at reinventing, reorganising, respeaking or redefining something. Rather than interpreting or documenting history, the emphasis is on creating new images from which different ways of seeing and understanding can emerge.

KB In order to gain access?

ZB It is not driven in that purposeful way.

ABH Is it a process of approximation then? You try to approach this history, which is very difficult to make sense of because it is so contradictory and because it is very difficult to assign responsibilities even though they exist. You try to come near to it by going back to these places, by looking at them, by sharing these places with us. In a way you want to know something, which in that sense of knowing, you actually cannot know. This is precisely where the potential of the aesthetic experience lies, in creating a space where you can intuitively grasp something, which evades the rationale of the single narrative, of saying this is how it was.

ZB Yes, and I like that about making art. I like the fact that you get hold of a bar of soap and then it slips away.

Works

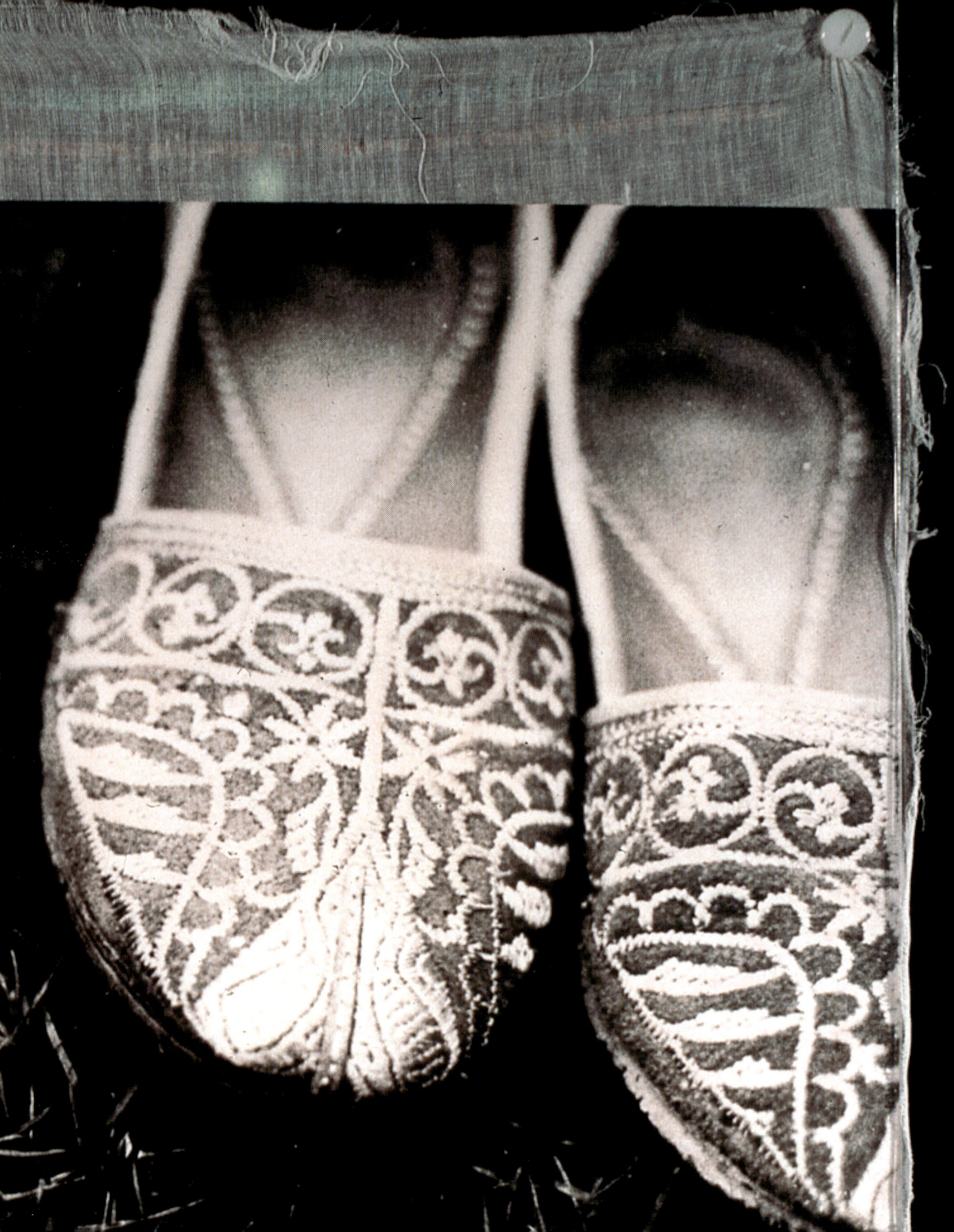

She Loved to Breathe – Pure Silence

This installation consists of eight photographic tinted images which are presented as double-sided pairs sandwiched between sheets of plexiglass and suspended from visible wire in a horizontal line that bisects the gallery space. In addition, one frame contains a pair of latex gloves encased in starched material. A field of turmeric and chilli scattered on the floor underneath adds an element of performance. *She Loved to Breathe – Pure Silence* refers to a scandalous chapter in British immigration history in which Asian women arriving at Heathrow airport in the 1970s were forced to undergo virginity tests at the request of Home Office officials, in order to determine whether they were allowed to enter the country on the grounds of marriage. Challenged by an Indian woman, such tests were subsequently found to be illegal.

She Loved to Breathe – Pure Silence, 1987
Installation consisting of eight hand-coloured gelatin-silver prints; text printed on muslin sandwiched between the photographs; latex gloves; plexiglass; photocopied passports on the muslin; turmeric and chilli powder scattered on the floor
Each image 49.7 × 51 cm | 19½ × 20 in, overall dimensions variable

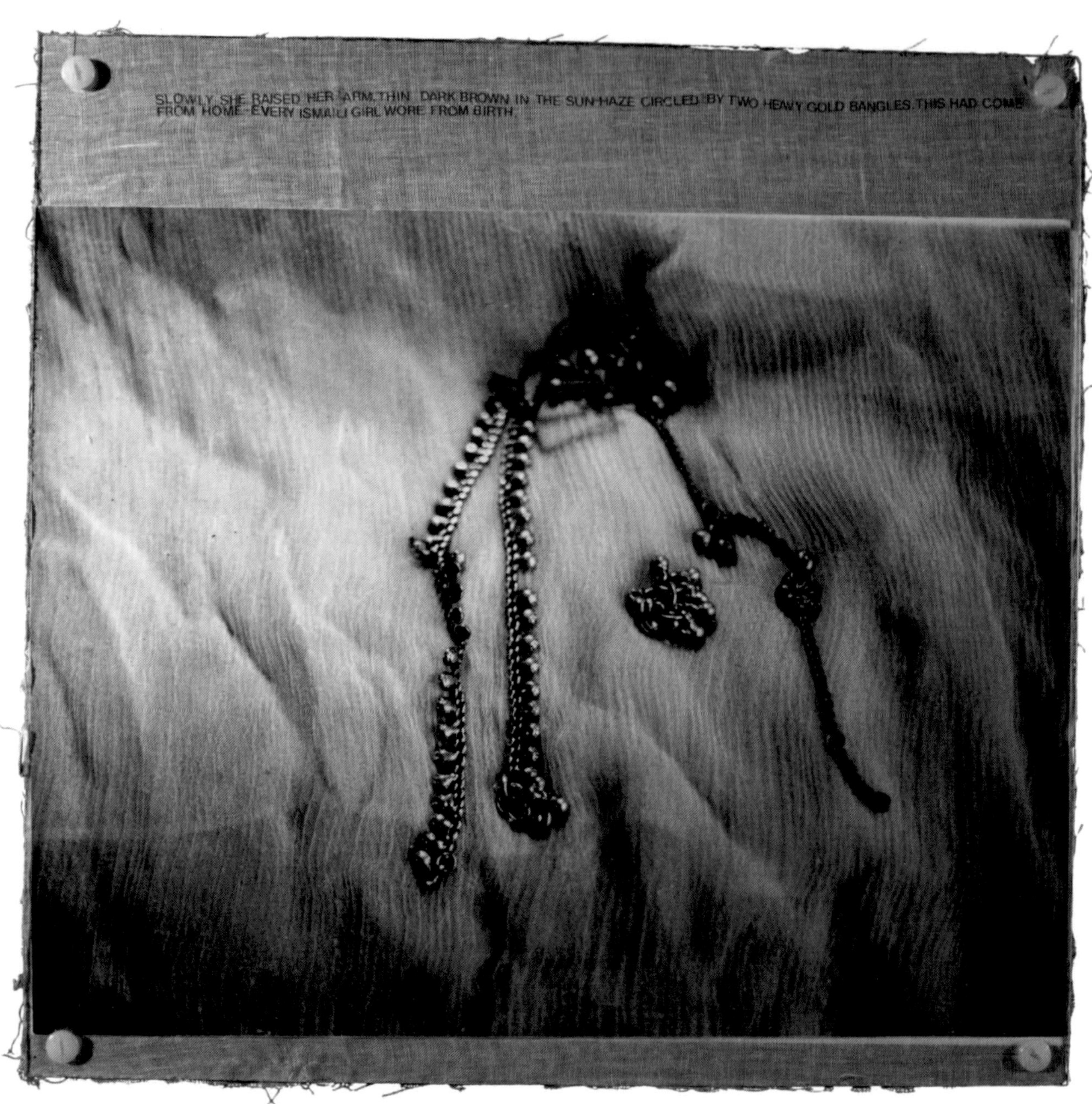
SLOWLY SHE RAISED HER ARM, THIN DARK BROWN IN THE SUN HAZE CIRCLED BY TWO HEAVY GOLD BANGLES. THIS HAD COME
FROM HOME. EVERY ISMAILI GIRL WORE FROM BIRTH.

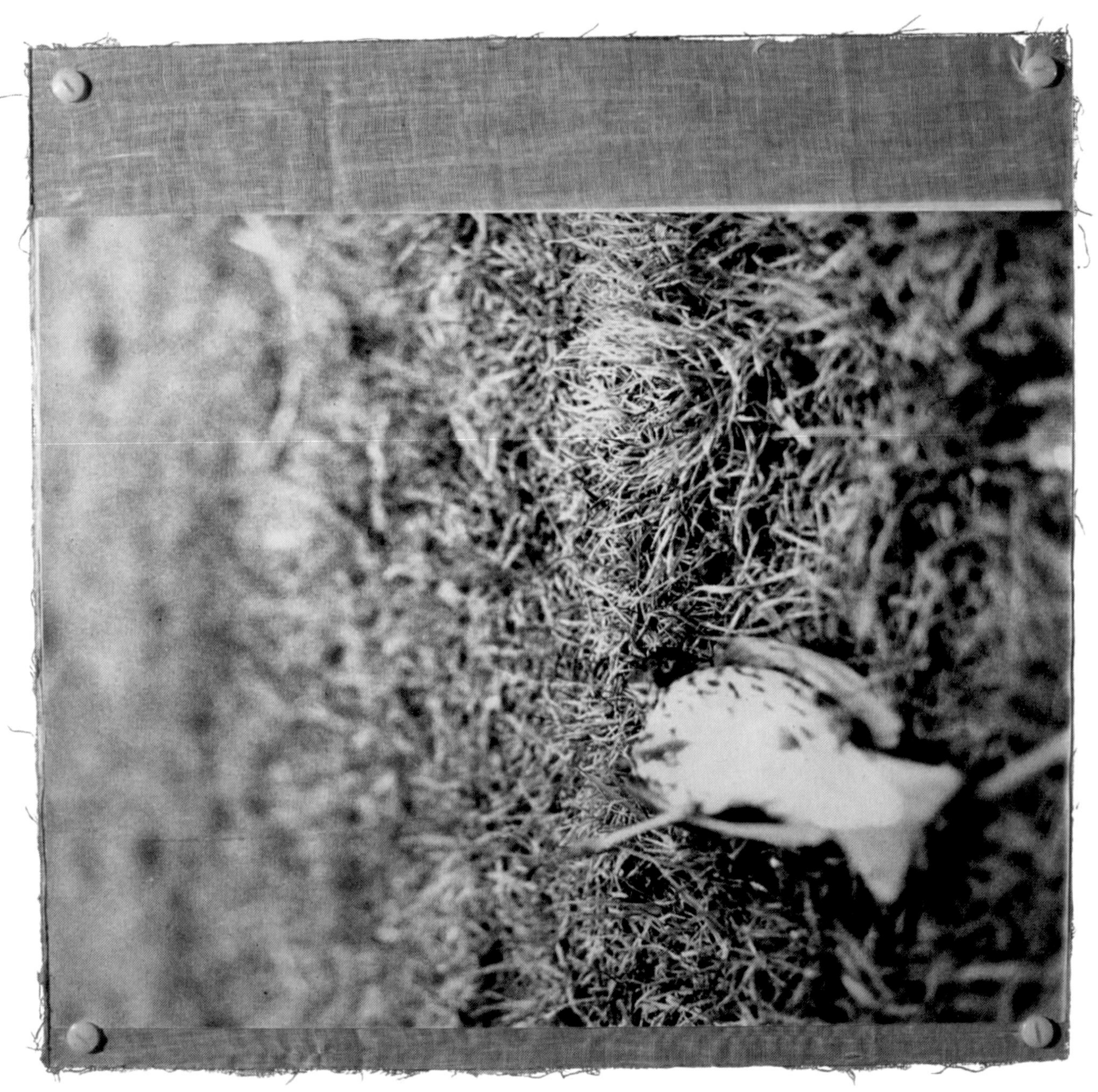

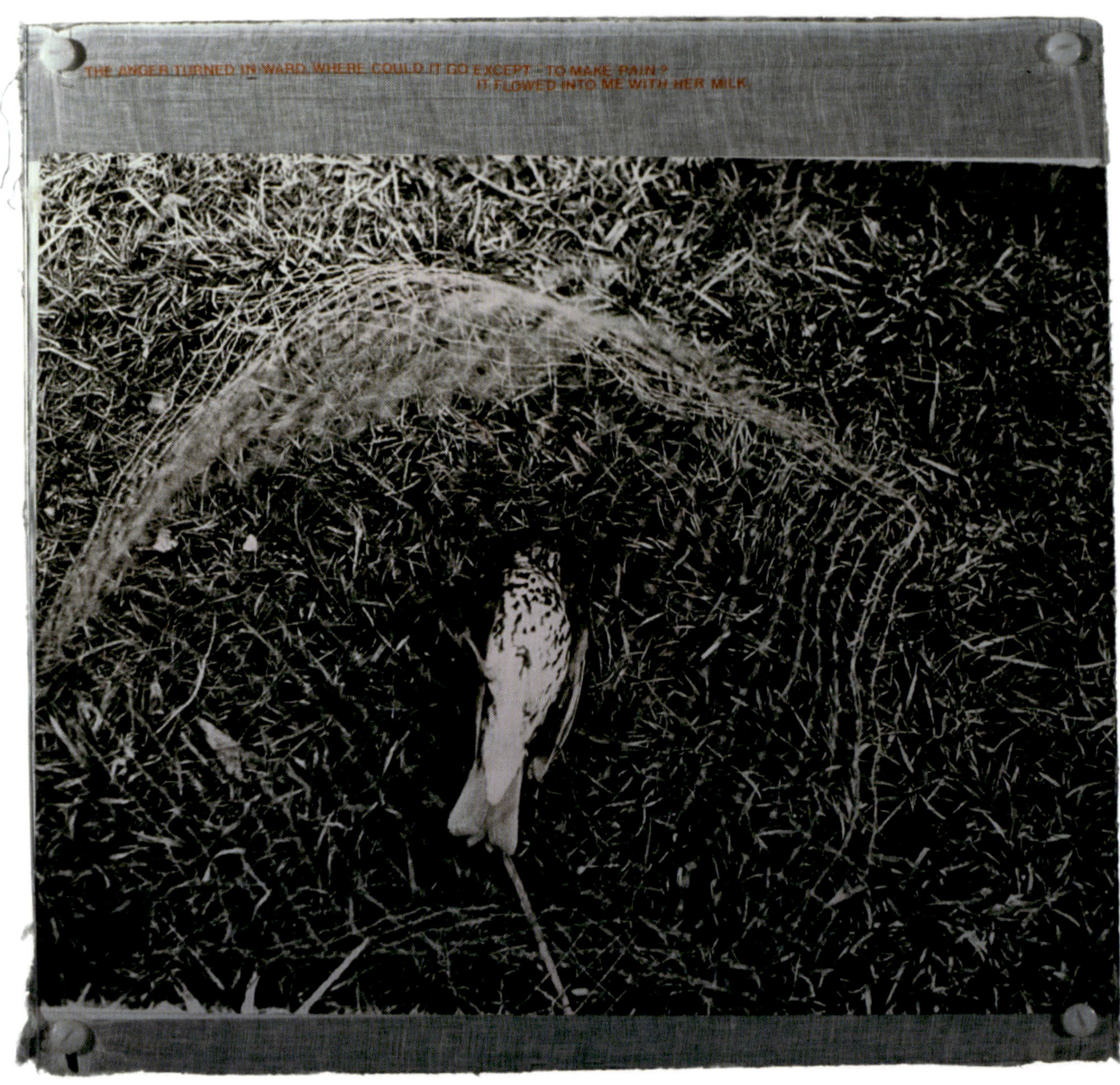
THE ANGER TURNED IN-WARD. WHERE COULD IT GO EXCEPT - TO MAKE PAIN ?
IT FLOWED INTO ME WITH HER MILK

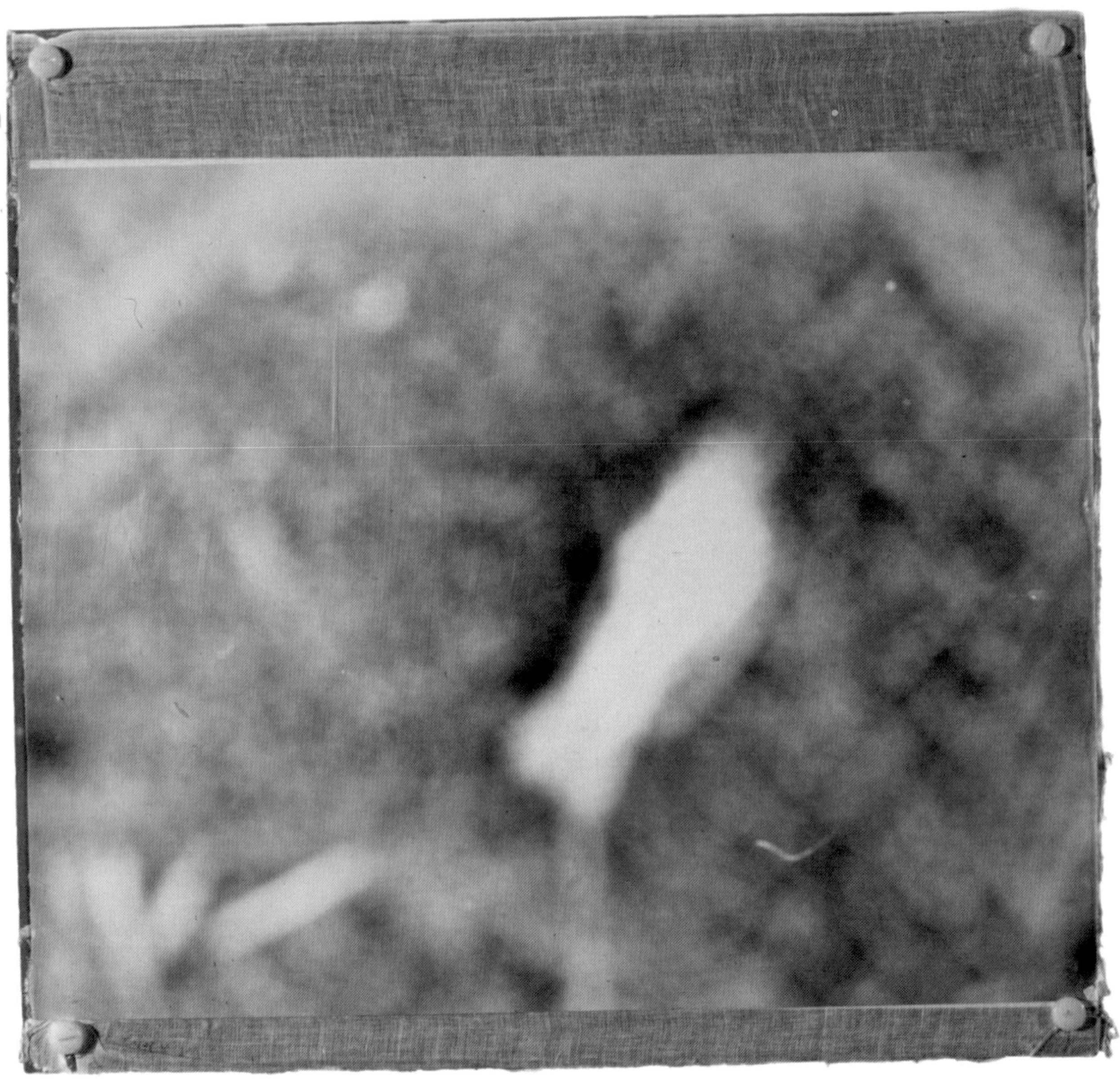

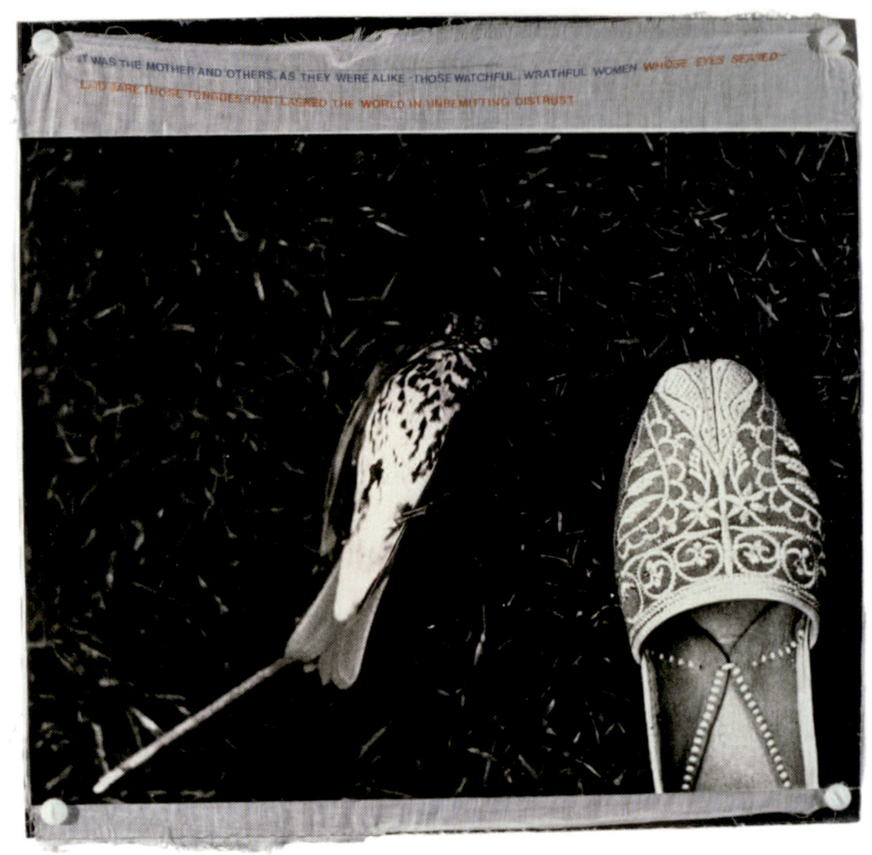
IT WAS THE MOTHER AND OTHERS, AS THEY WERE ALIKE -THOSE WATCHFUL, WRATHFUL WOMEN WHOSE EYES SEARED-
LAID BARE THOSE TONGUES THAT LASHED THE WORLD IN UNREMITTING DISTRUST

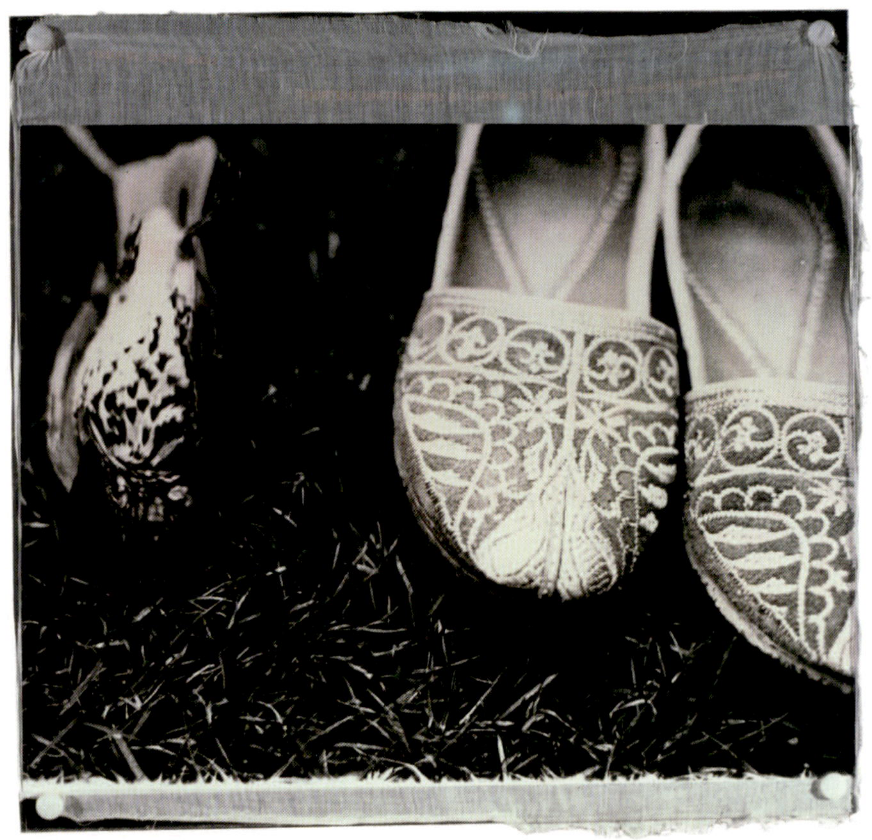

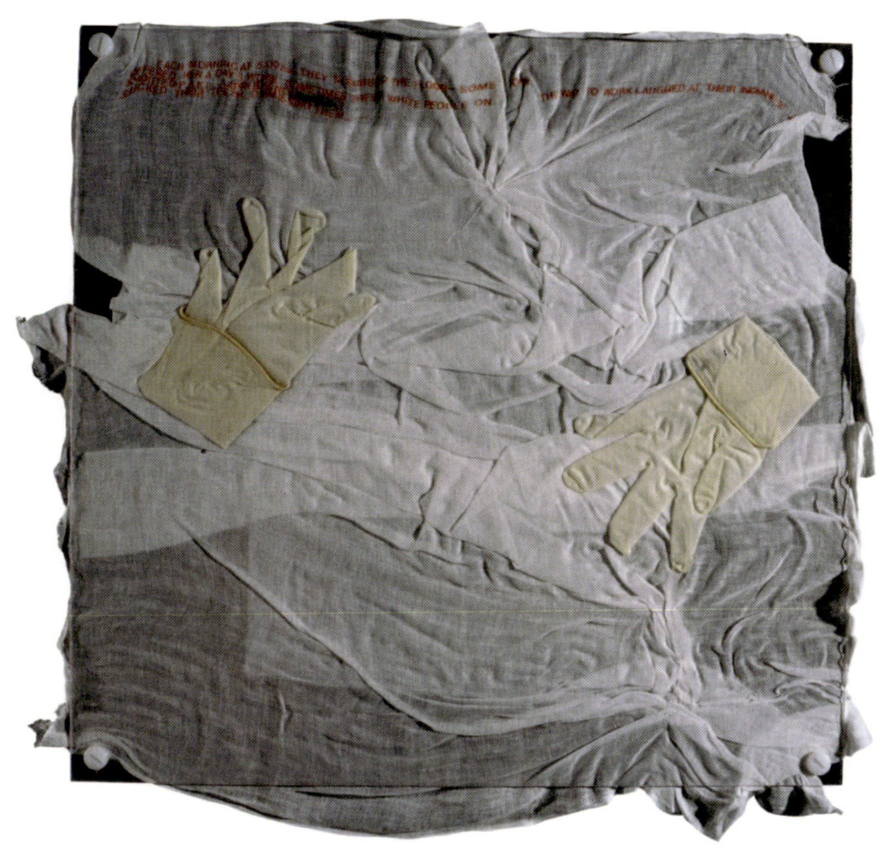

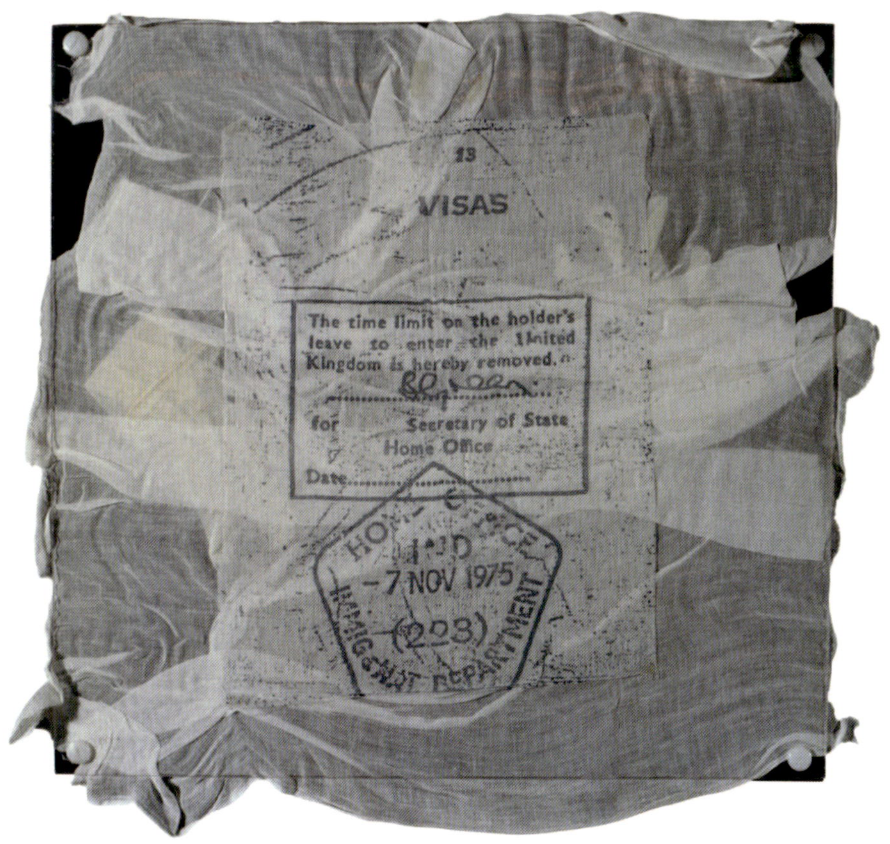
13
VISAS
The time limit on the holder's leave to enter the United Kingdom is hereby removed.
for Secretary of State
Home Office
Date
-7 NOV 1975

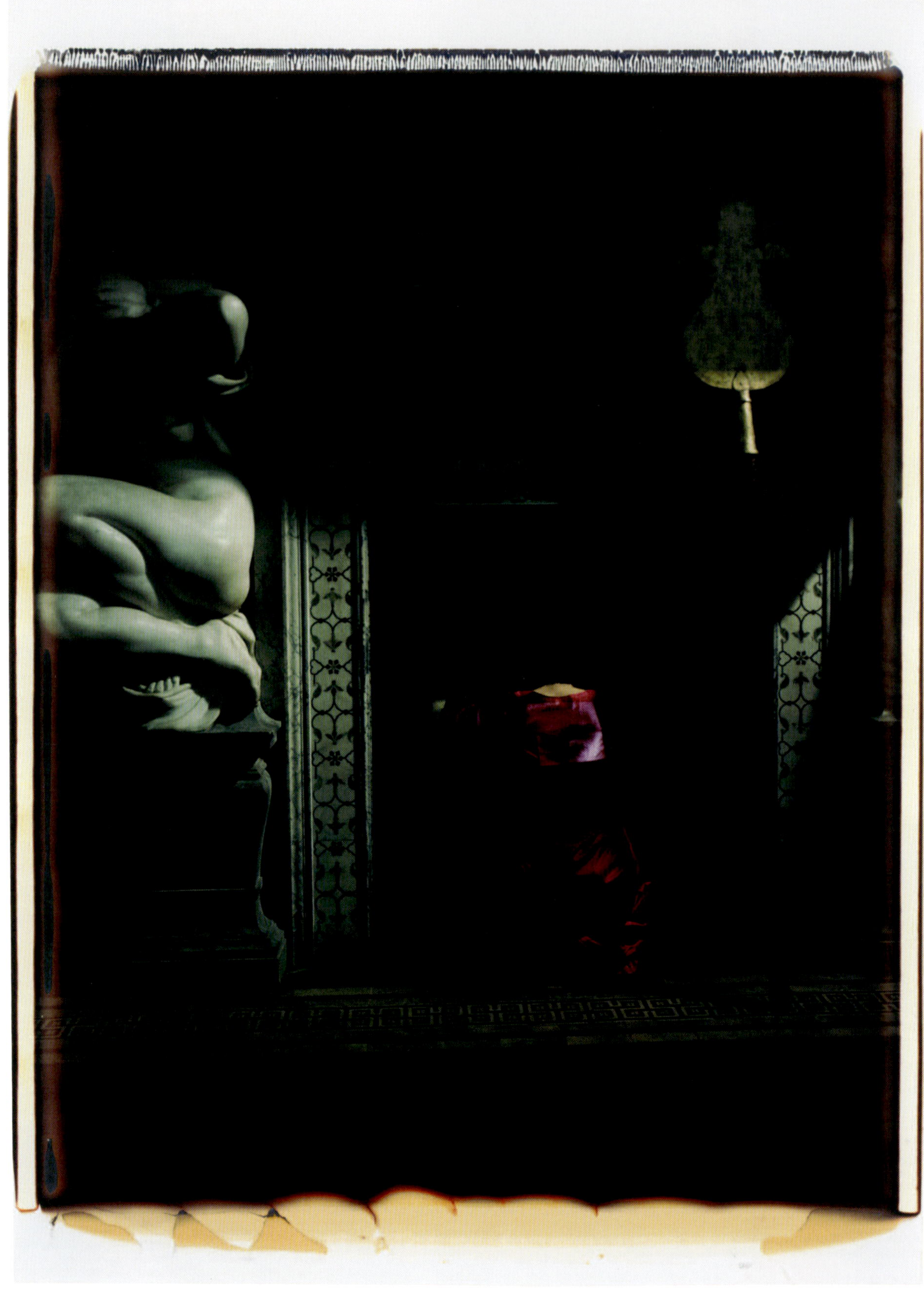

Untitled

This series of large-scale Polaroid photographs are the outcome of a two-day residency at the Victoria & Albert Museum where they were first shown as part of *Photography Now* (1989). Using a rare Polaroid Corporation large-format camera – at the time only two existed in the world – the images focus on the museum's high Victorian architecture including the lavish Gamble Room, in which ornate mirrors extol the values of 'Truth' and marble statues embody late nineteenth-century ideals of 'Beauty'. The images focus upon details such as chiffon, hair, ripped postcards and tulips to evoke a sense of pleasure, exposure and grief. Each photograph is unique and the exposed edge of the Polaroid image forms an integral part of the work.

Untitled, 1989
Polaroid photographs
Each 60 × 50 cm | 23 3/5 × 19 7/10 in

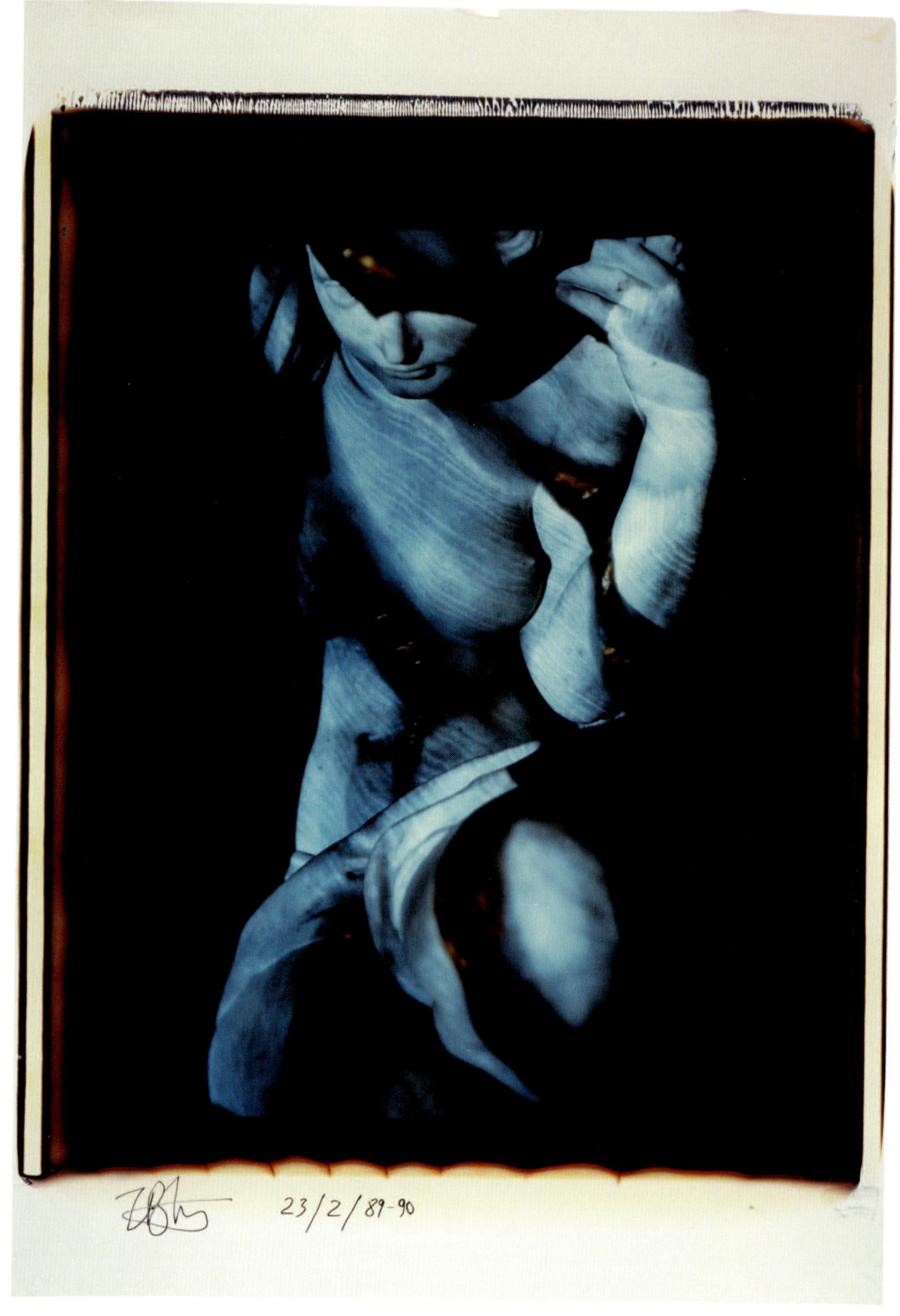
23/2/89-90

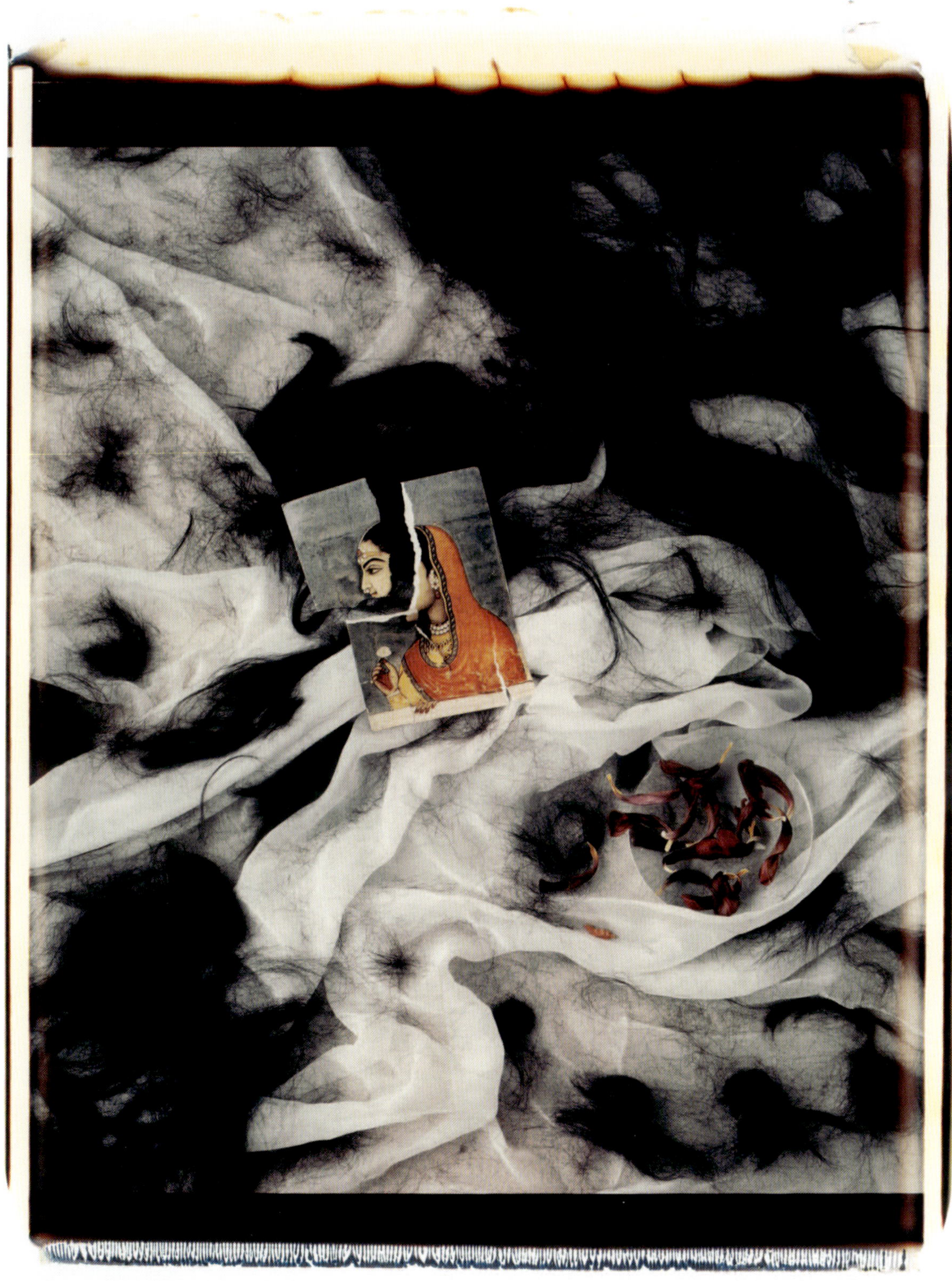

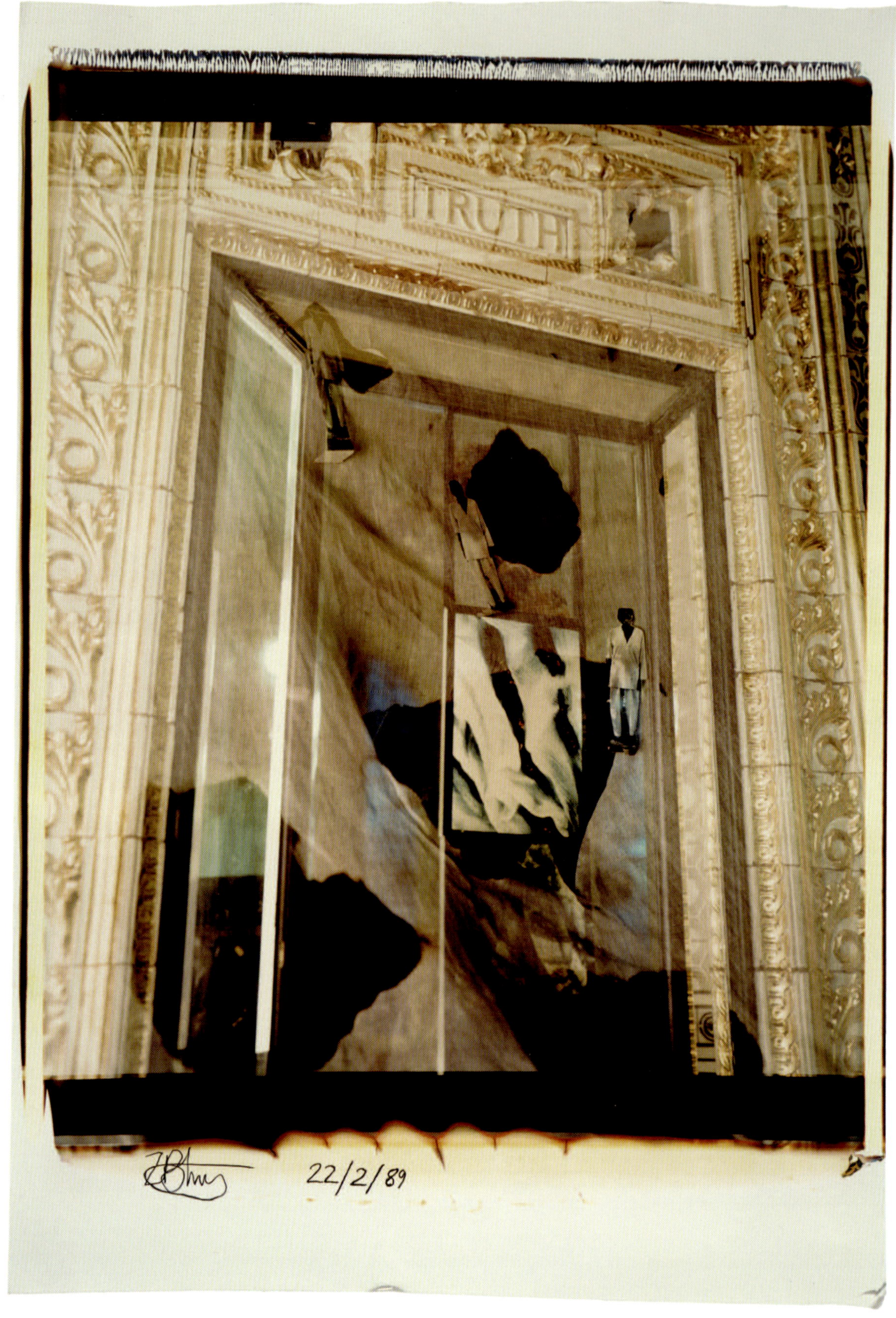
TRUTH
22/2/89

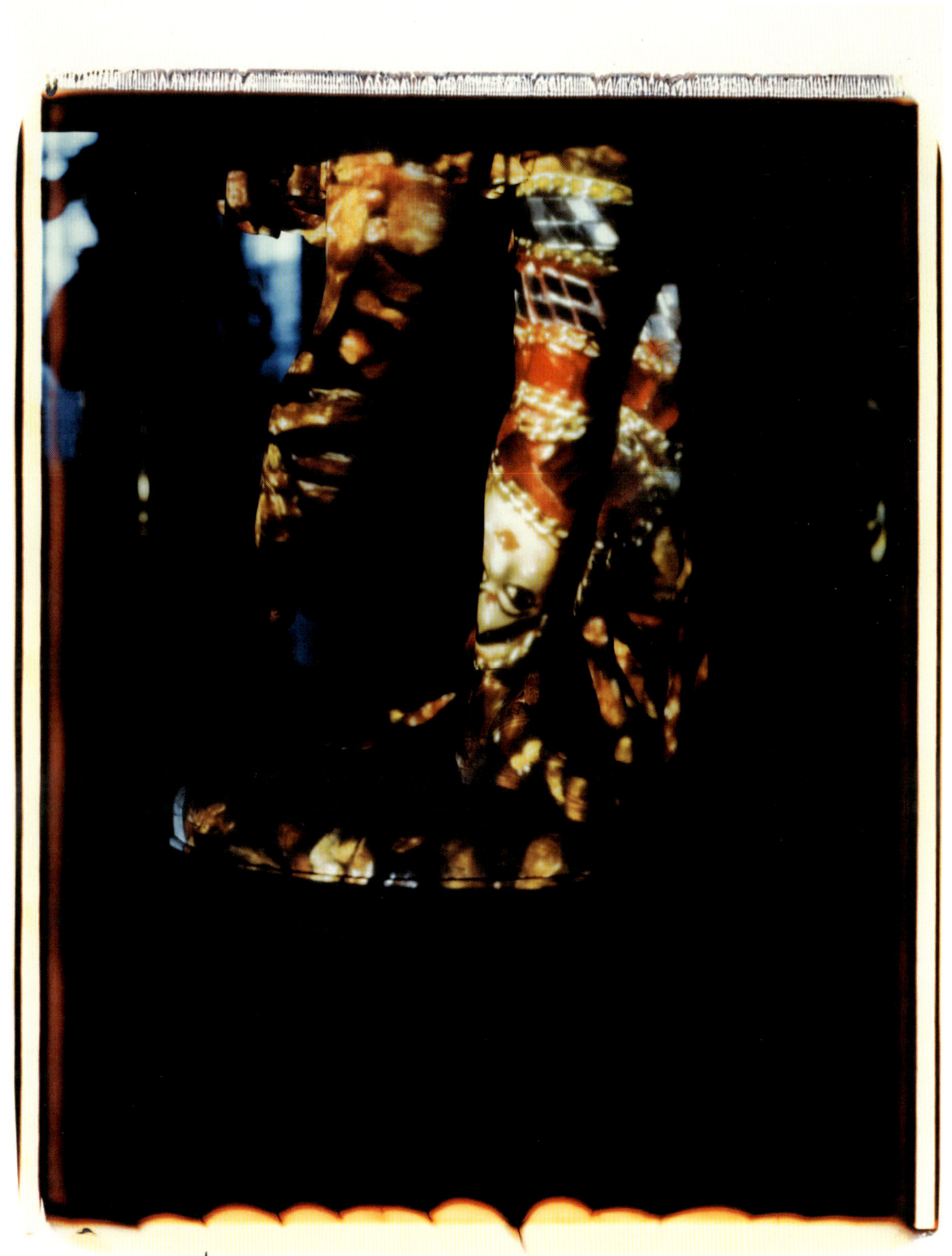

23/2/89

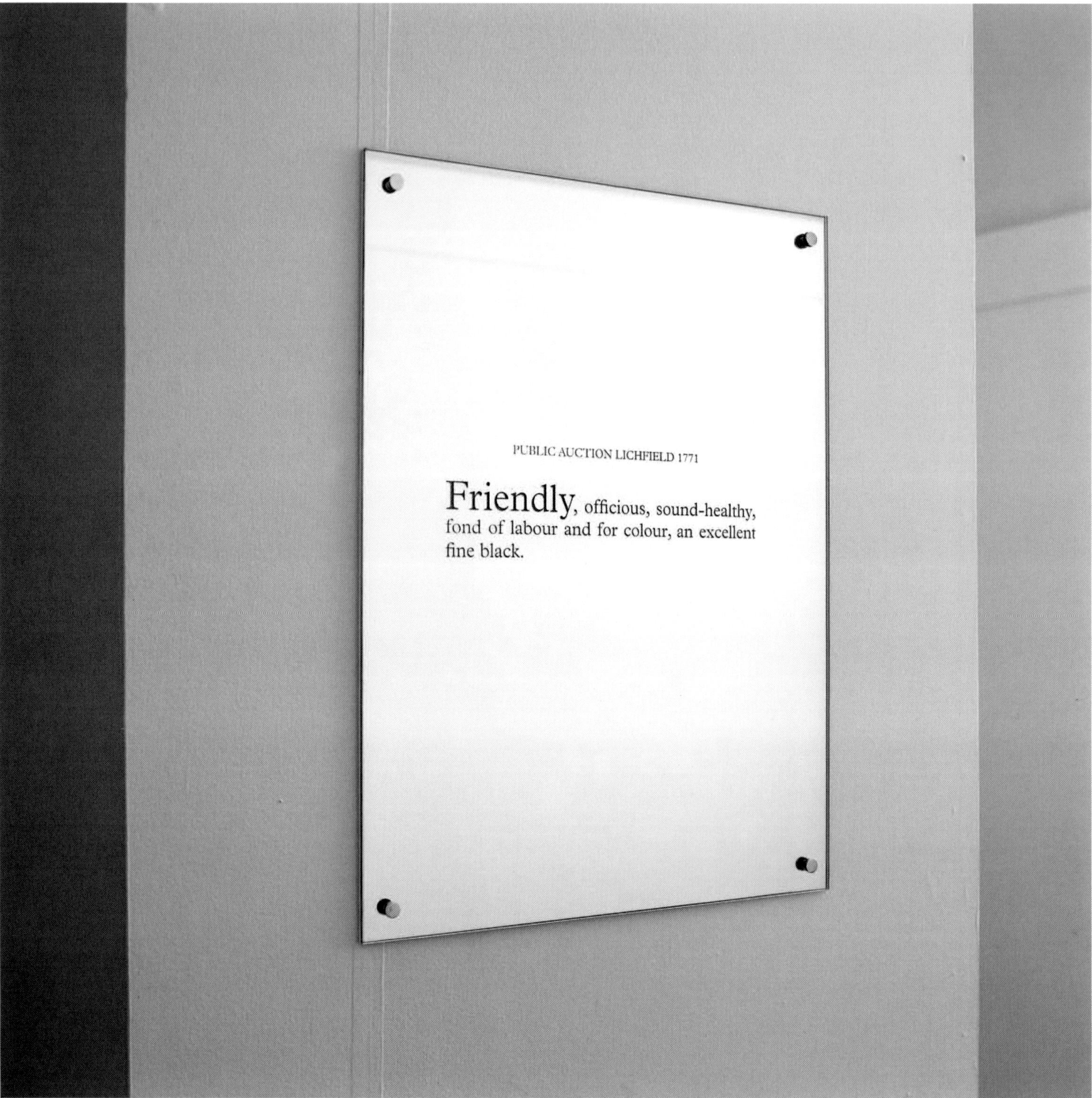

Friendly, 1998

Cleaning the Garden

Cleaning the Garden is an exploration of formal garden traditions in Britain and Spain as cultural metaphors. This series of lightboxes, photographic prints and etched mirrors considers the hidden politics at play behind two different types of gardens. The first shows the grounds of Harewood House, an opulent eighteenth-century stately home near Leeds, UK, built from the wealth generated by sugar plantations and with gardens designed by renowned landscape architect Capability Brown. A series of mirrors etched with the wording of eighteenth-century newspaper advertisements reflects this history. These works are contrasted with images from the Islamic gardens of the Alhambra in Granada, Spain, a palace and fortress built in the fourteenth century by the North African rulers of what was then the 'Emirate of Granada'. The images capture various landscapes from both sites honing in on details such as pomegranates, pollen, furniture, saffron, chiffon and pubic hair. The resulting series is a dual investigation of the ways in which power imprints itself on nature as well as the relationship between sexuality and power.

Cleaning the Garden, 1998
Installation consisting of six Cibachrome transparency lightboxes,
each 88 × 105 × 16 cm | 34⅘ × 41⅓ × 6⅓ in;
four Cibachrome photographs on aluminium,
122.4 × 173.4 cm | 48⅗ × 68 3/10 in and 120.4 × 157.5 | 48⅖ × 62 in
and four etched mirrors, each 61.2 × 51 cm | 24 × 20 in

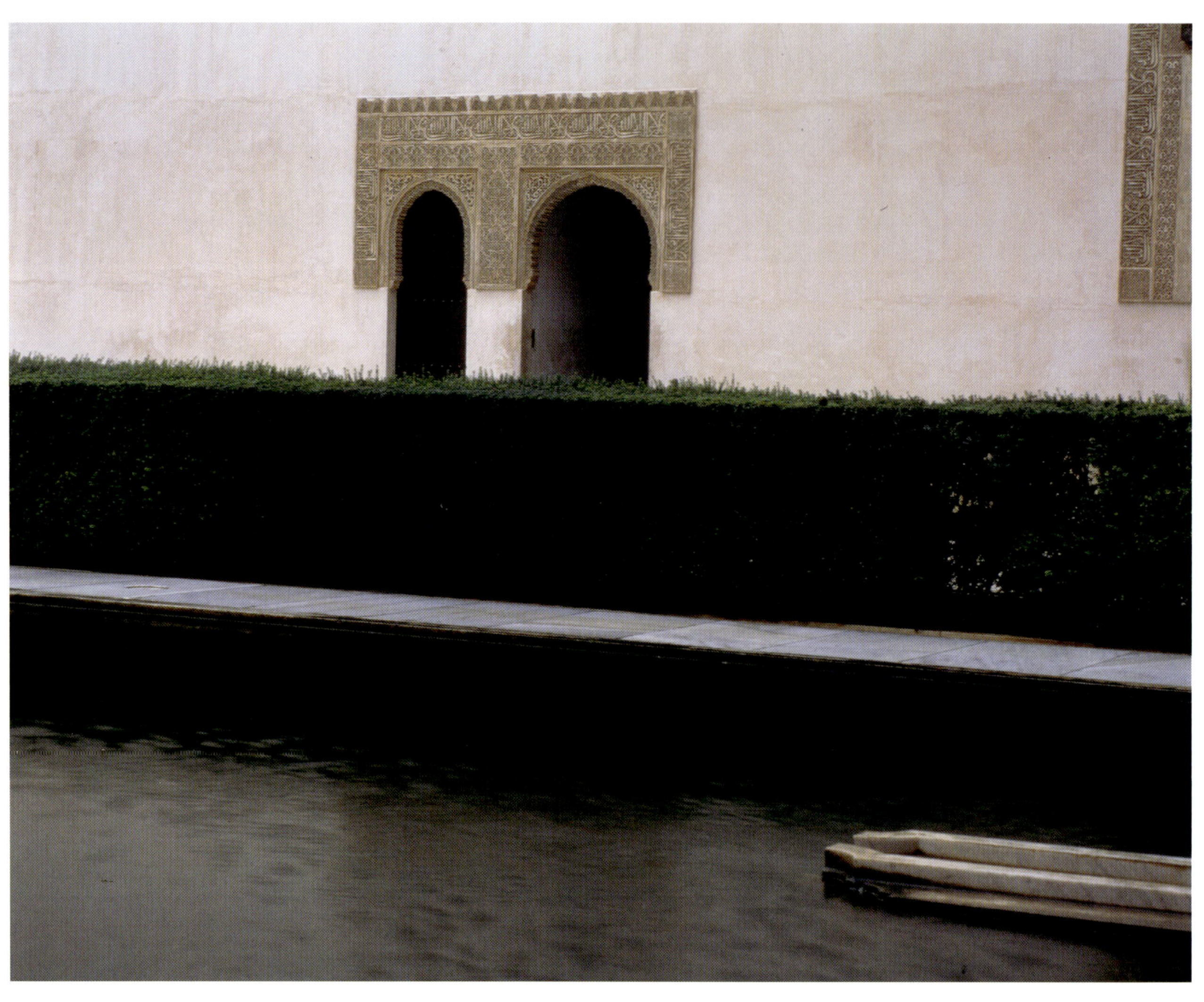

 Alcazar, 1998

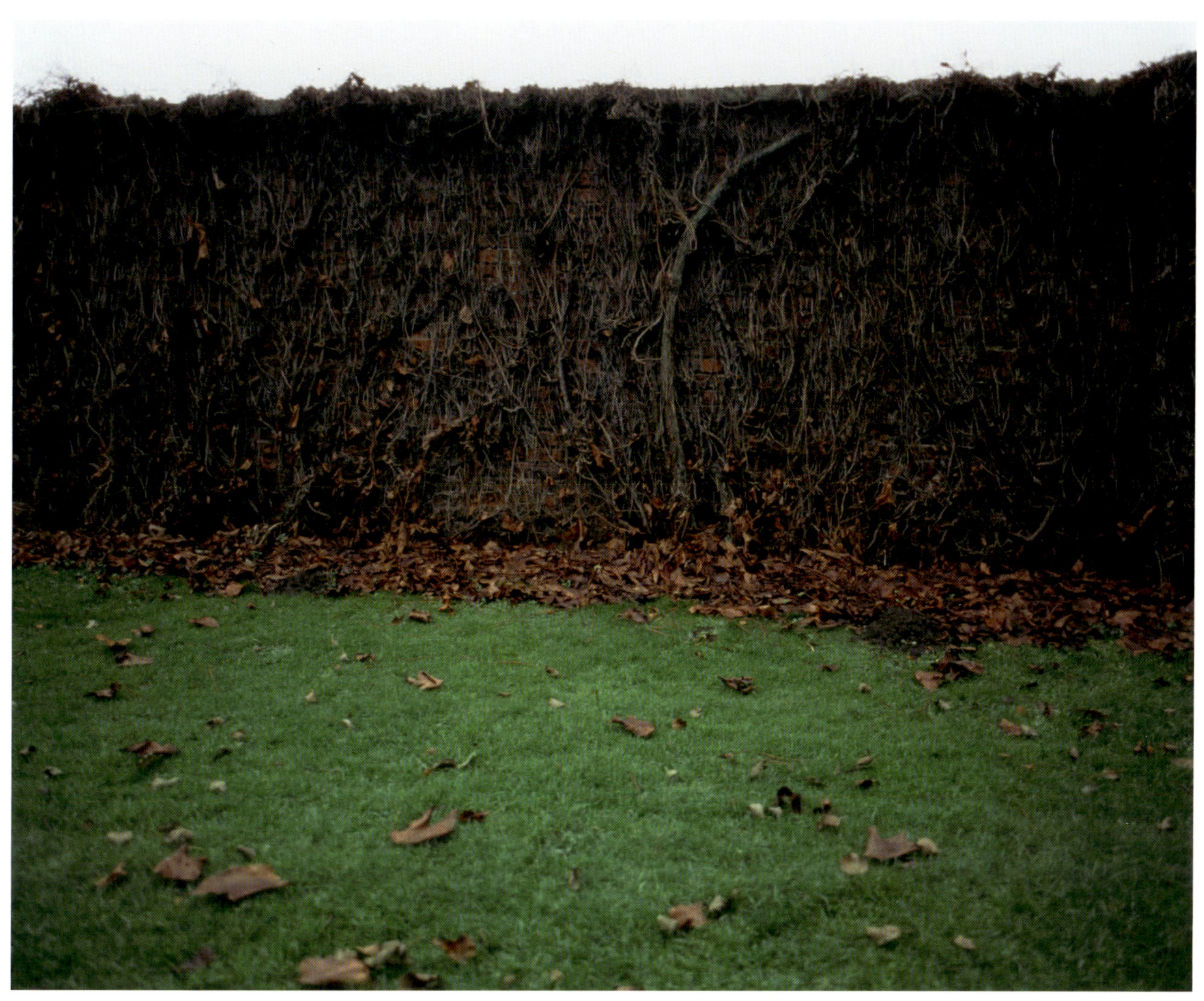

Wallings, 1998

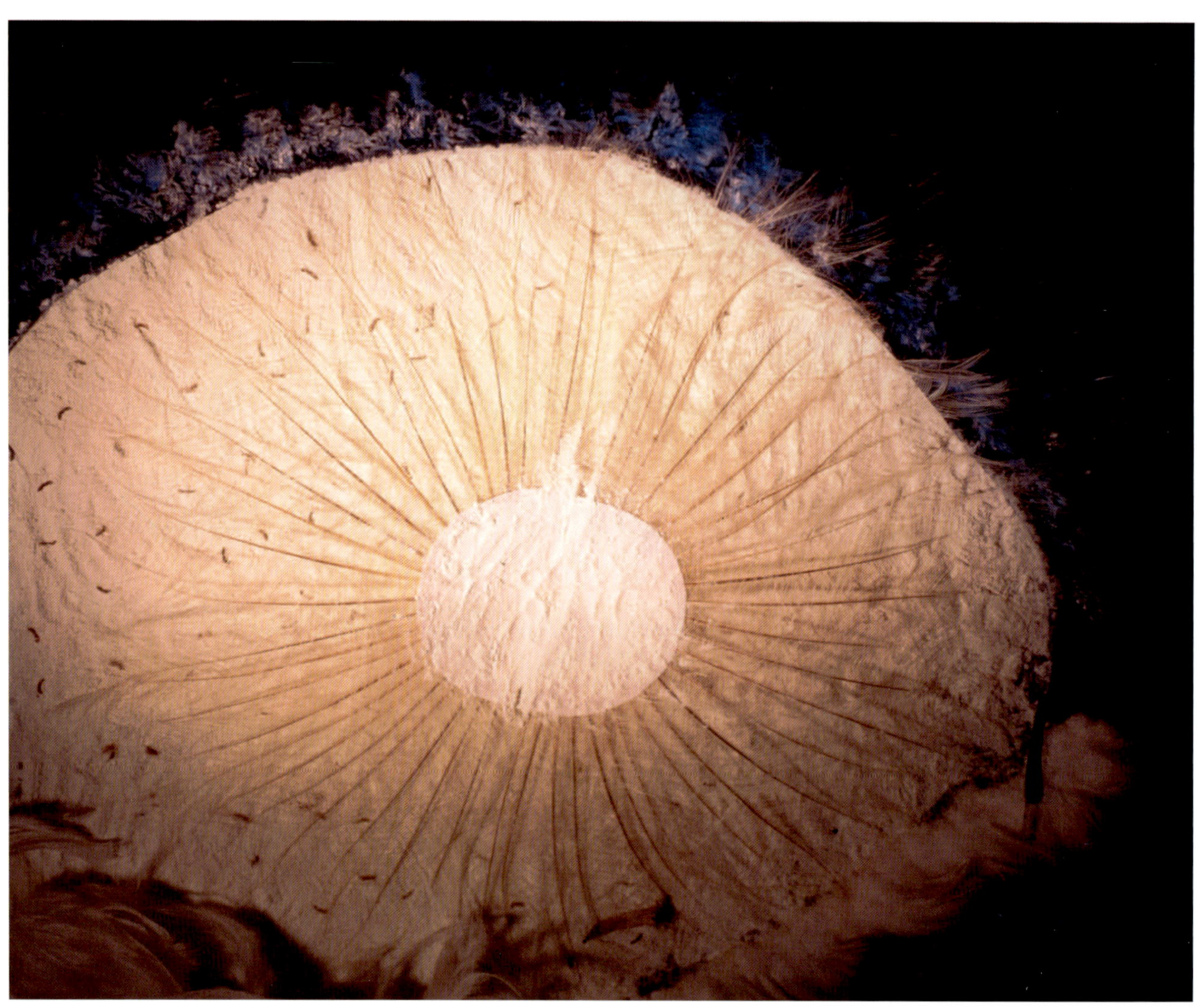

 Something concealed, 1998

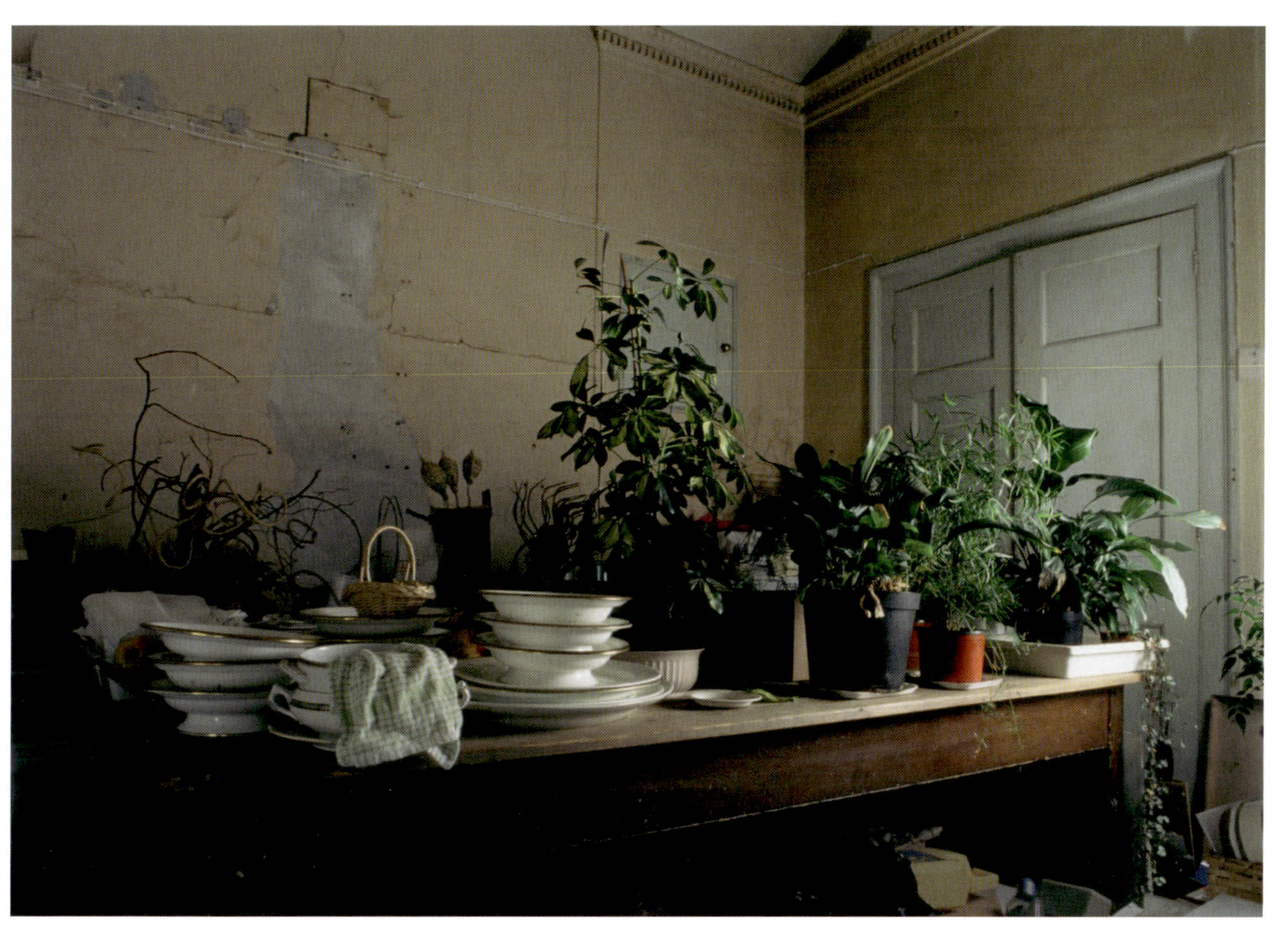

Female government, 1998

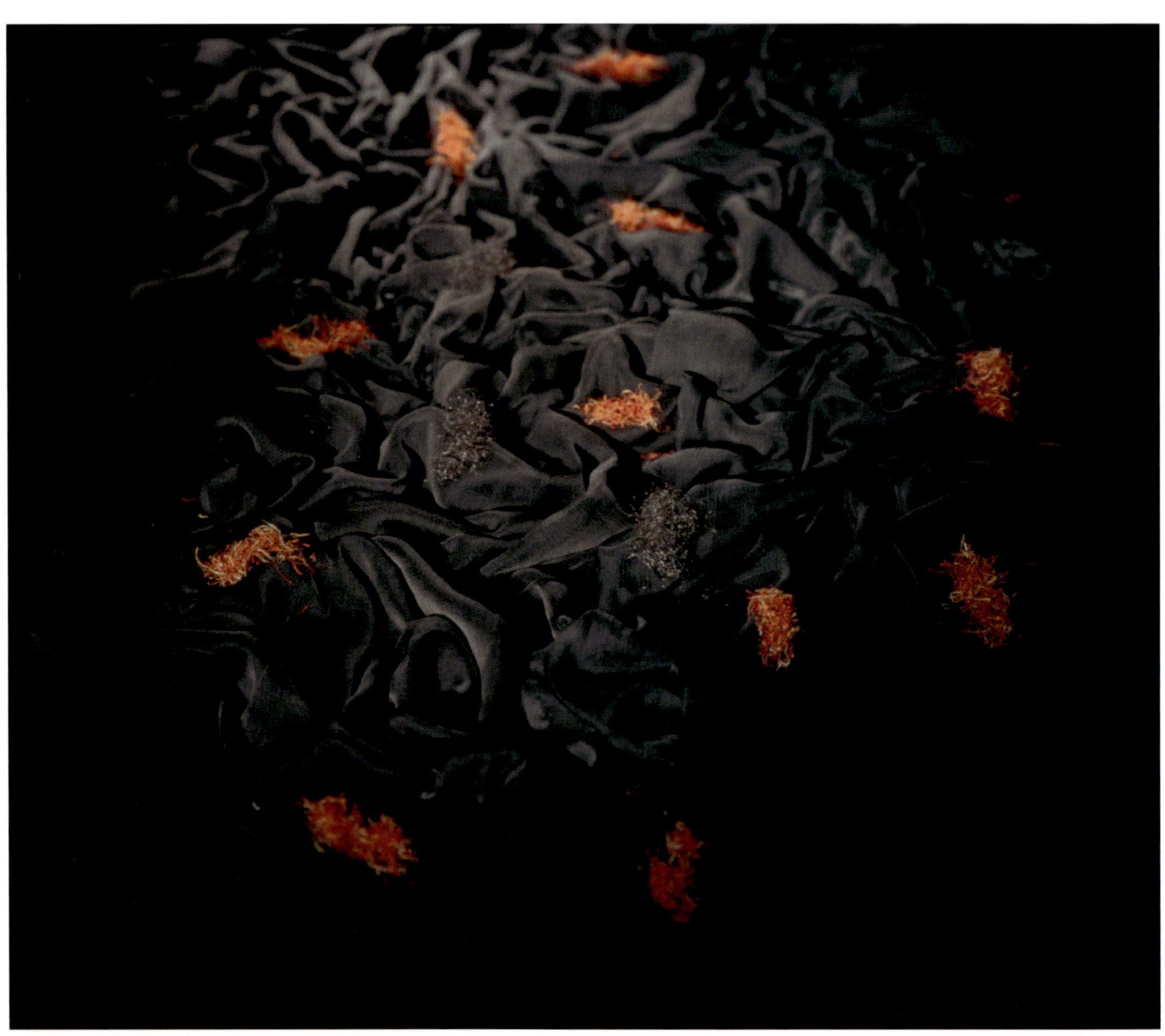

 Harsh pubic hair, 1998

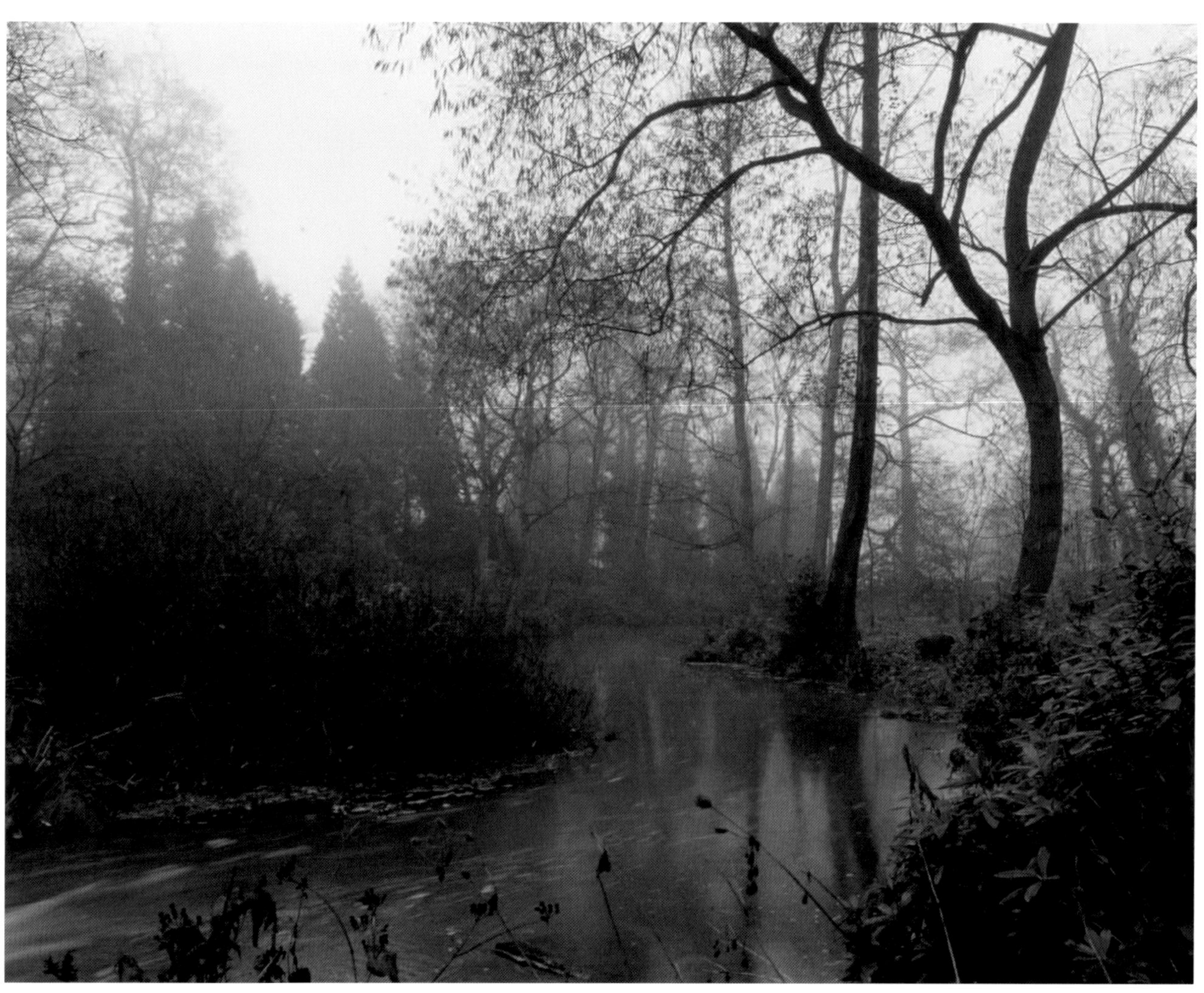

WHEREAS a BLACK SERVANT BOY, 1998

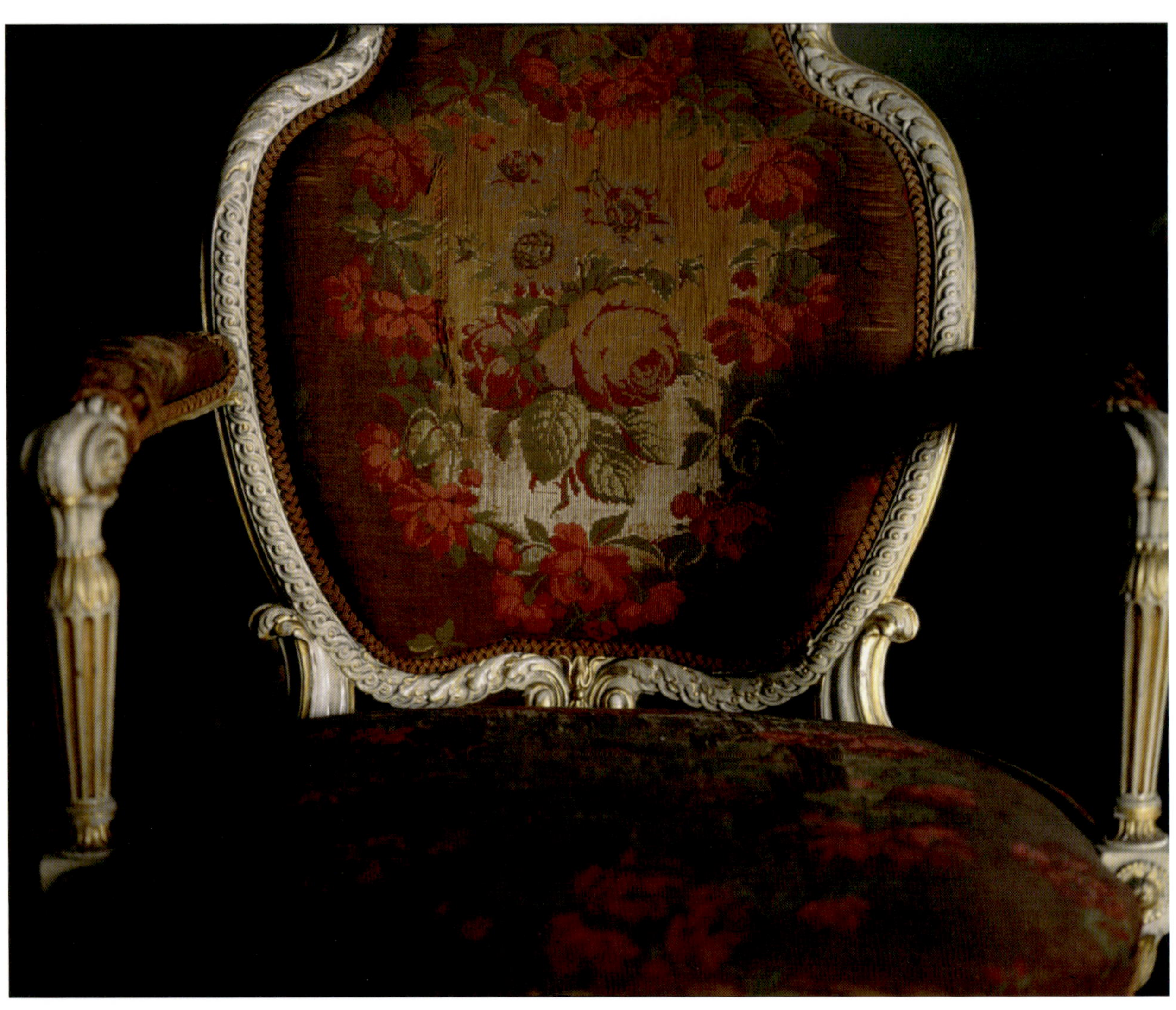

 Strange domineering tenderness, 1998

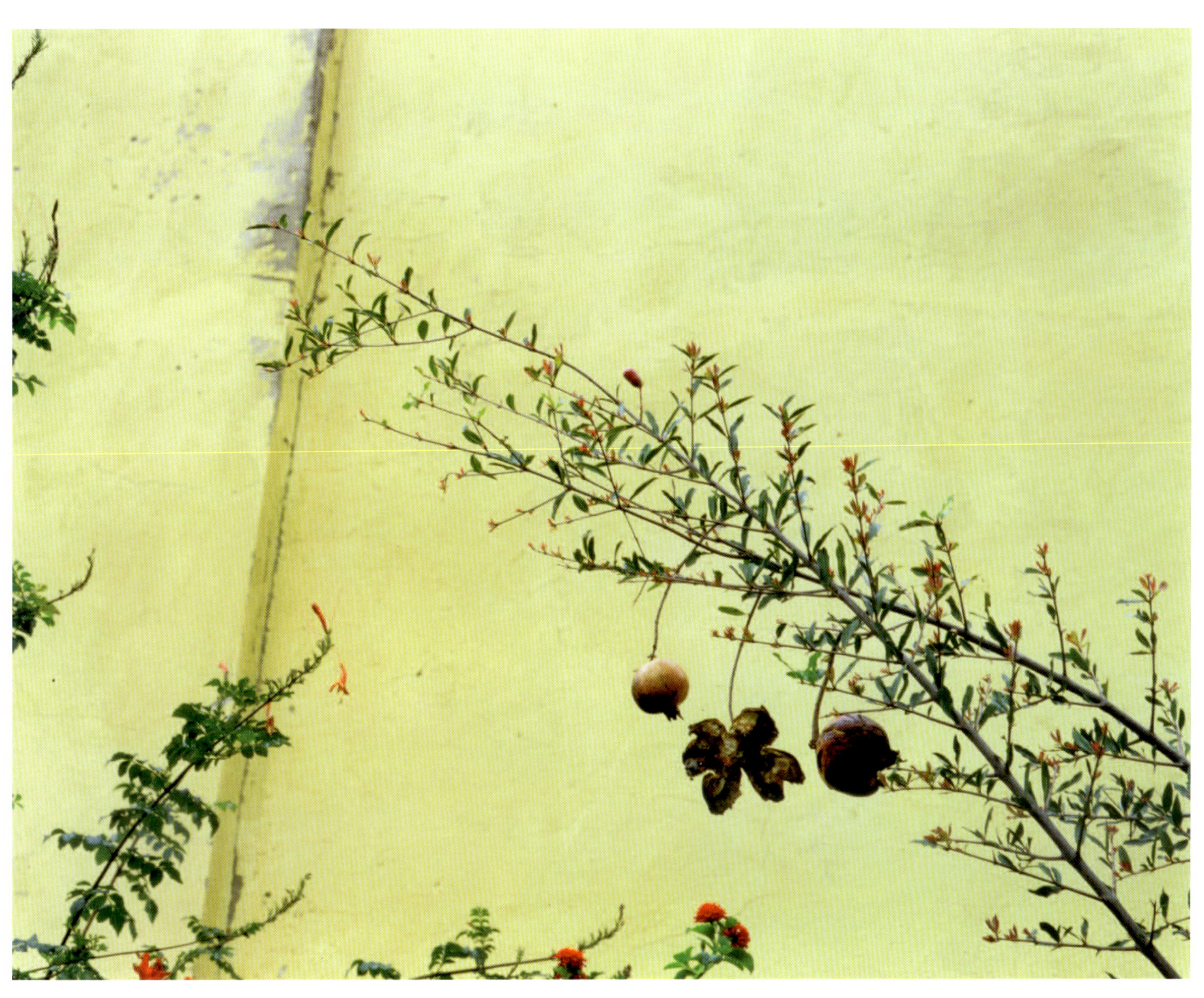

Musâlimûn, 1998

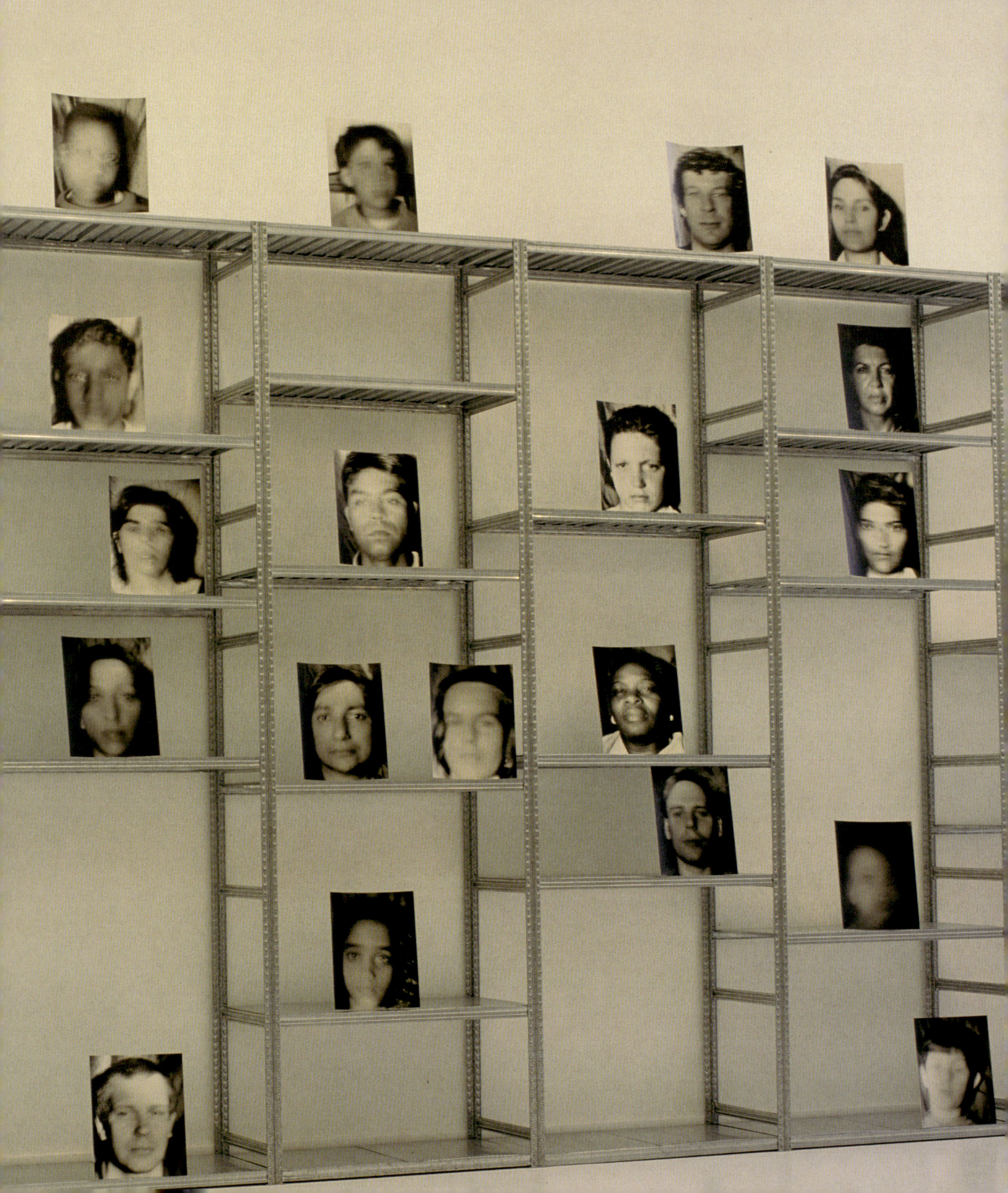

1822 – Now

1822 – Now consists of over 100 black and white and colour portraits installed opposite one another in an imposing library-like setting. Two long bookshelves flank an empty scholar's desk with chair. Commissioned by Antwerp '93, MuKHA, the work was inspired by a year-long residency at Kettle's Yard and Darwin College, University of Cambridge, UK, and the artist's concurrent research into the theory of eugenics. Invented by Sir Francis Galton, who was born in 1822, eugenics was a quasi-scientific theory that attempted to explain the implications of genetic variation through crossbreeding. The term soon became synonymous with the eugenics movement which categorised people based on racial characteristics, thus enabling colonial powers to sustain the myth of racial superiority. For her project, Bhimji invited people who were either of mixed-race origin or involved in mixed-race relationships to sit for portraits. Visually imitating the nineteenth-century belief that photography captured the soul, Bhimji used a 5 × 4 camera, employing a long exposure time of approximately half an hour which resulted in a blurry image. Subverting the essentialist nature of eugenics and critiquing its artificial construct, the portraits share more similarities than they are divided by differences.

1822 – Now, 1993
Installation consisting of 200 black and white and colour photographs, metal shelving, table and chair;
Dimensions variable

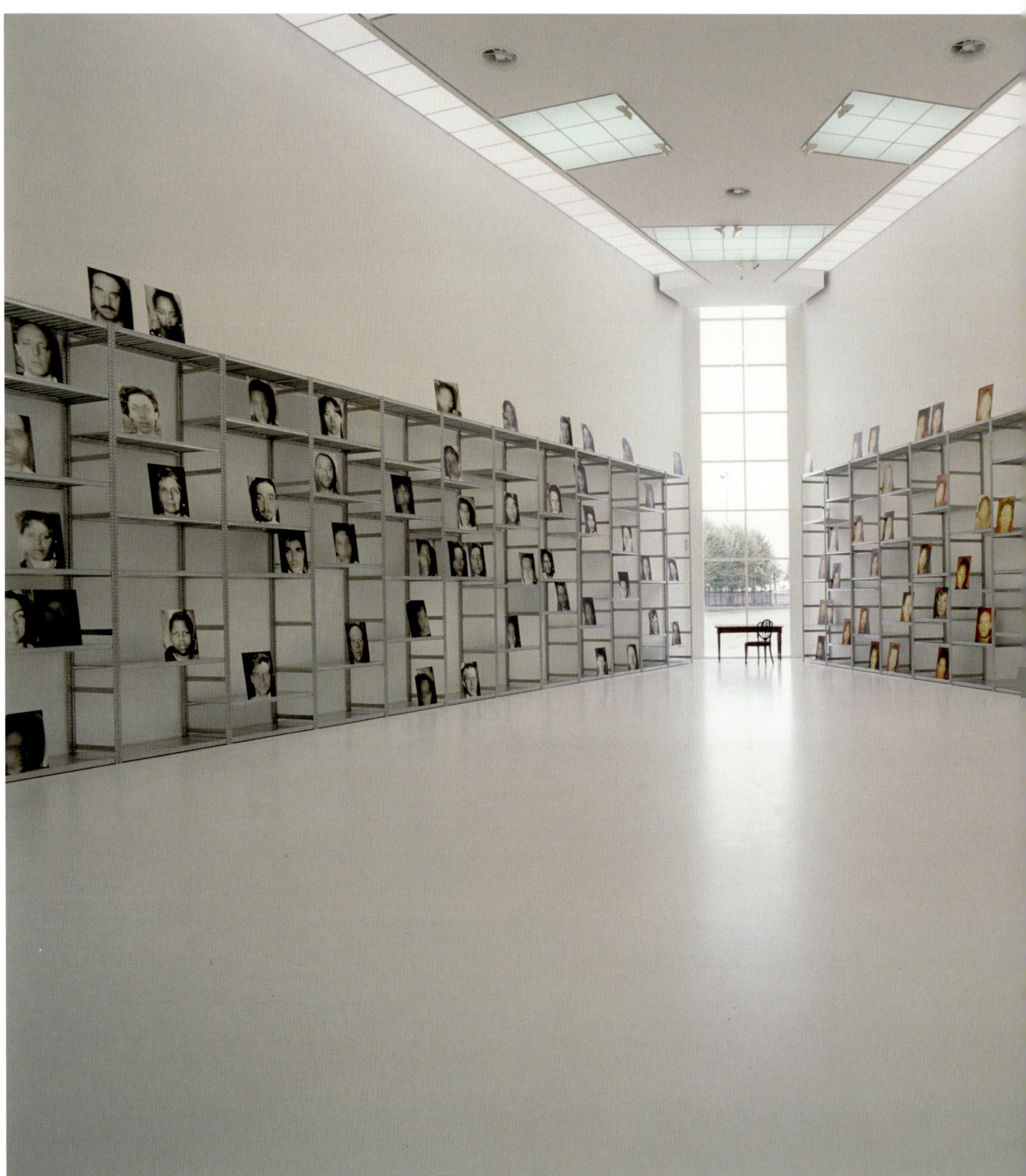

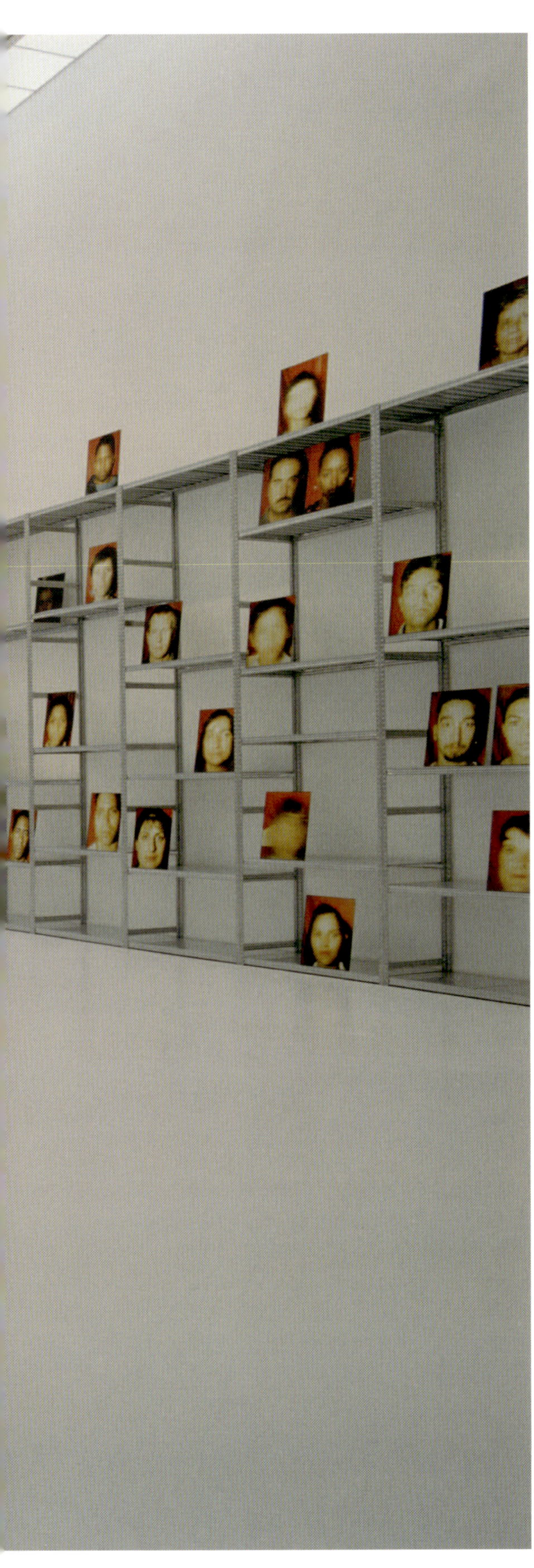

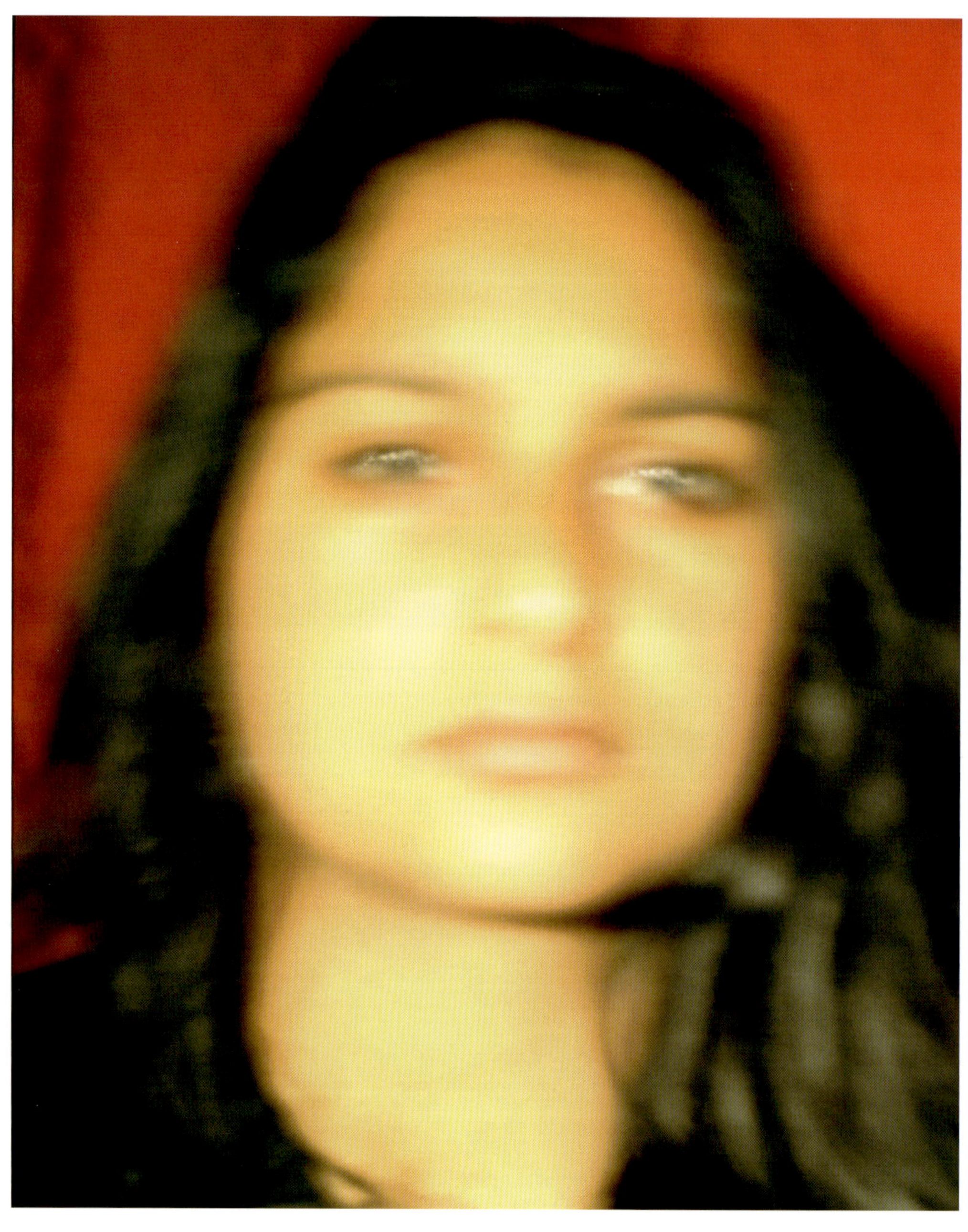

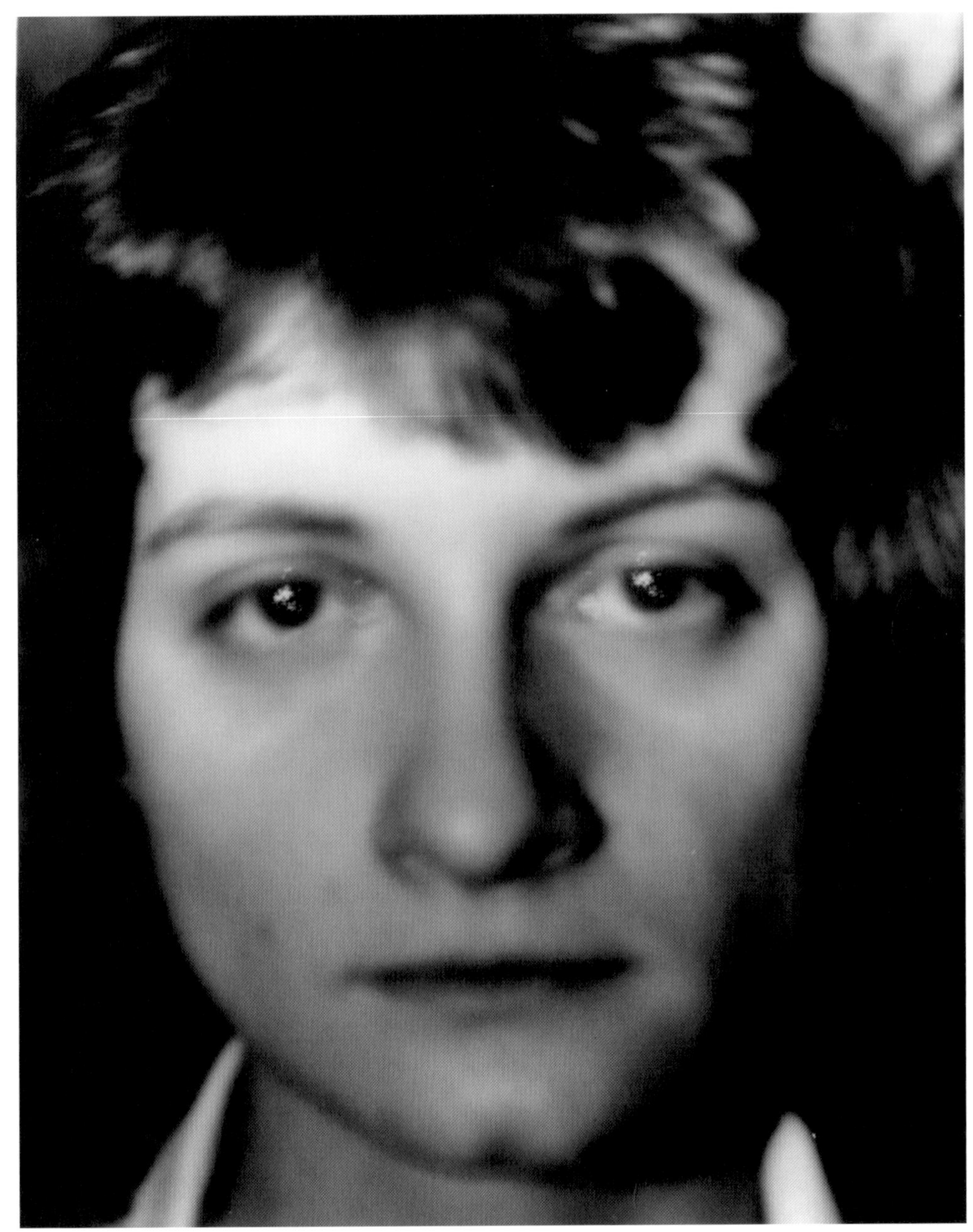

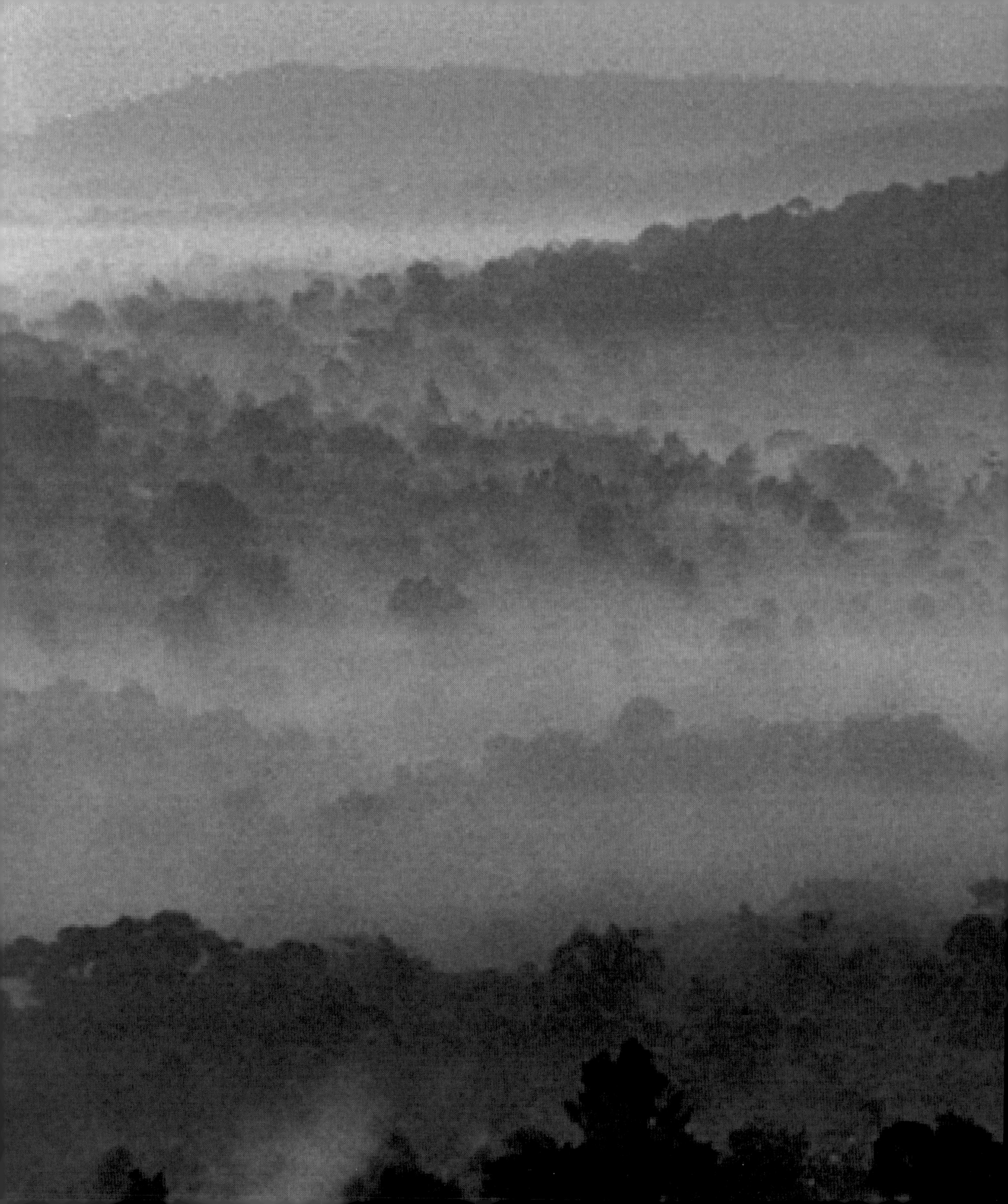

Out of Blue

Bhimji's first major film installation, *Out of Blue* was commissioned for Documenta 11. Concerned with issues of elimination, extermination and erasure, the film is the result of several prolonged visits to the artist's country of birth, Uganda, from which she was expelled at the age of 11 along with her family. They shared the fate of 80,000 residents of Asian descent, who were forced to leave Uganda in the wake of dictator Idi Amin's 1972 decree expelling all Asians from the country. Bhimji extends the currency of these events by linking them, albeit not explicitly, to subsequent ethnically motivated conflicts such as the ones in Rwanda and former Yugoslavia. Deserted landscapes and decaying interiors are noticeable for the absence of the human figure. Each scene is purposefully non-narrative and non-documentary, distancing the images from personal and historical specifics. Footage of an abandoned home, for example, segues the stained walls of an unrelated prison cell. Likewise, the crumbling facade of Entebbe airport is coupled with spiders weaving webs in bullet-ridden windows. Shot on super 16 mm film, the dense images are accompanied by a richly layered soundtrack, which forms a central component of the work.

Out of Blue, 2002
Single screen installation
Super 16 mm colour film, DVD transfer
24 min 25 sec

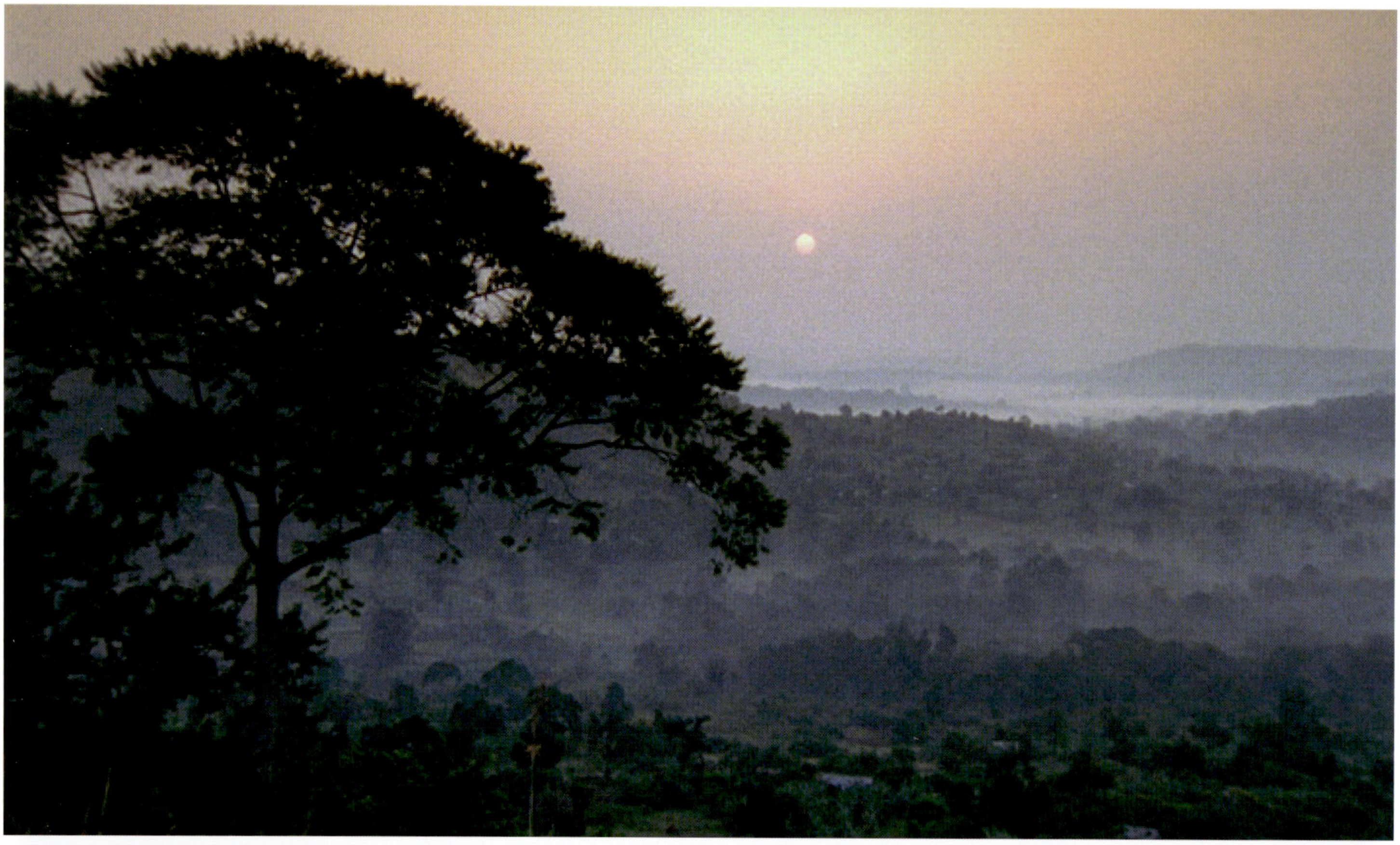

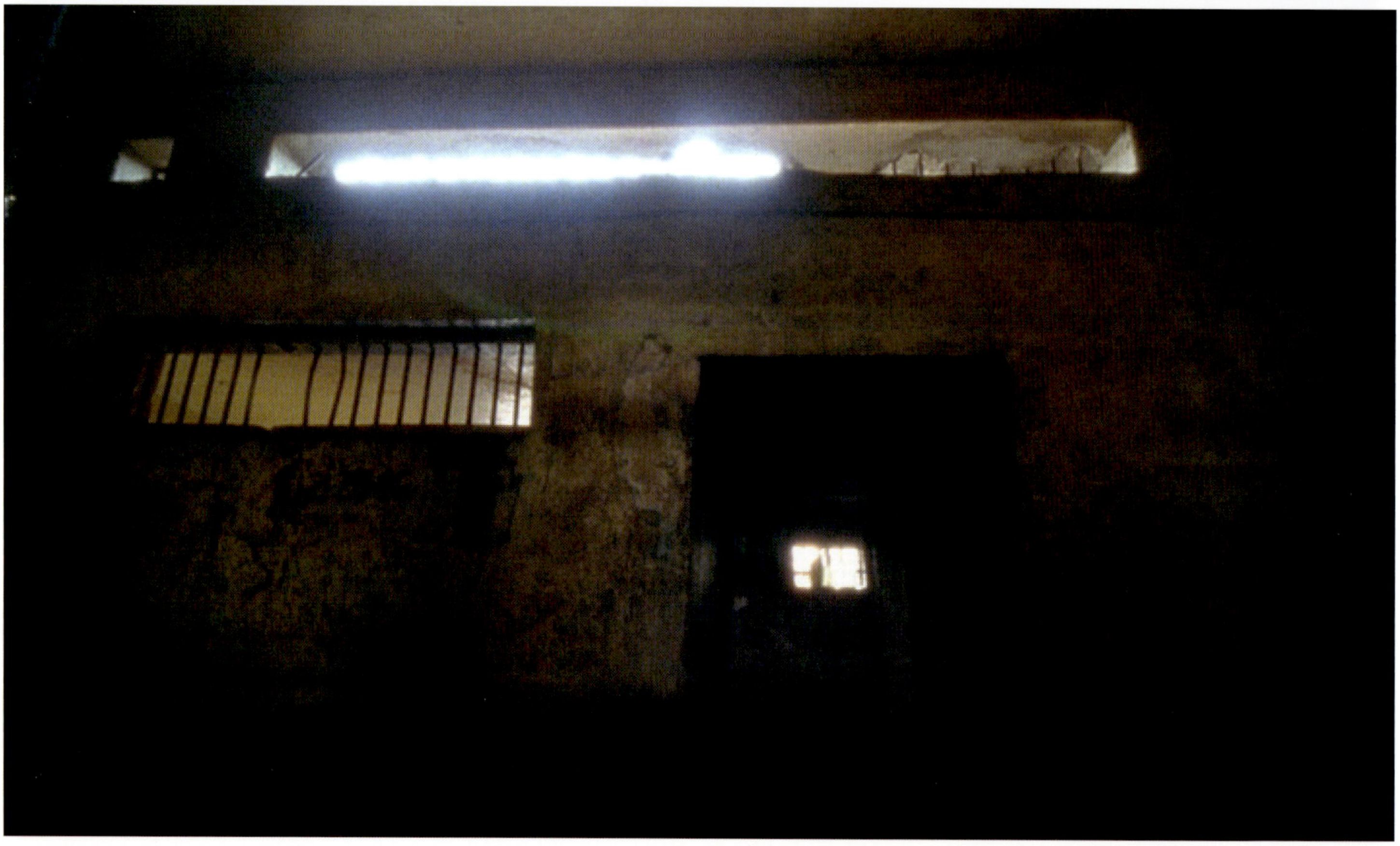

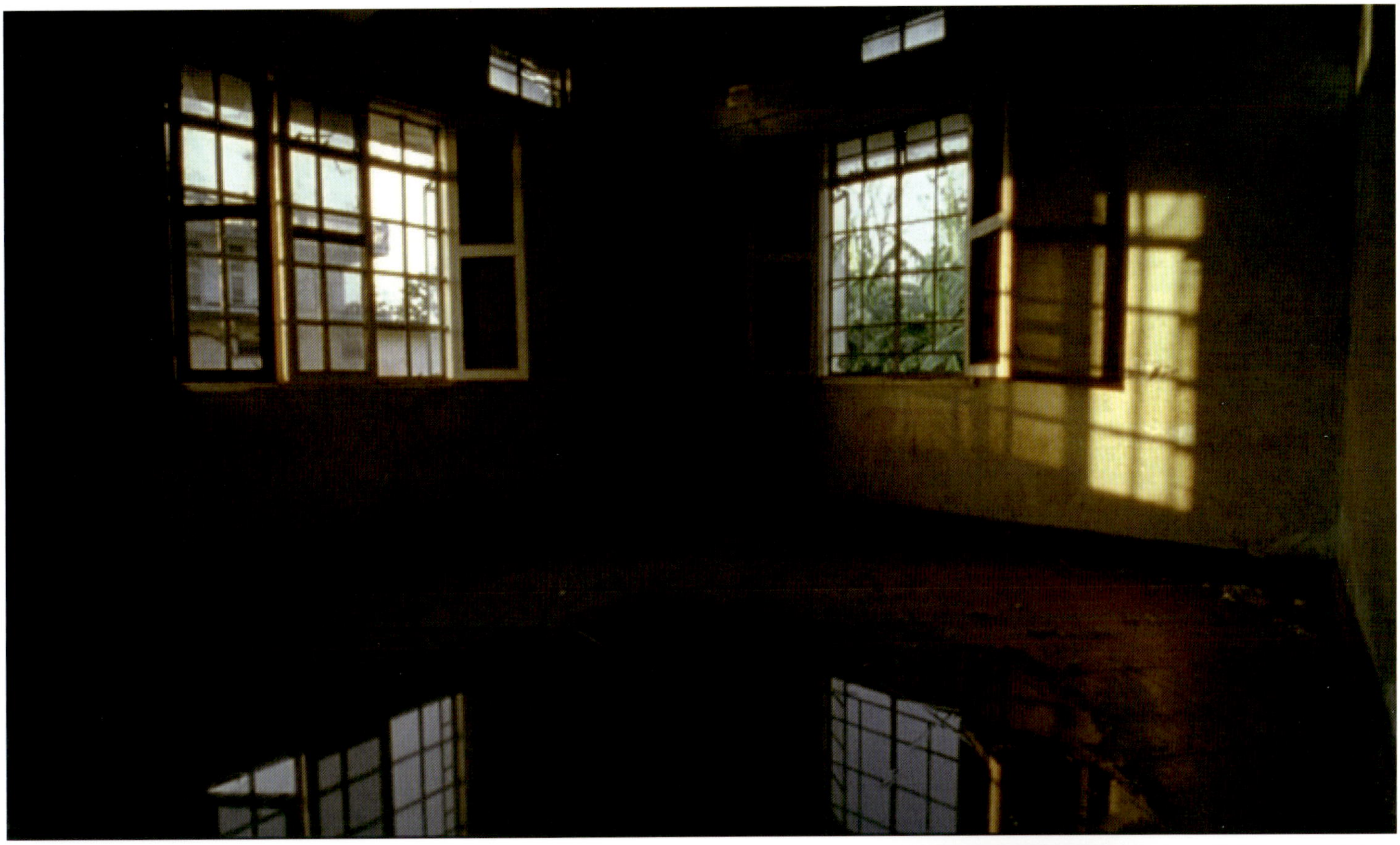

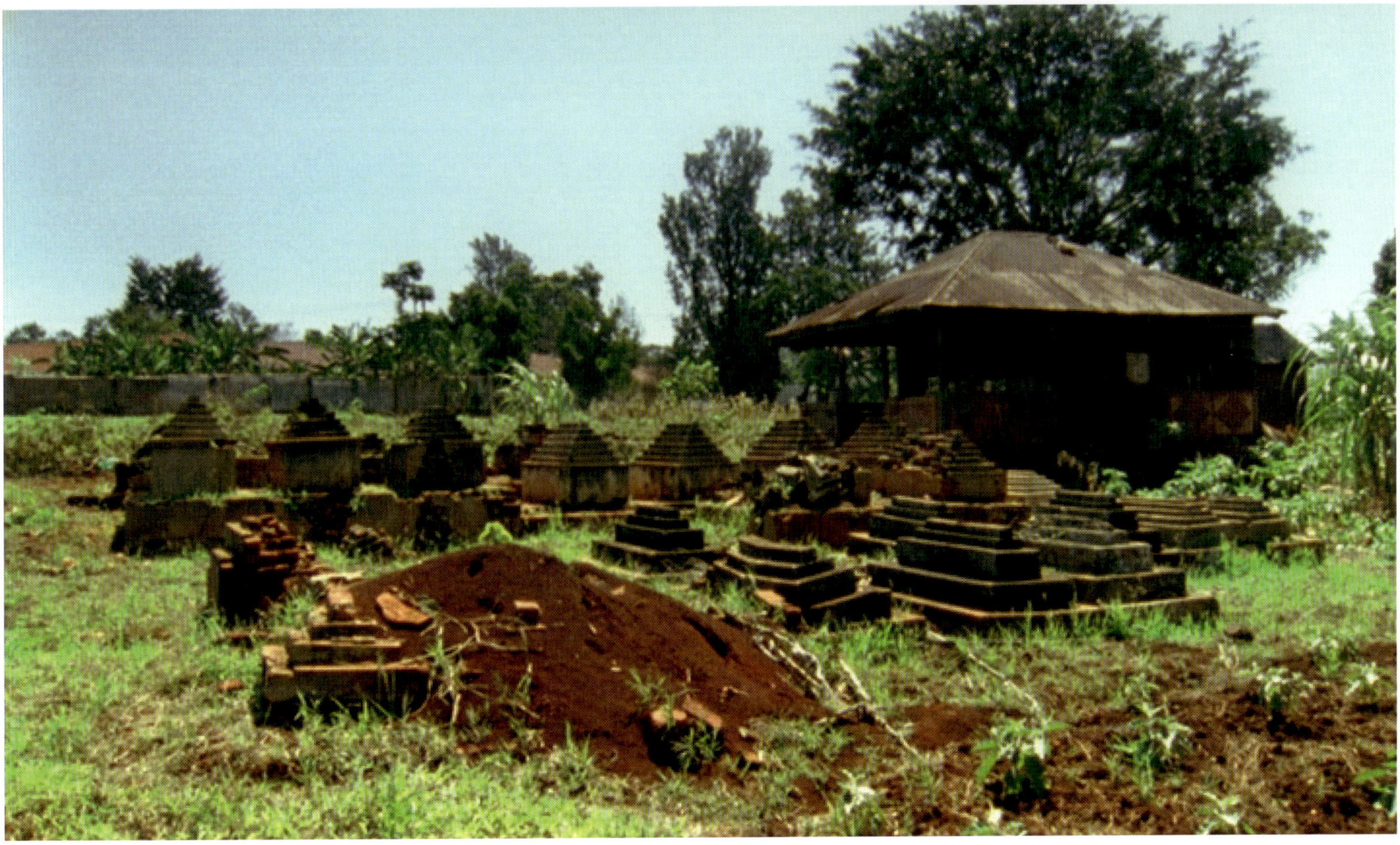

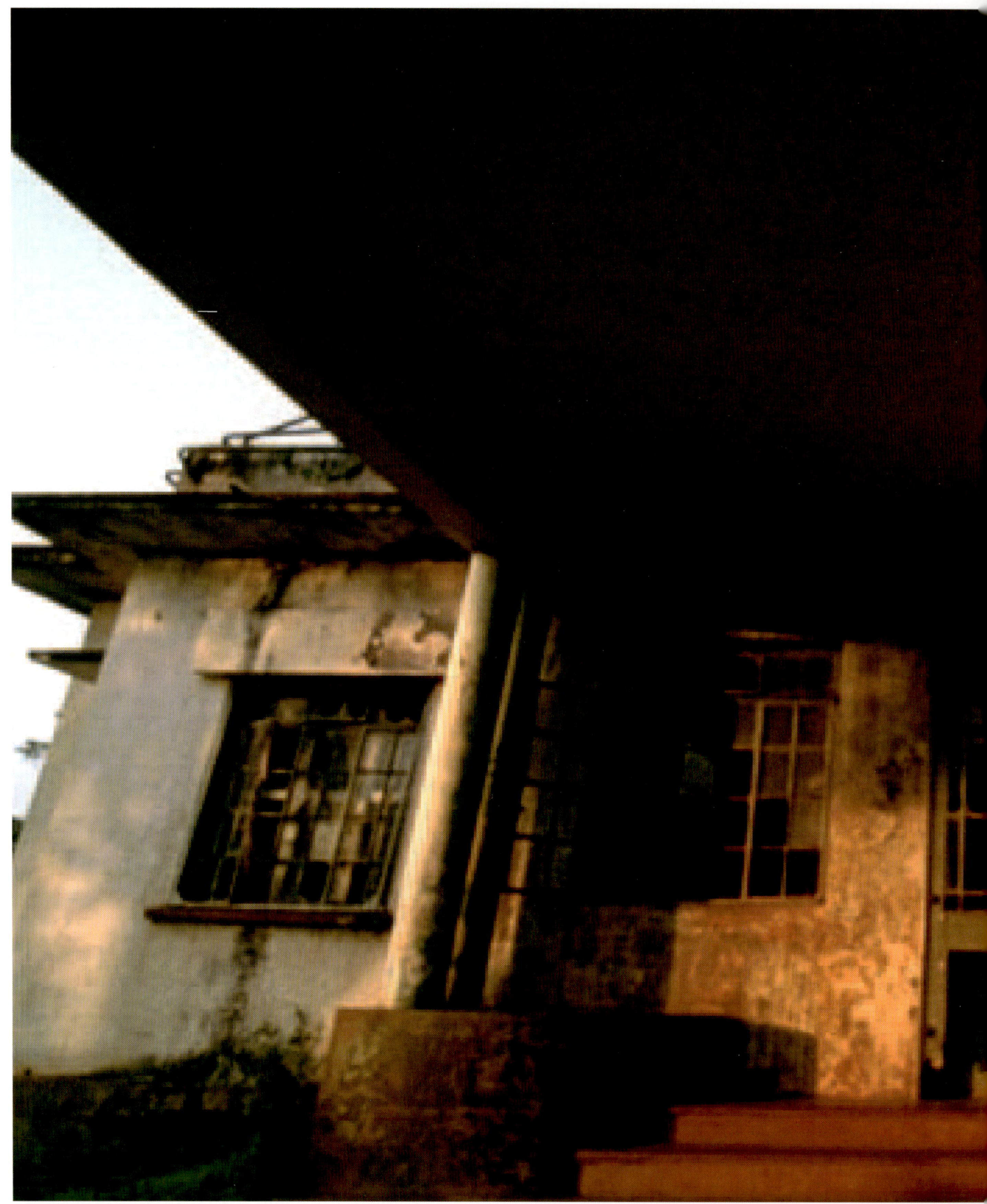

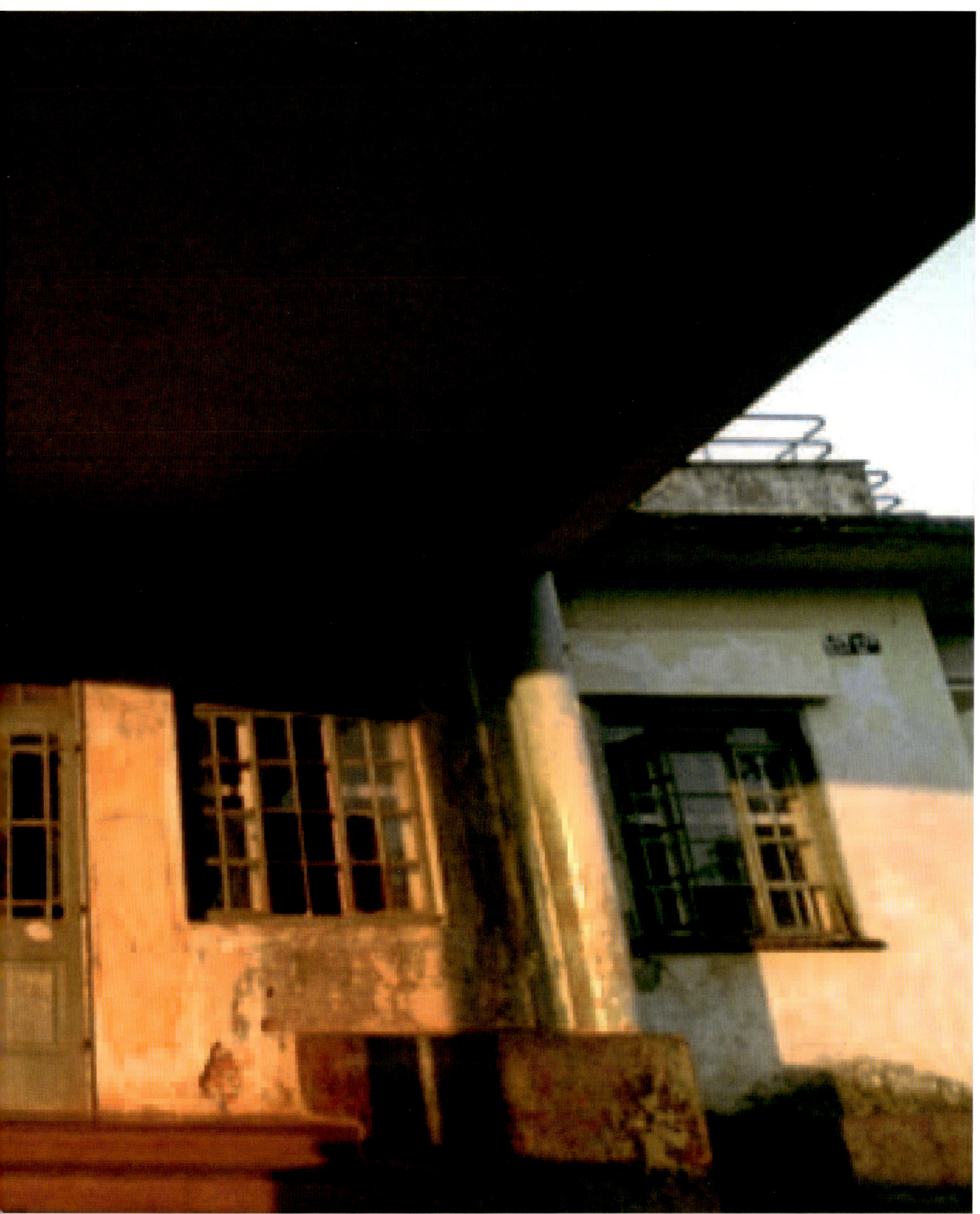

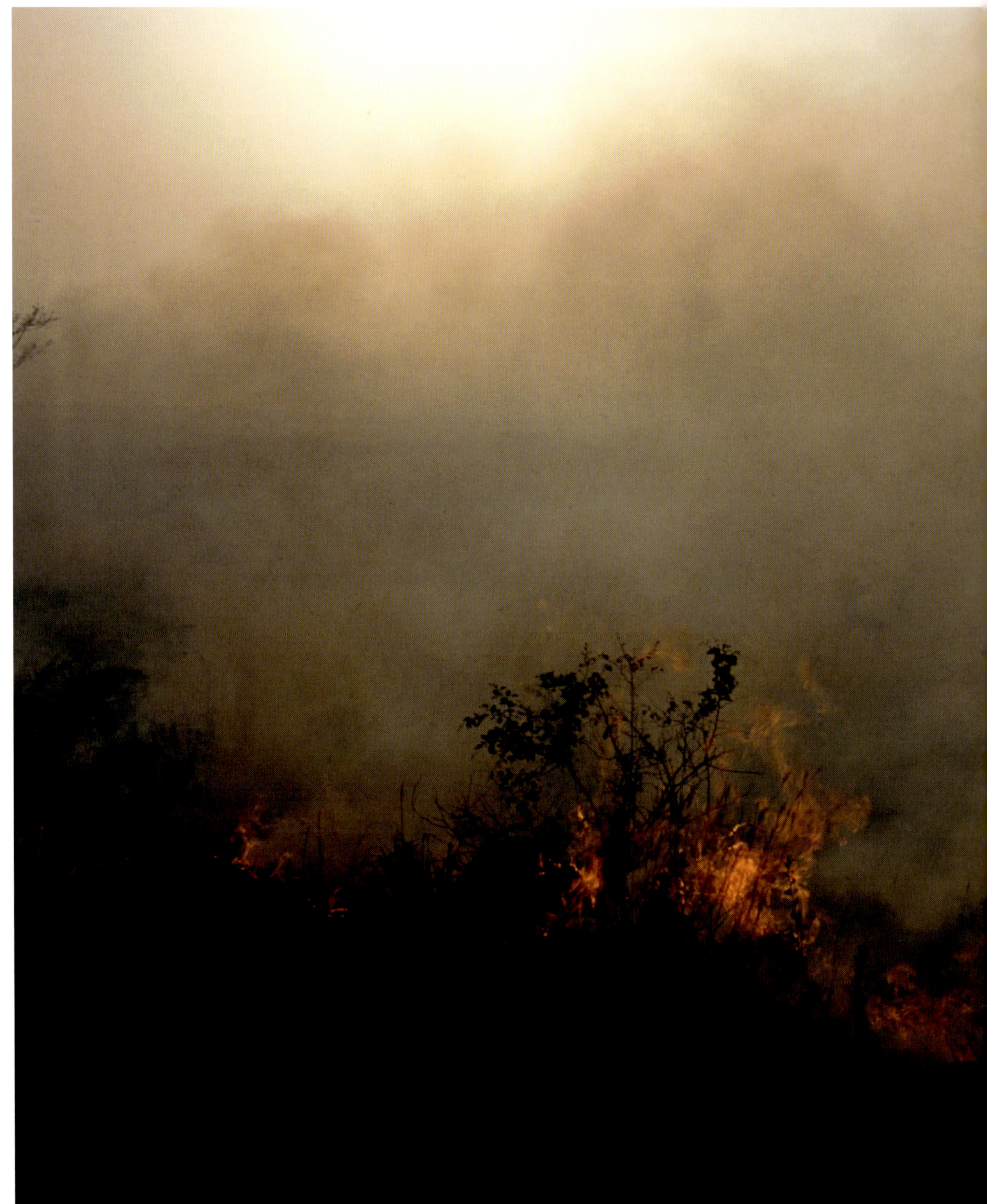

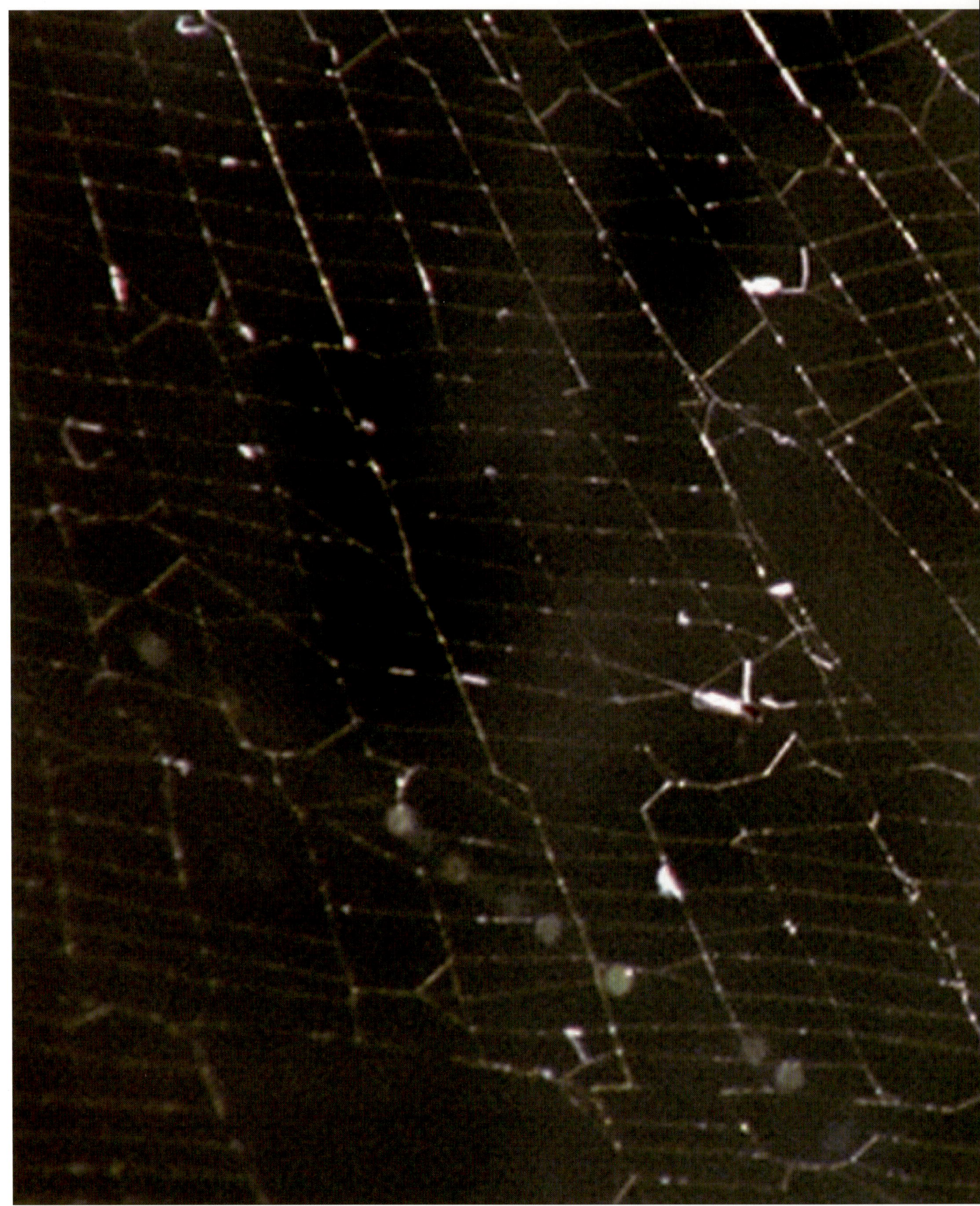

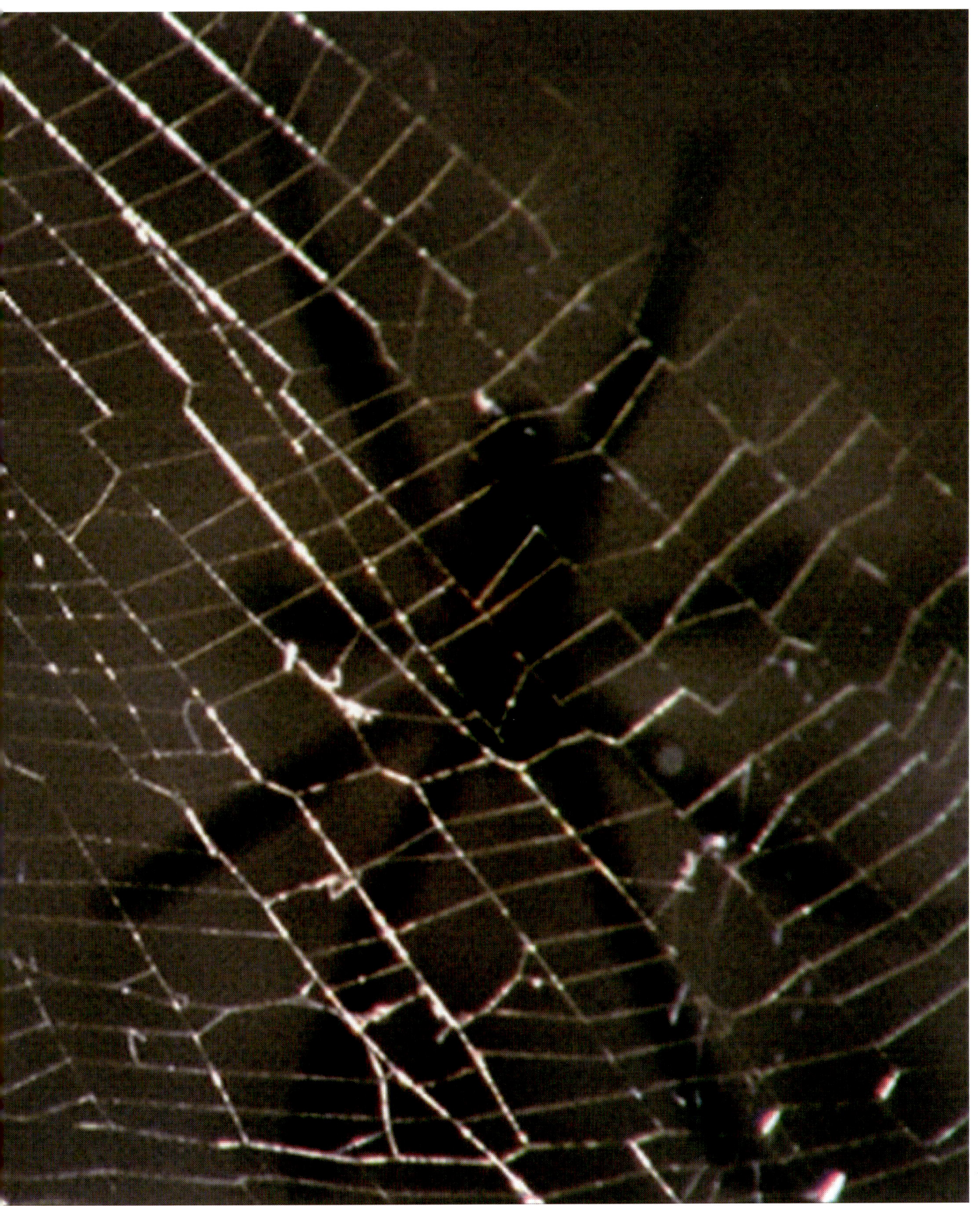

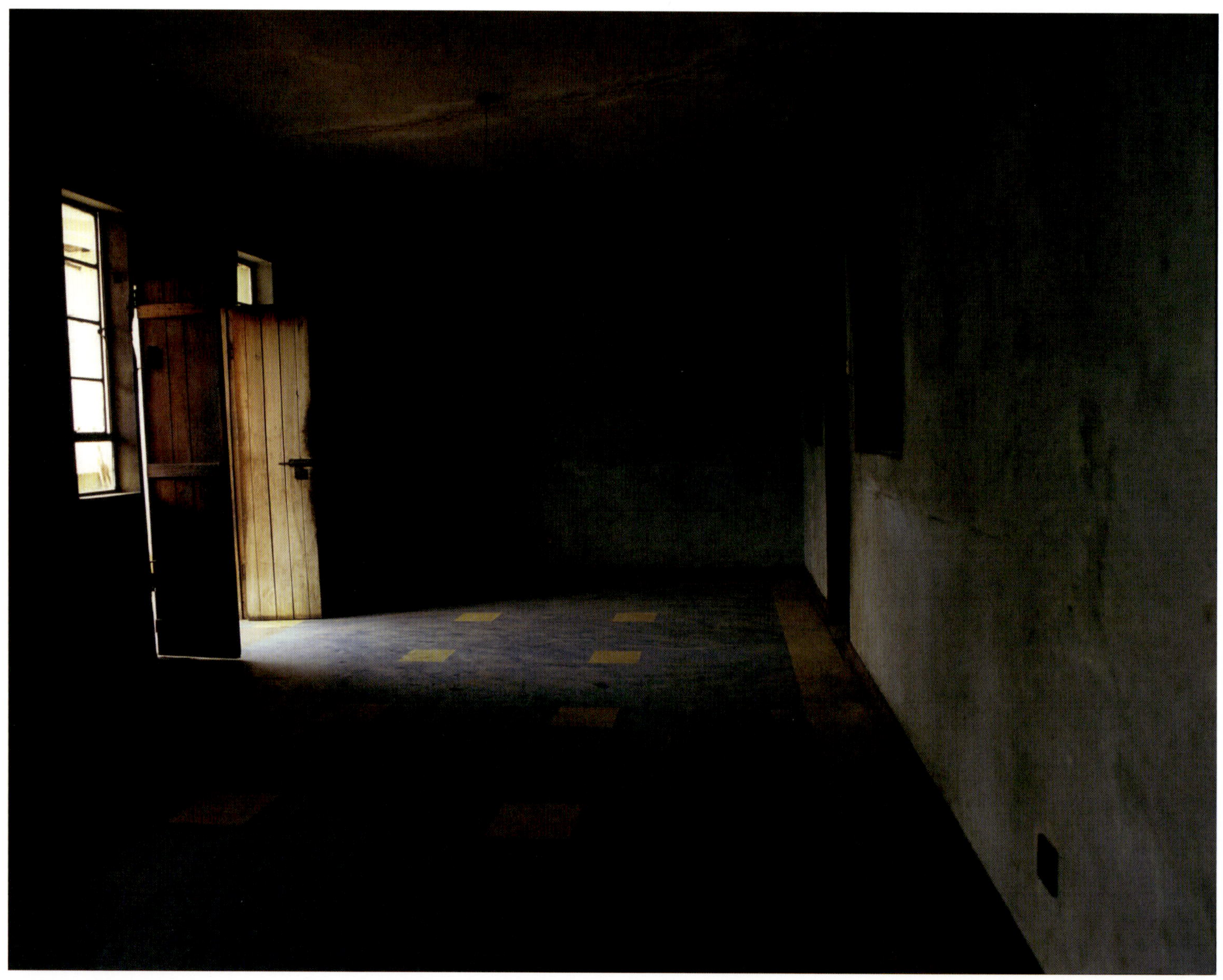

Grenade, 1998–2003

Love

This series of 40 photographs was taken as part of ongoing research into Uganda, which also led to the making of *Out of Blue* (2002; p.77). The photographs capture deserted landscapes and empty buildings which were primarily chosen for their strong visual qualities. Whether taken in or out of doors, all images share a sense of human absence. Although grounded in meticulous research, the resulting photographs are distanced from historic and political specificity characterised instead by Bhimji's sensitive attention to composition and light. Evocative titles such as *This Unhinged Her* and *Howling Like Dogs, I Swallowed Solid Air* extend the images' poetic resonance into psychological narrative. Trying, in the artist's own words, to 'speak the unspeakable that wants to be spoken', the images can be seen as transferences of emotional states through visual language.

Love, 1998–2007
Ilfochrome Ciba classic prints, 127 × 160 cm | 50 × 63 in (framed)
and transparency lightboxes, 130 × 170 × 12.5 cm | 51⅕ × 67 × 5 in

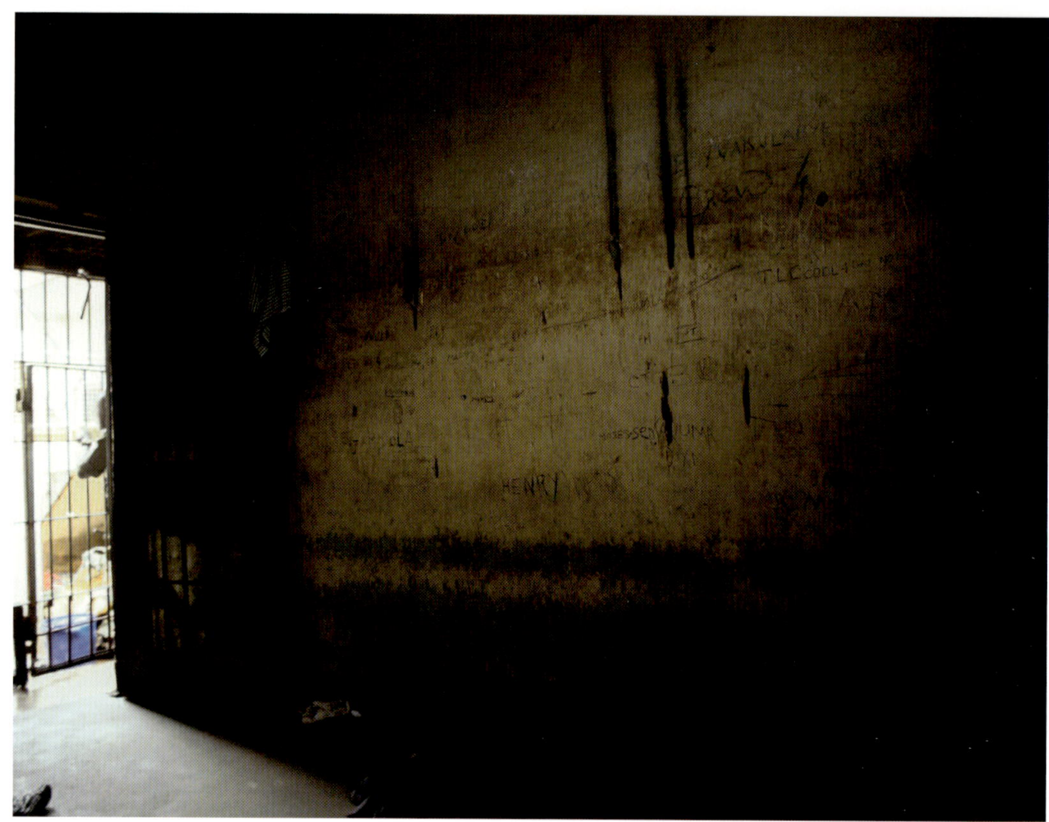

Bullet Riddled, 2001–2006

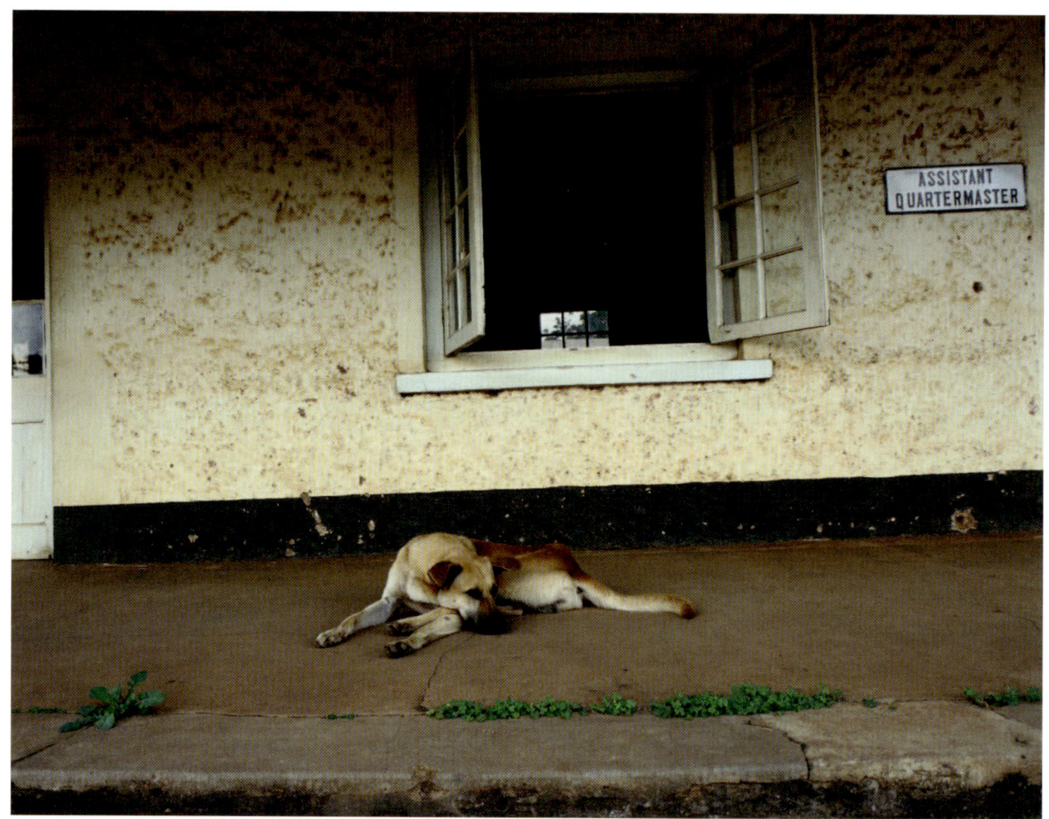

Rado Watch, Such Western Precision, 2001–2006

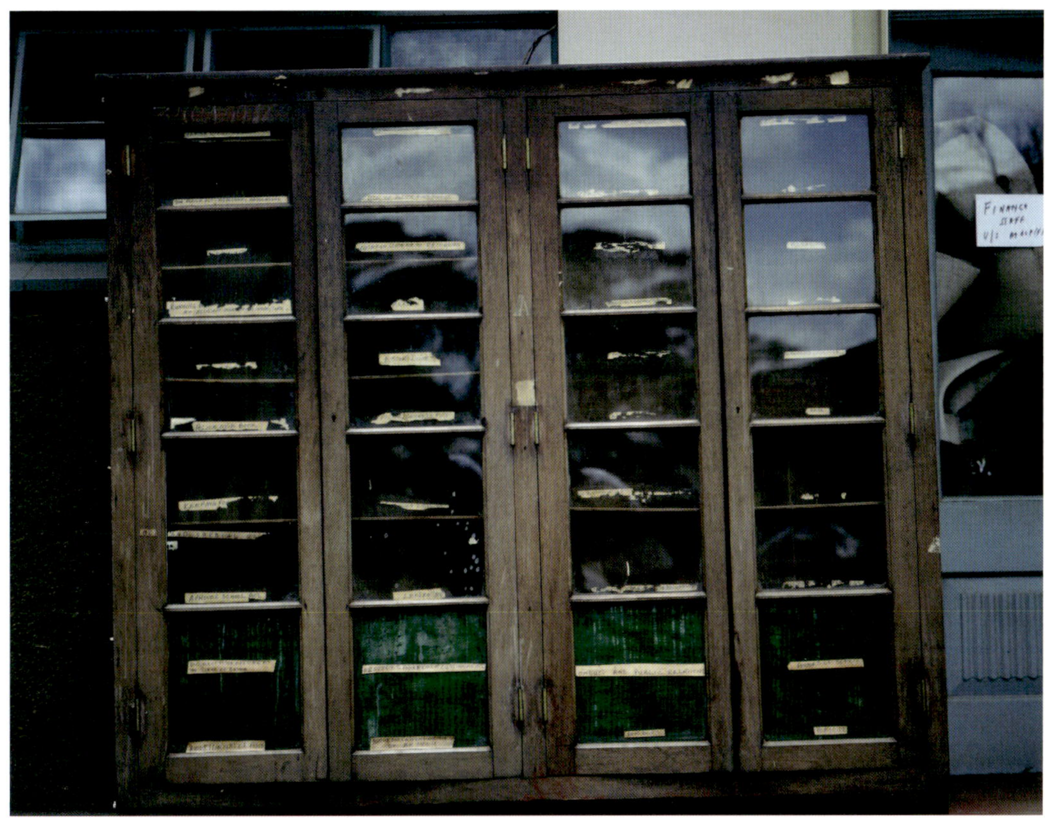

Indispensable Monument, 2001–2006

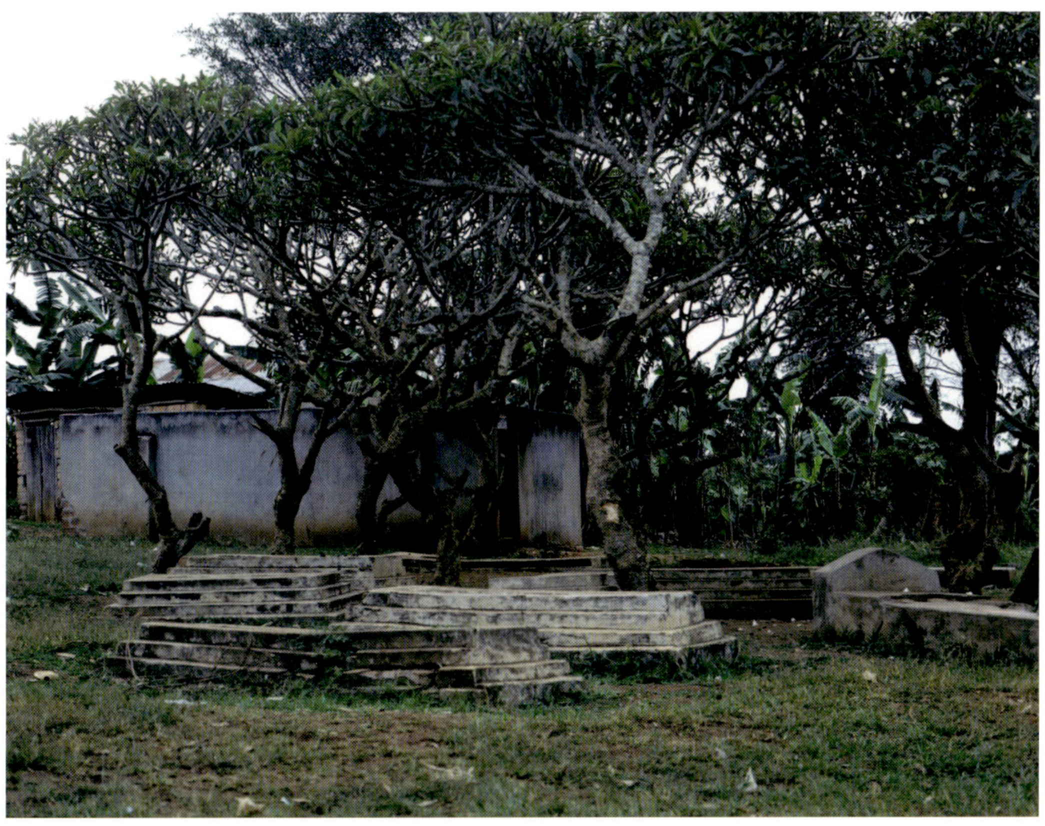

Frightened Goats, 2001–2006

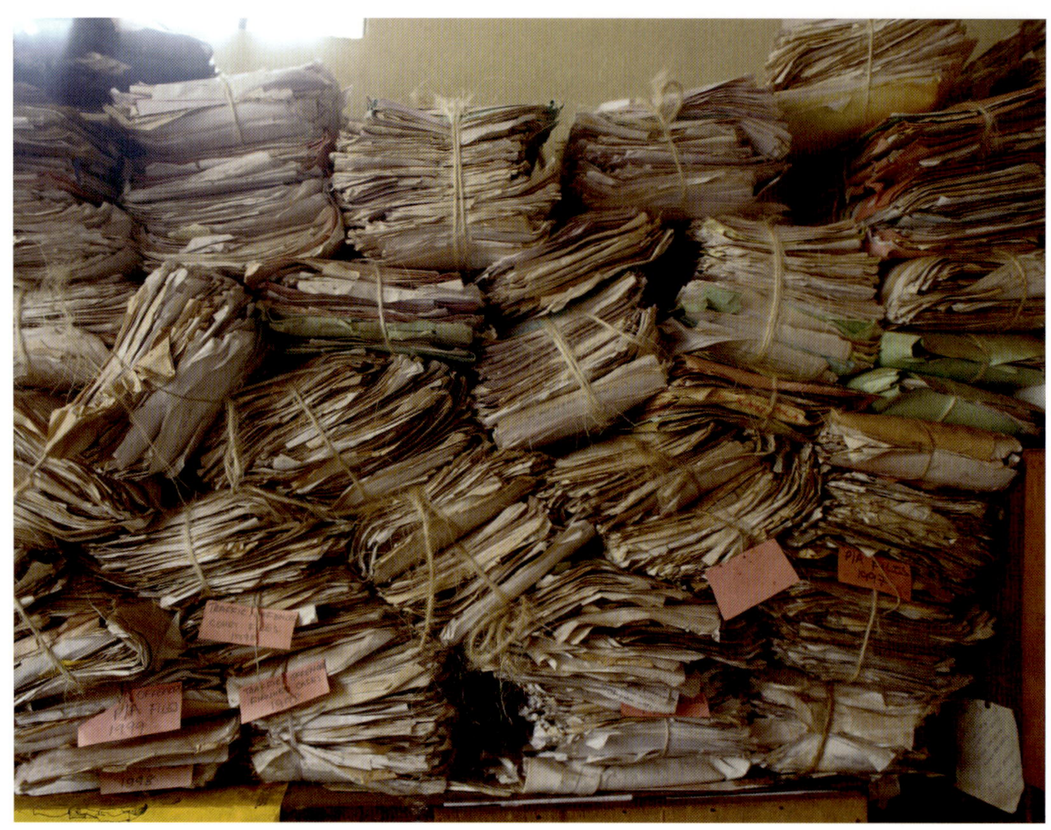

No Border Crossing, 2001–2006

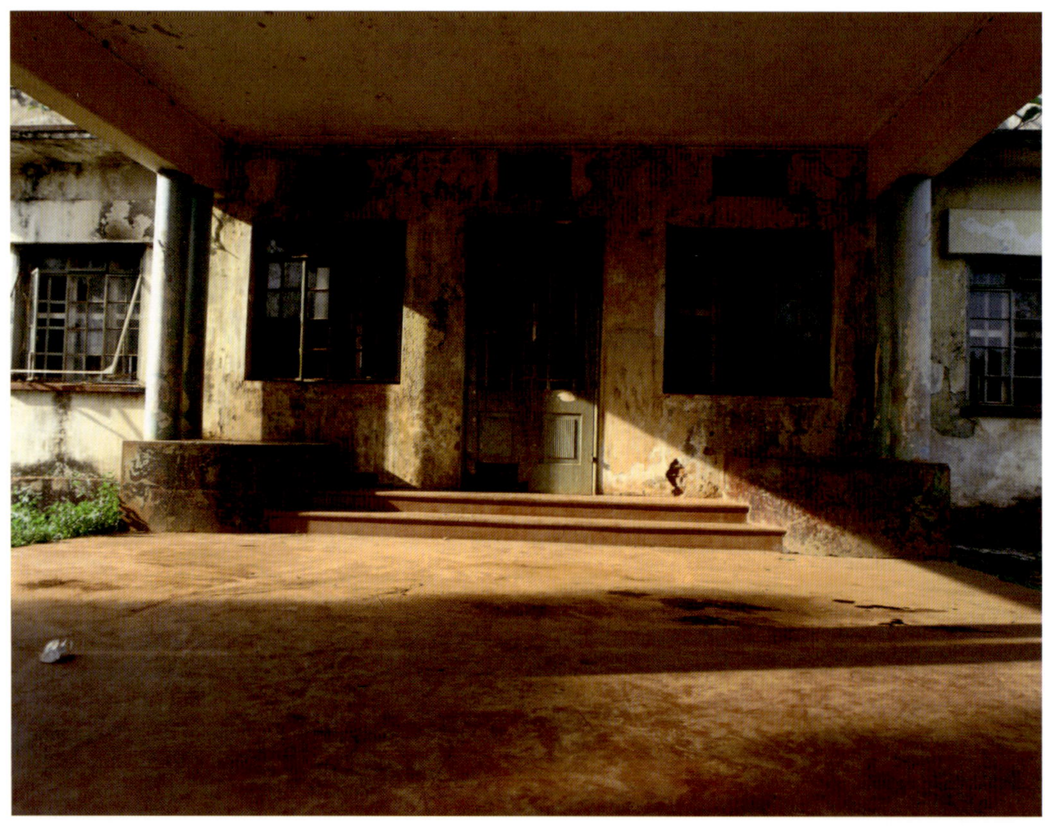

Forgotten Us, 2001–2006

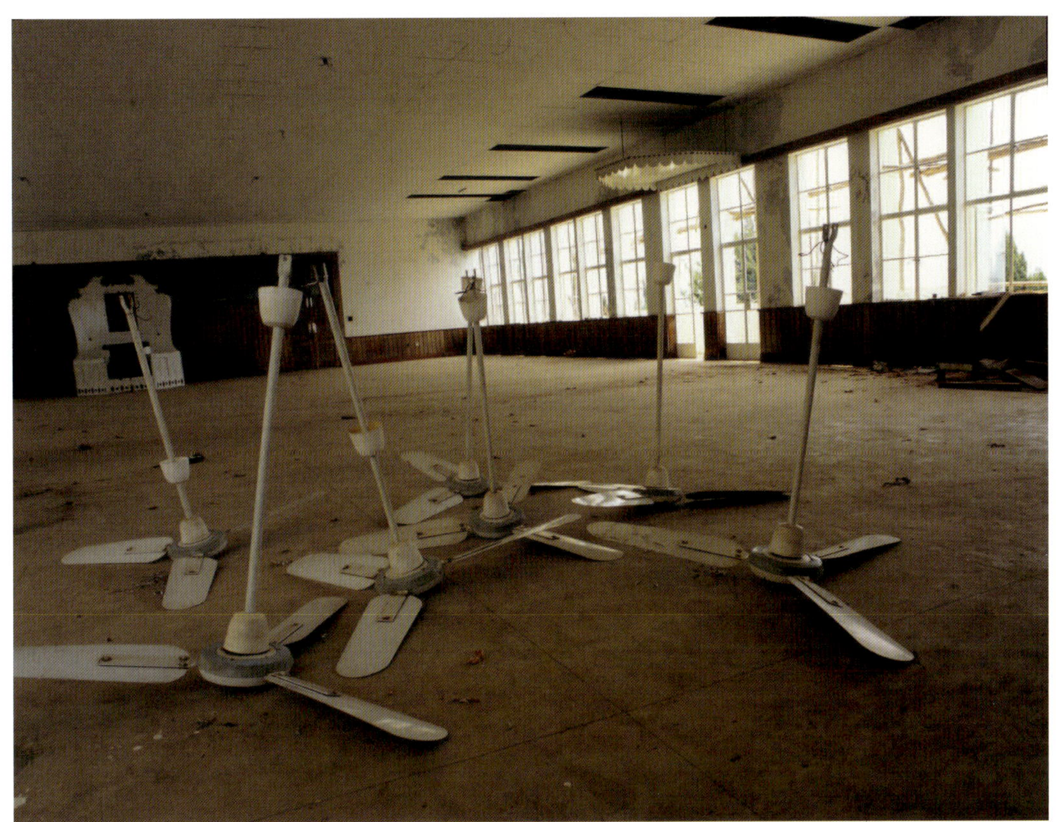

Howling Like Dogs, I Swallowed Solid Air, 1998–2003

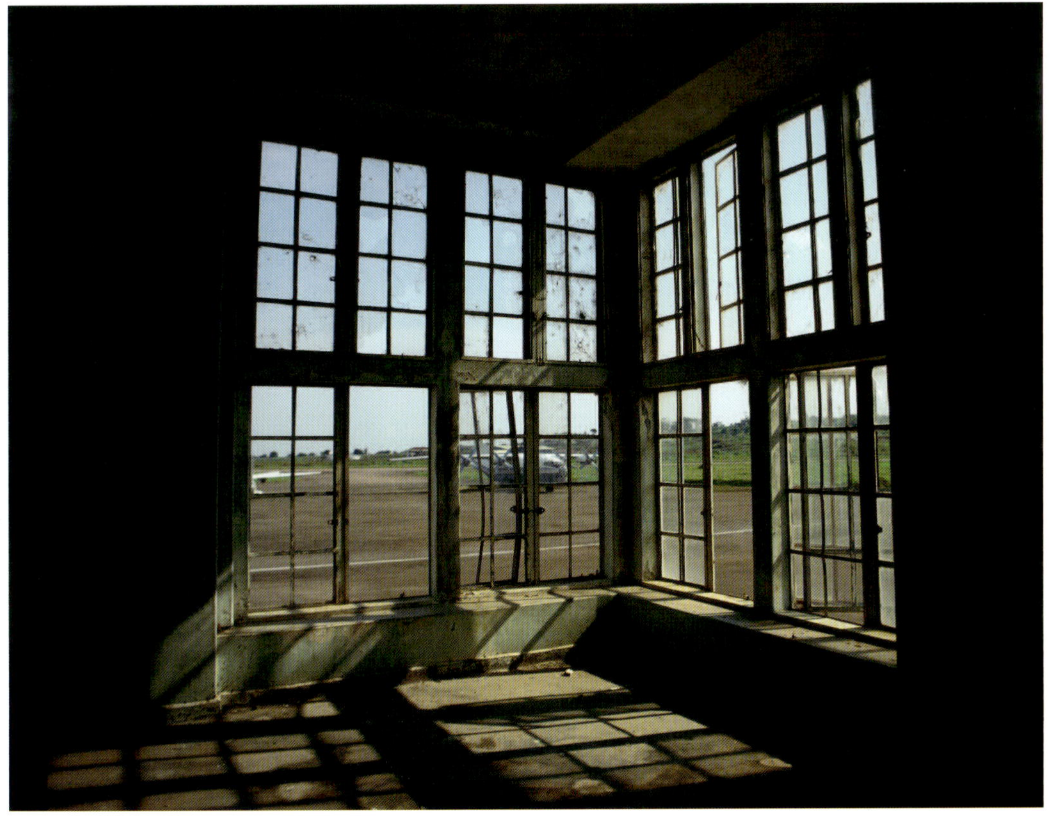

Bapa Closed His Heart, It Was Over, 2001–2006

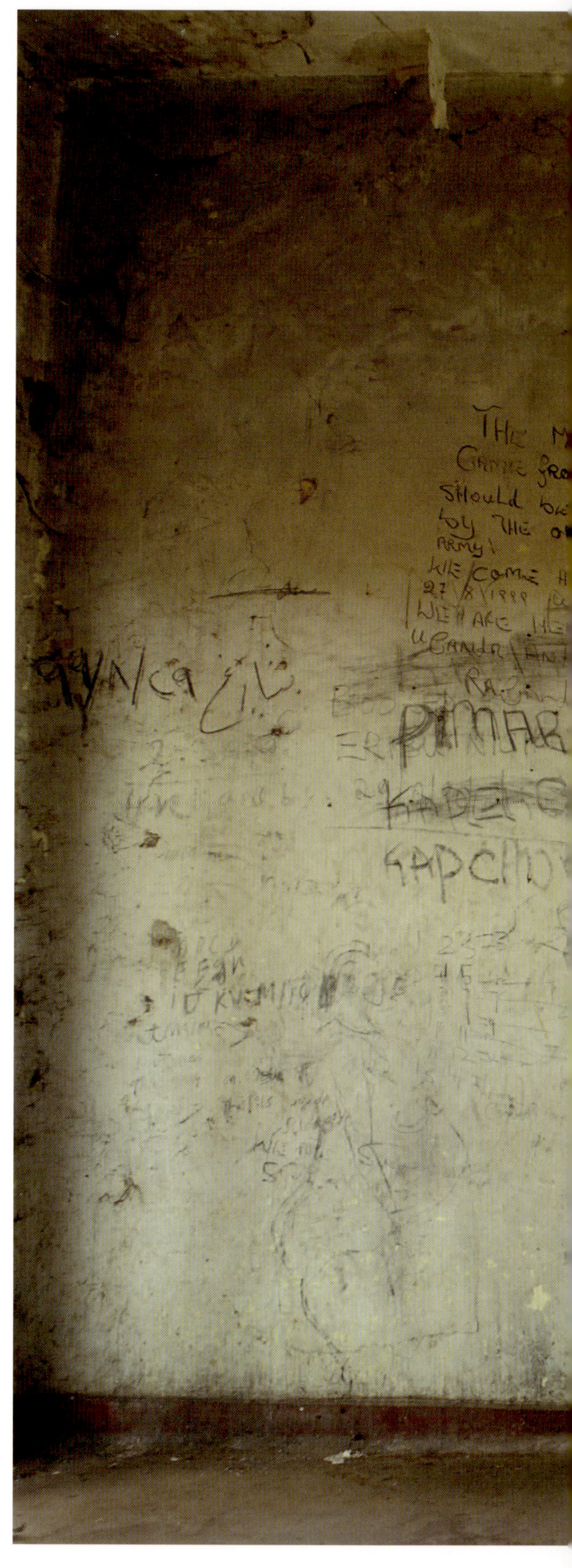

Echo, 2007

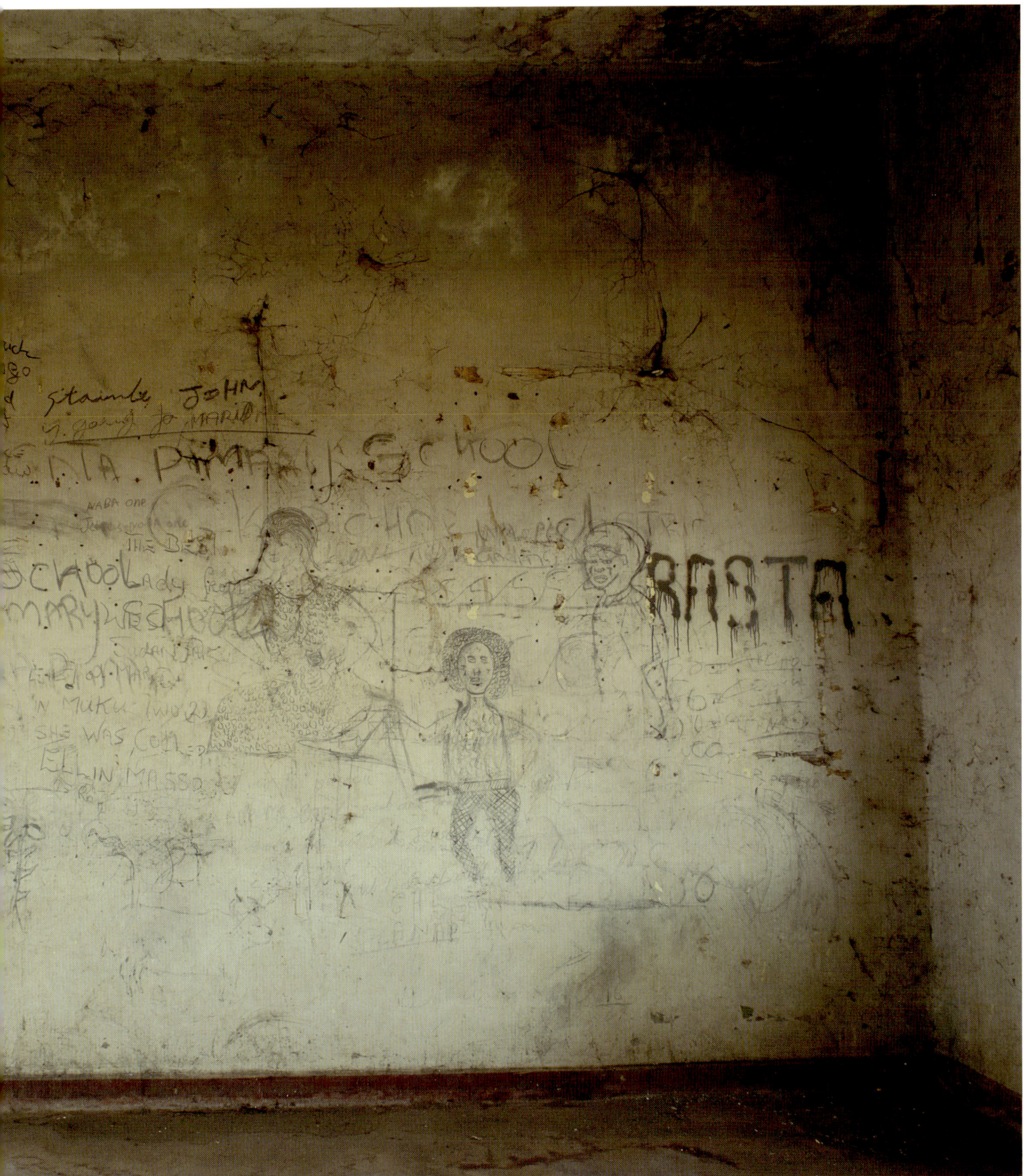
JOHN
THE BEST
RASTA

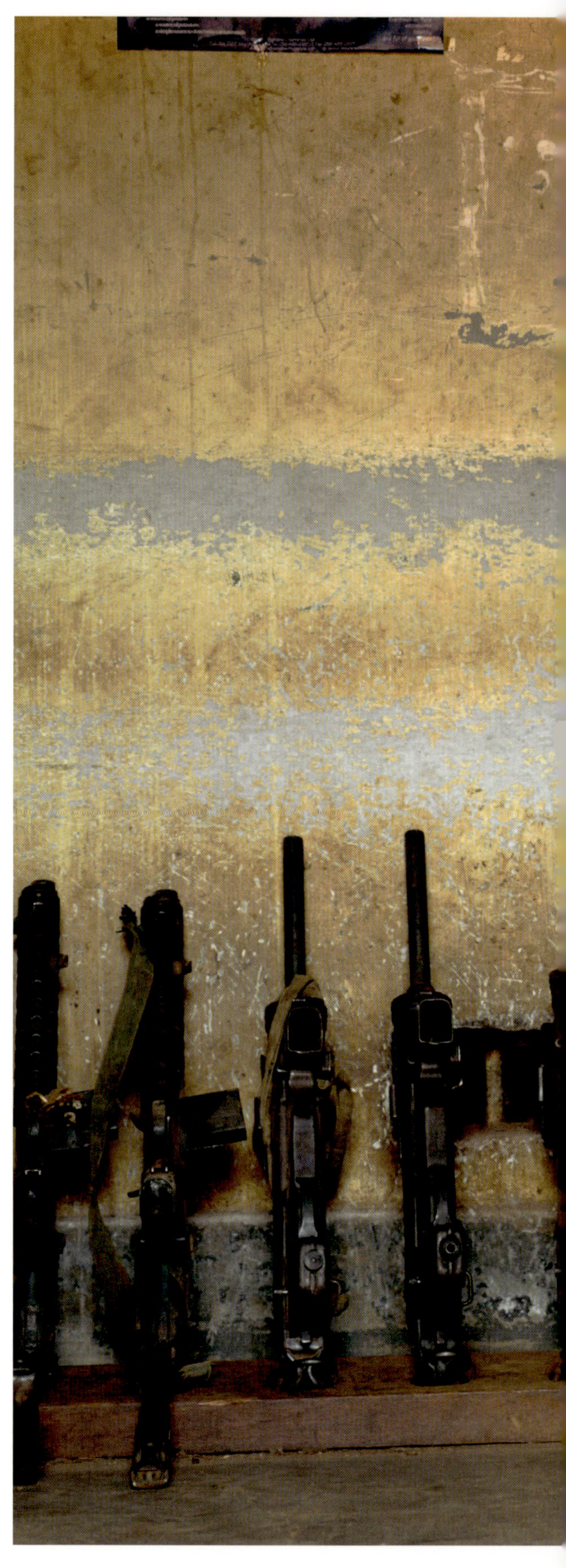

Illegal Sleep, 2007

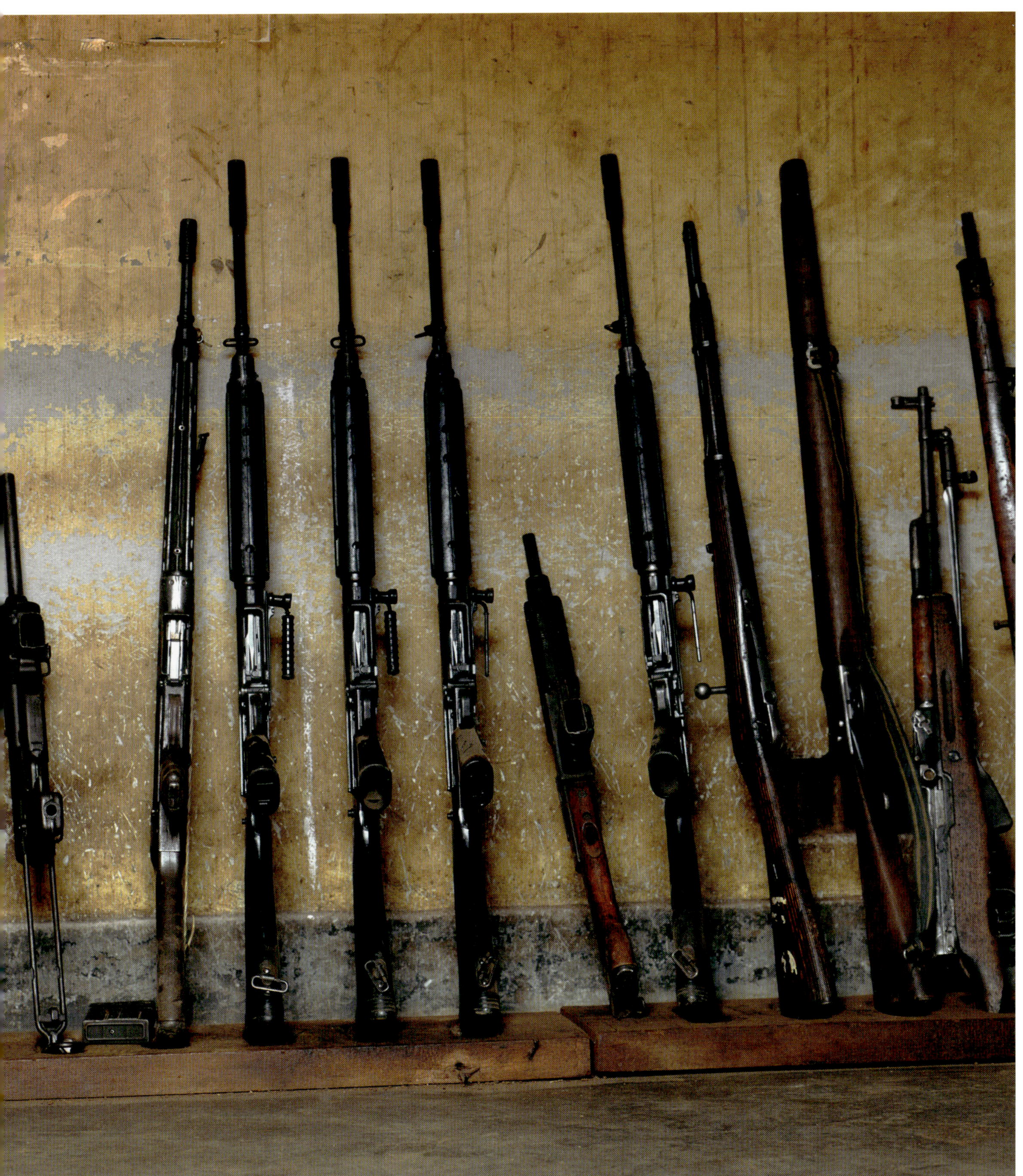

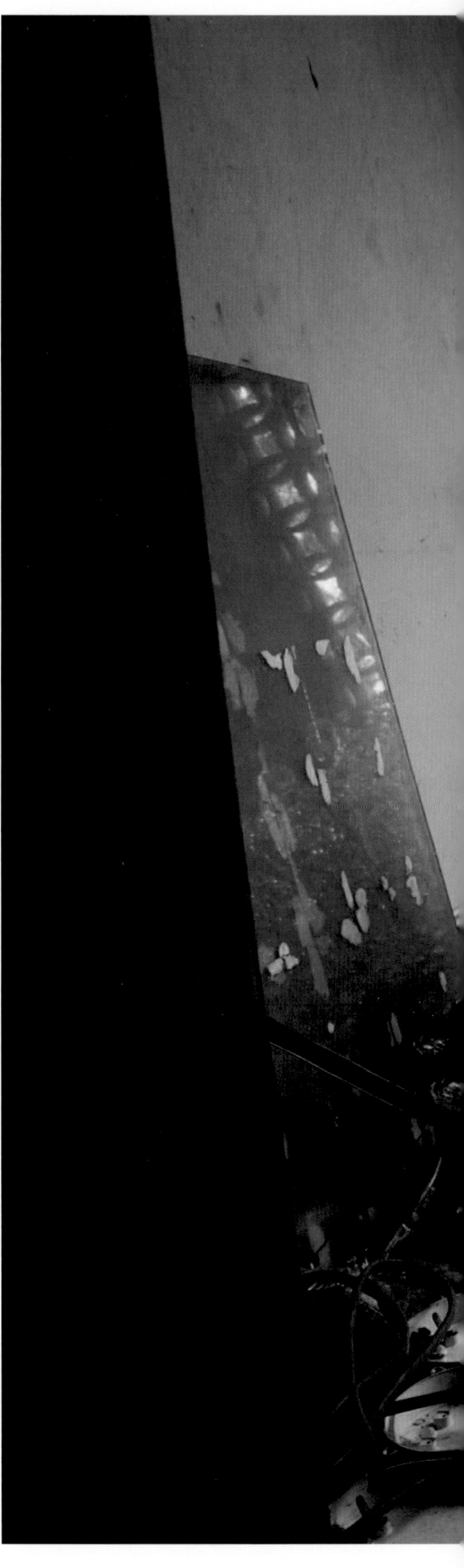

This Unhinged Her, 1998–2006

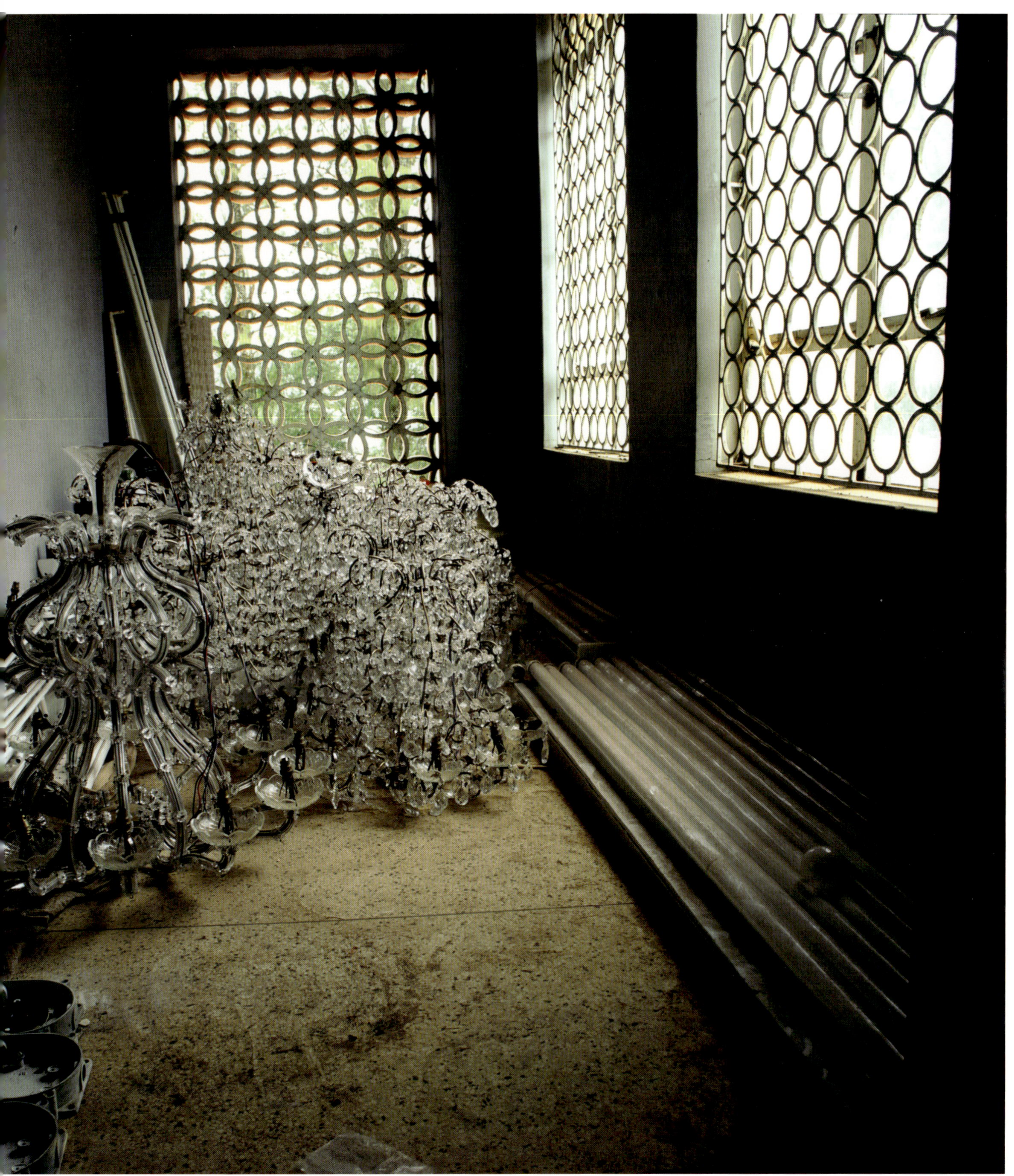

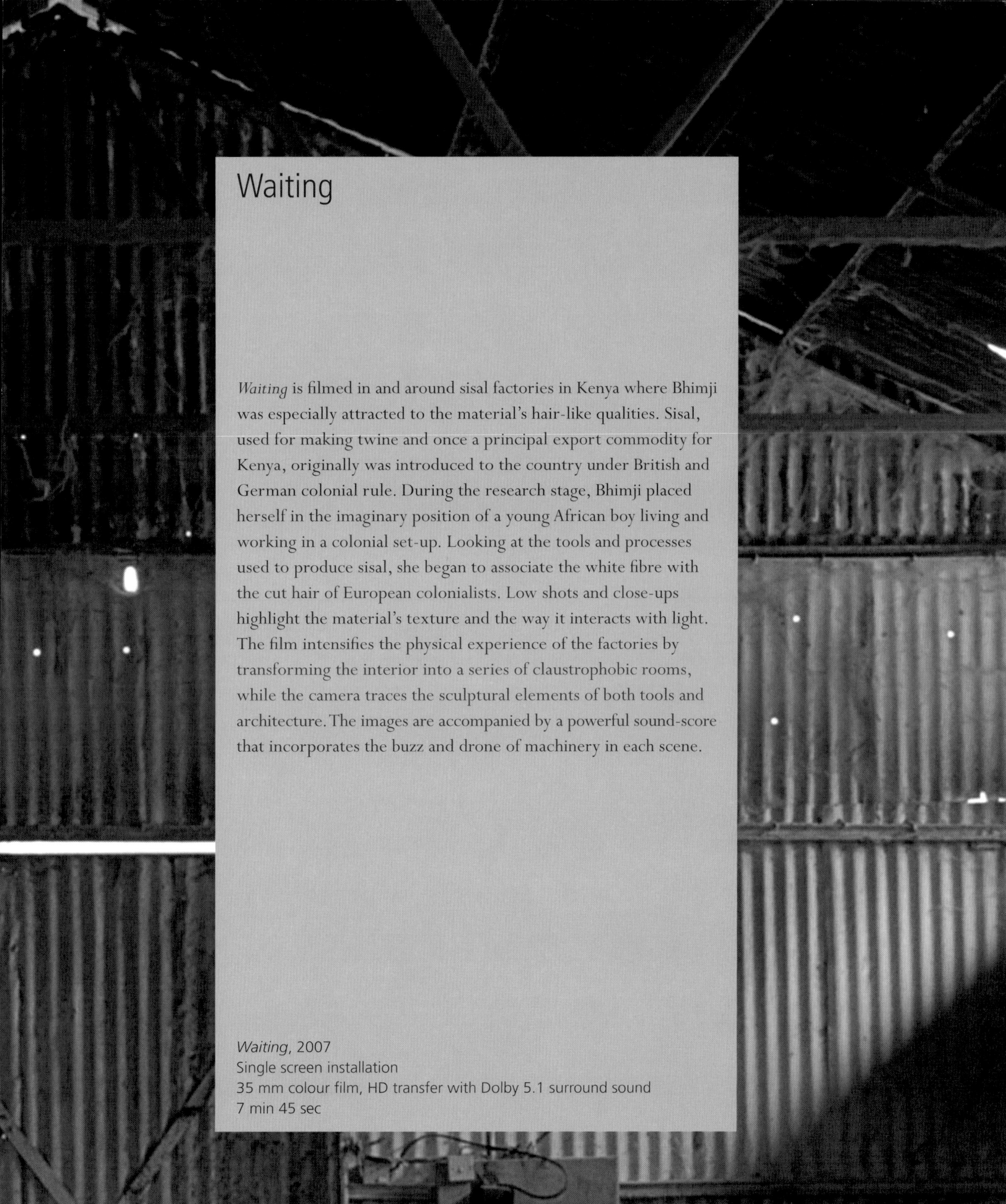

Waiting

Waiting is filmed in and around sisal factories in Kenya where Bhimji was especially attracted to the material's hair-like qualities. Sisal, used for making twine and once a principal export commodity for Kenya, originally was introduced to the country under British and German colonial rule. During the research stage, Bhimji placed herself in the imaginary position of a young African boy living and working in a colonial set-up. Looking at the tools and processes used to produce sisal, she began to associate the white fibre with the cut hair of European colonialists. Low shots and close-ups highlight the material's texture and the way it interacts with light. The film intensifies the physical experience of the factories by transforming the interior into a series of claustrophobic rooms, while the camera traces the sculptural elements of both tools and architecture. The images are accompanied by a powerful sound-score that incorporates the buzz and drone of machinery in each scene.

Waiting, 2007
Single screen installation
35 mm colour film, HD transfer with Dolby 5.1 surround sound
7 min 45 sec

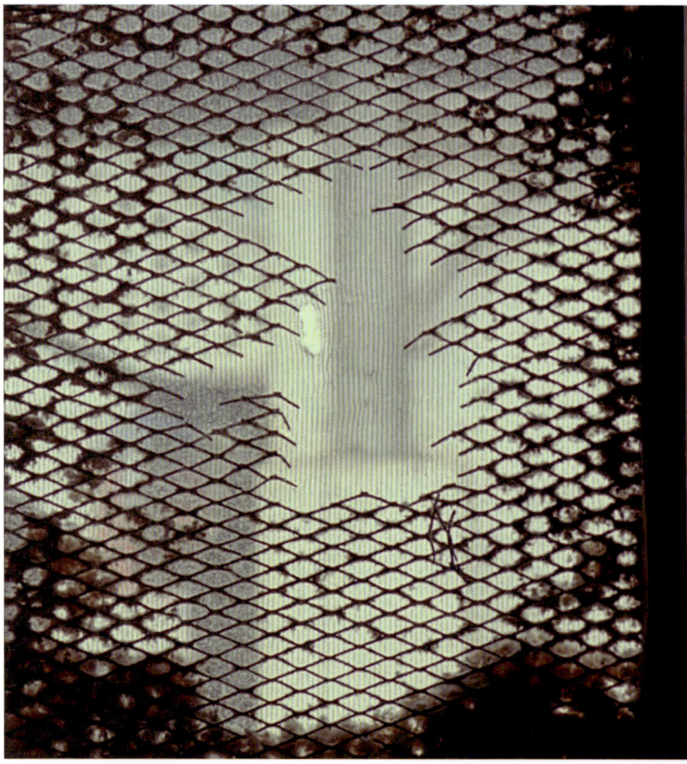

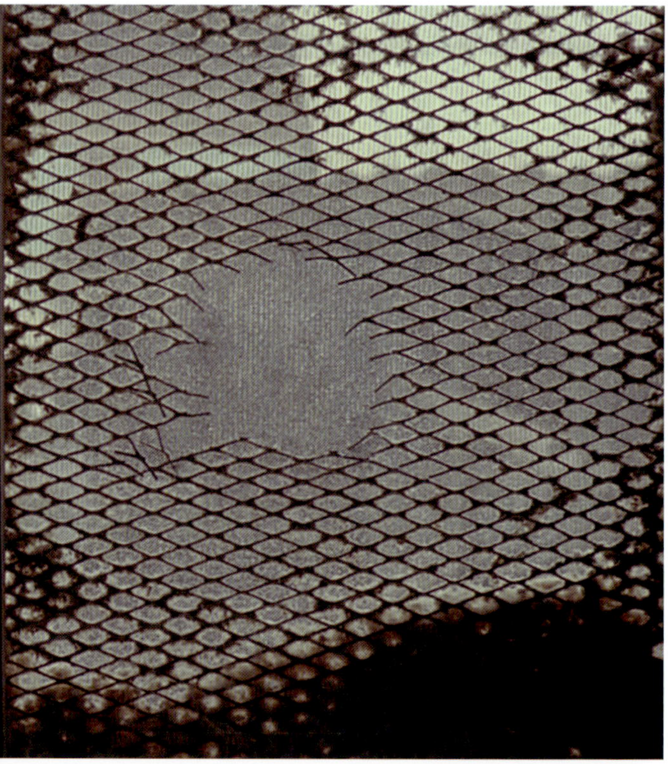

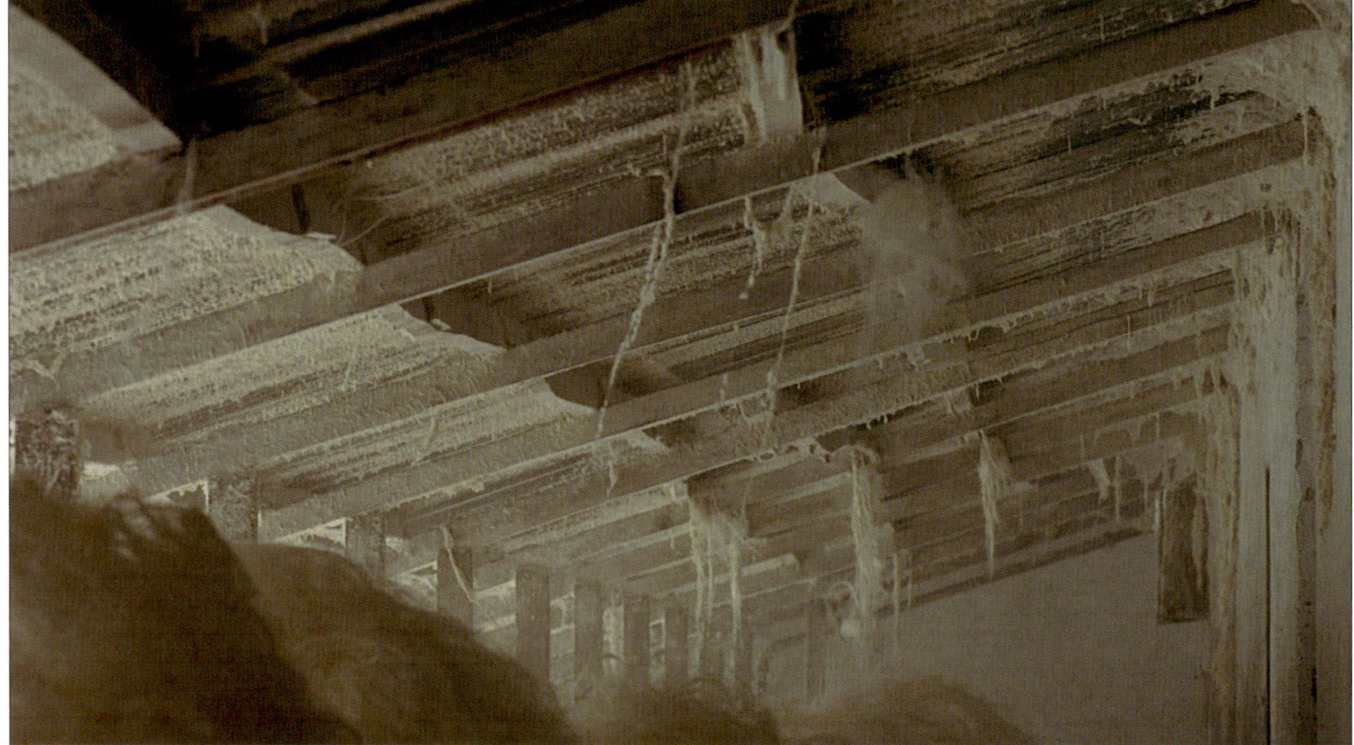

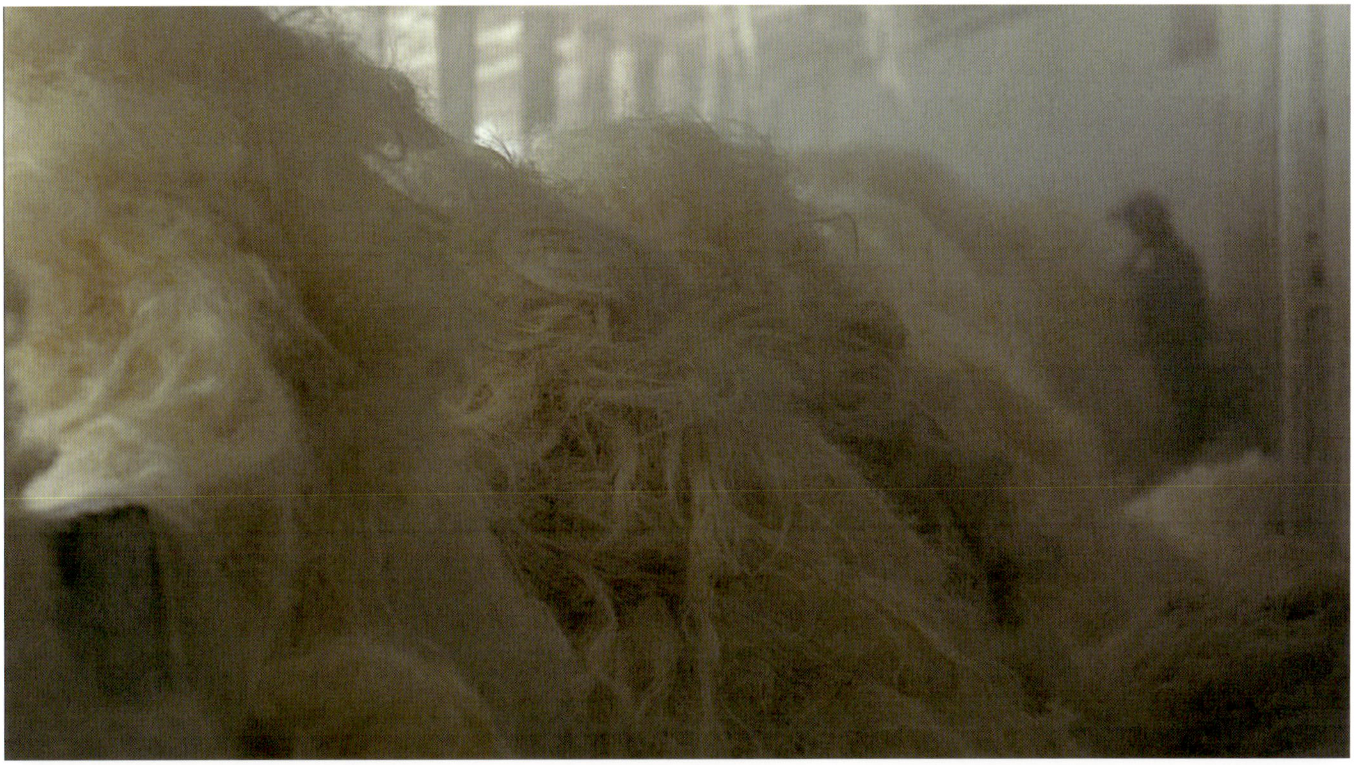

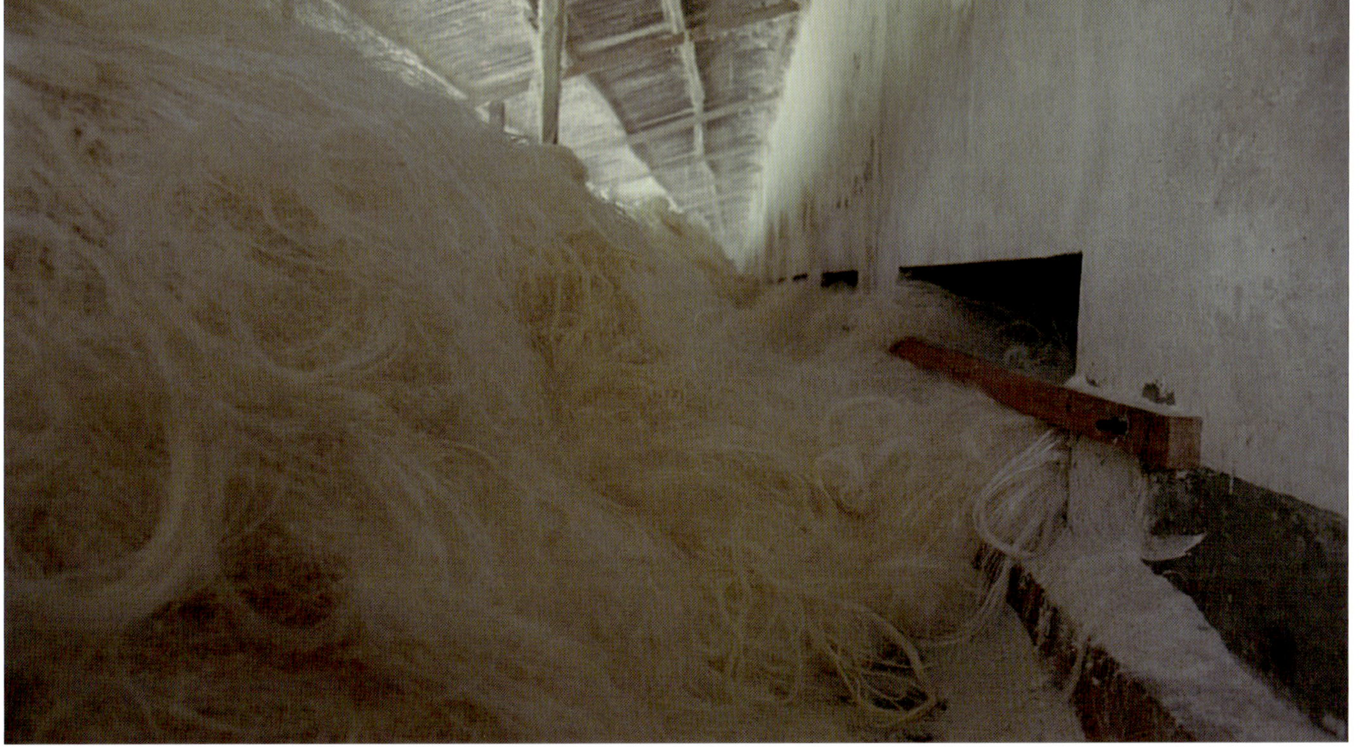

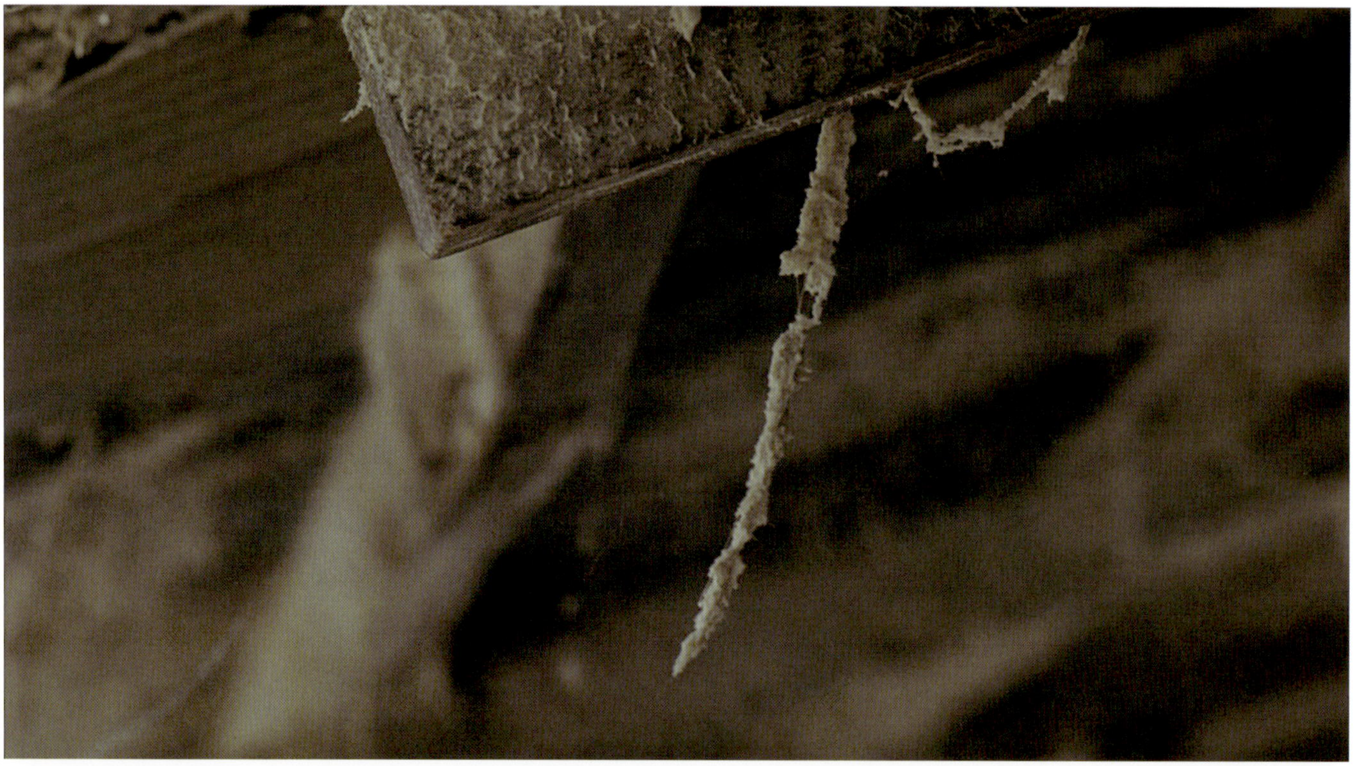

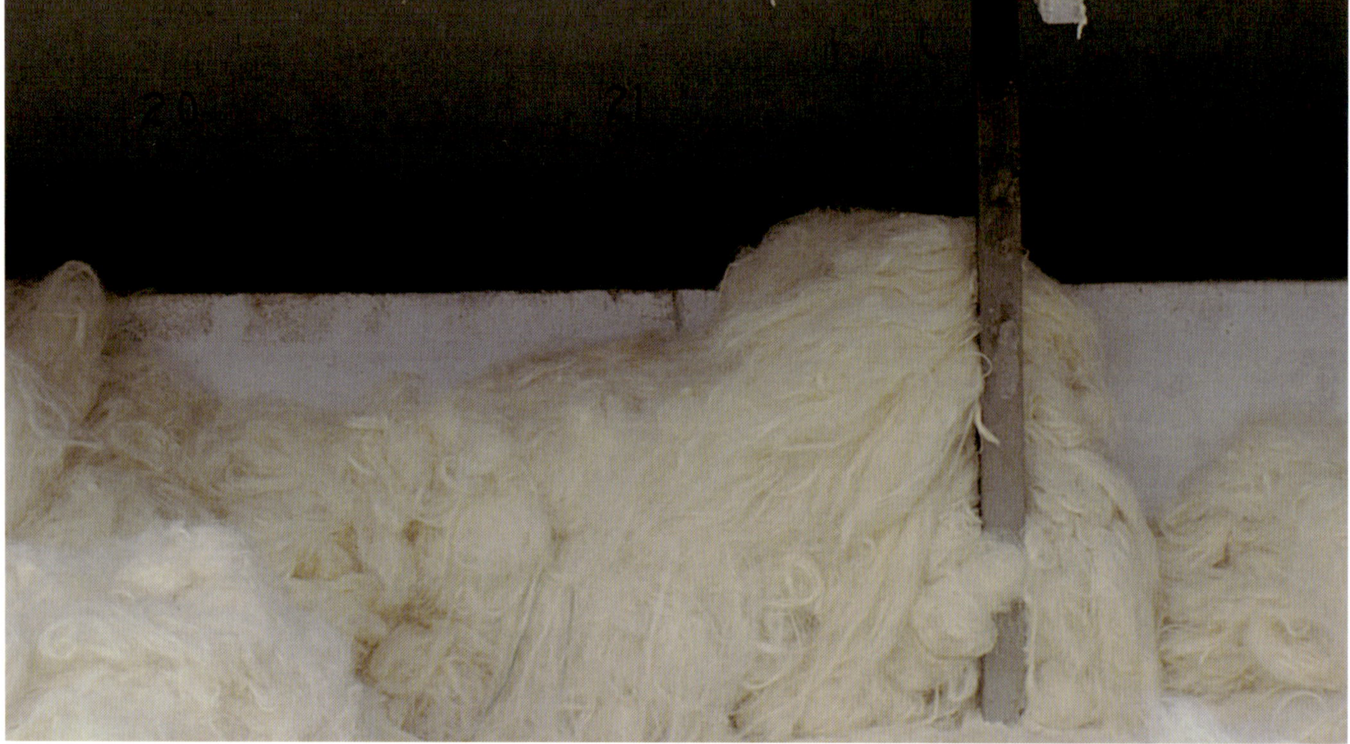

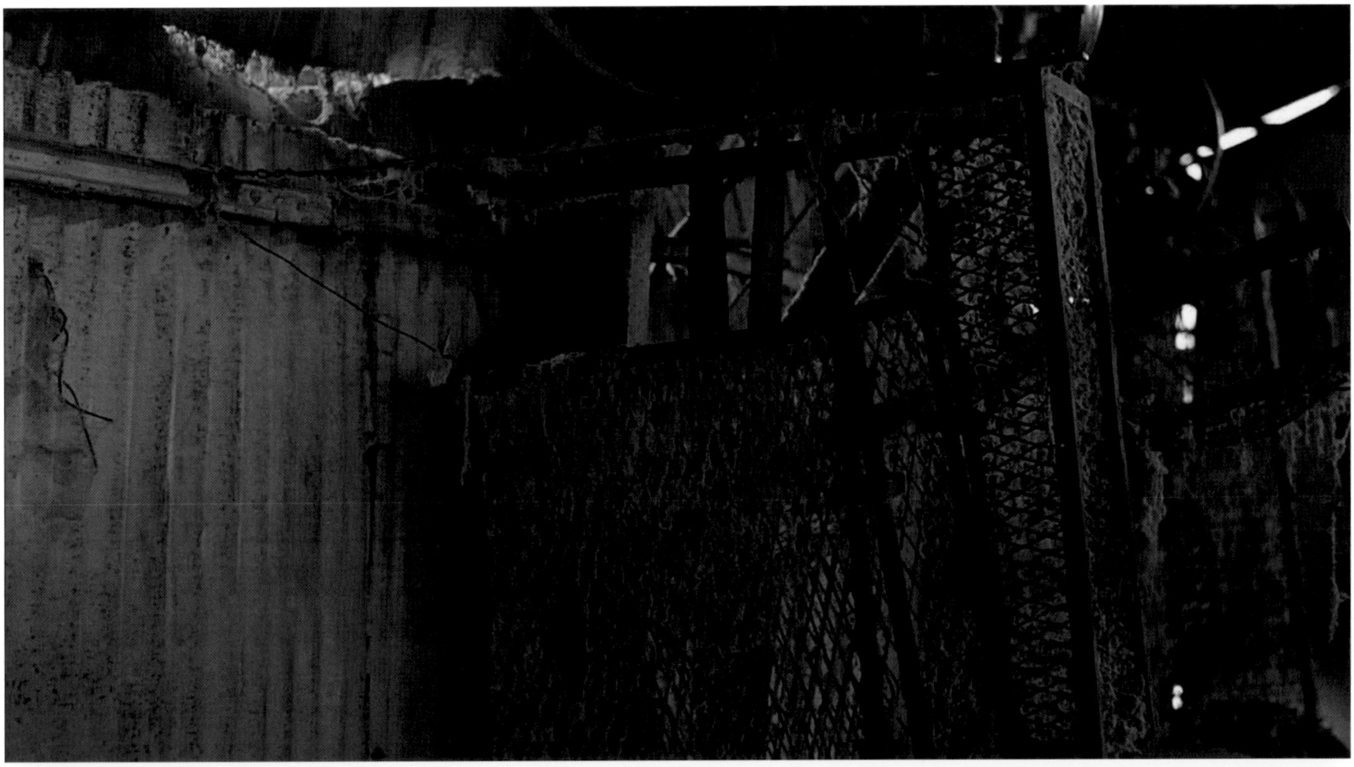

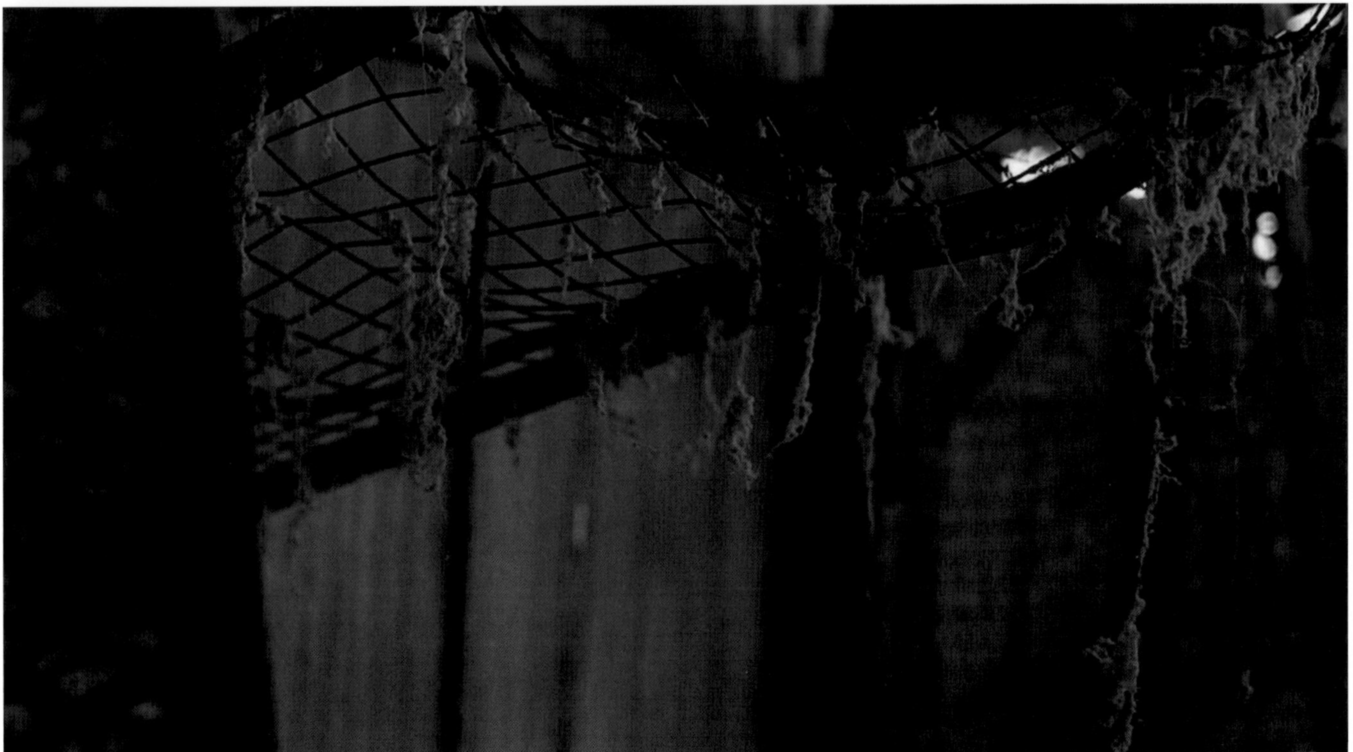

Yellow Patch

Taking as its starting point the history of trade and migration between India and Africa, *Yellow Patch* is filmed in four main locations across the Indian sub-continent: the old Victorian offices in the Port Trust of Bombay, the desert landscape of the Rann of Kutch, the Indian Ocean near the port of Mandvi and various houses and structures in the Western region of Gujarat. The film is the result of extensive research, although Bhimji approaches her various locations with a painterly approach that relinquishes information and factual presentation in favour of highlighting the aesthetic qualities and poetic potential of each image. As much as for the traces of history they carry, each location was chosen for its distinct quality of light, the details of its architecture and the particular character of the landscape. Sumptuous images of sea, desert, domestic and administration buildings are accompanied by a soundtrack of waves, birdsong, typewriters and voices that provoke impressions of dread, loss, passion, love and tenderness.

Yellow Patch, 2011
Single screen installation
35 mm colour film, HD transfer with Dolby 5.1 surround sound
29 min 43 sec

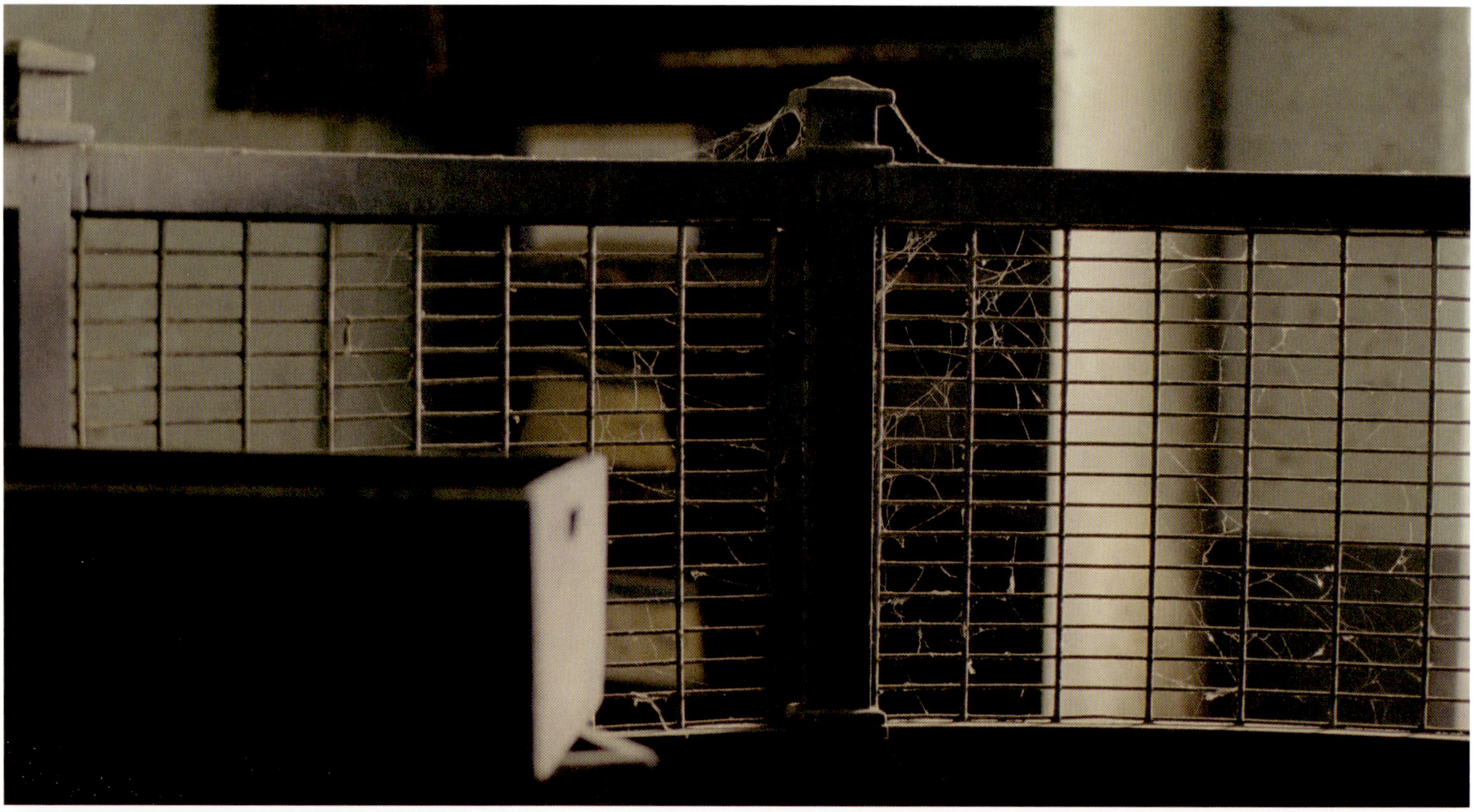

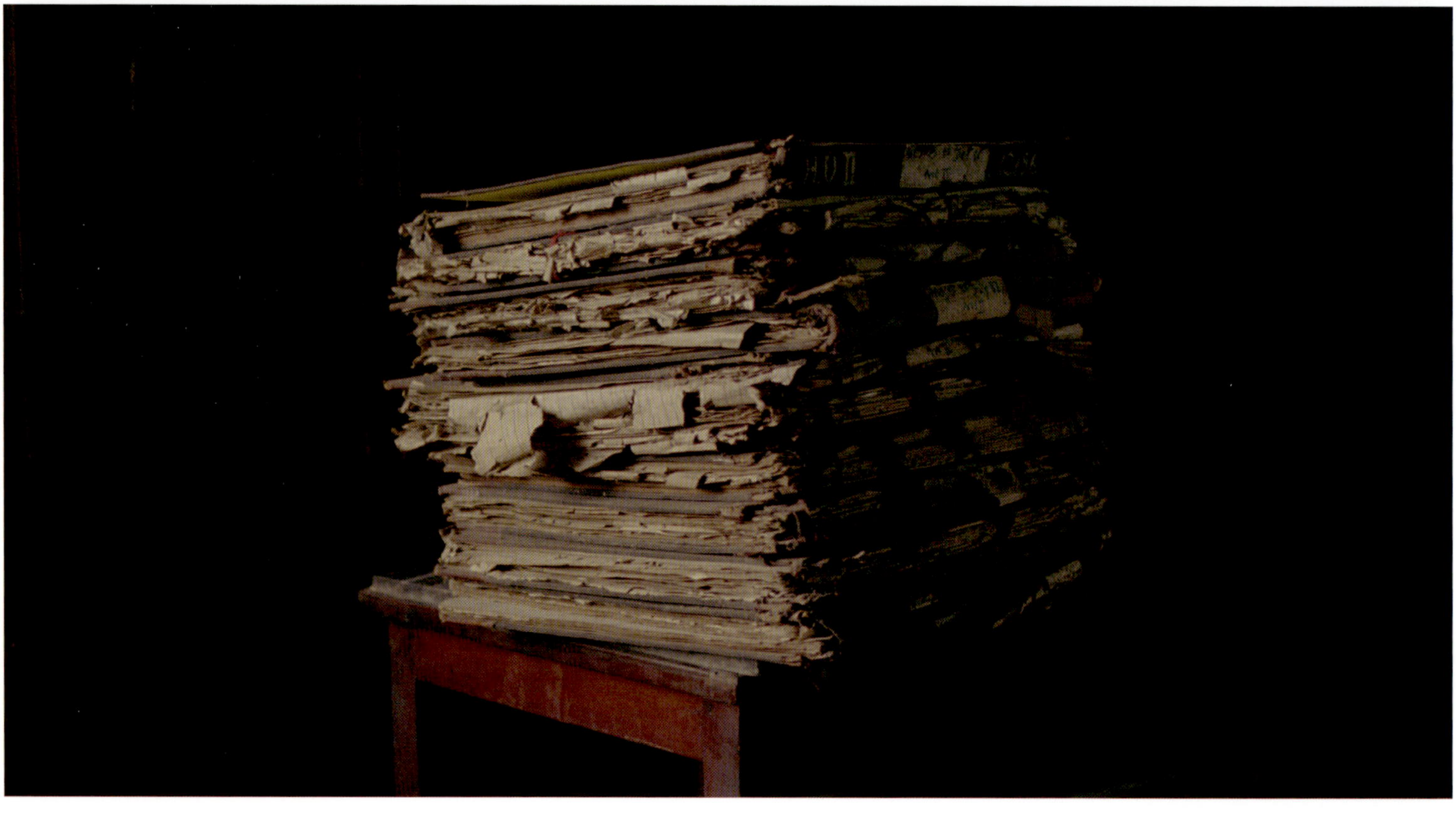

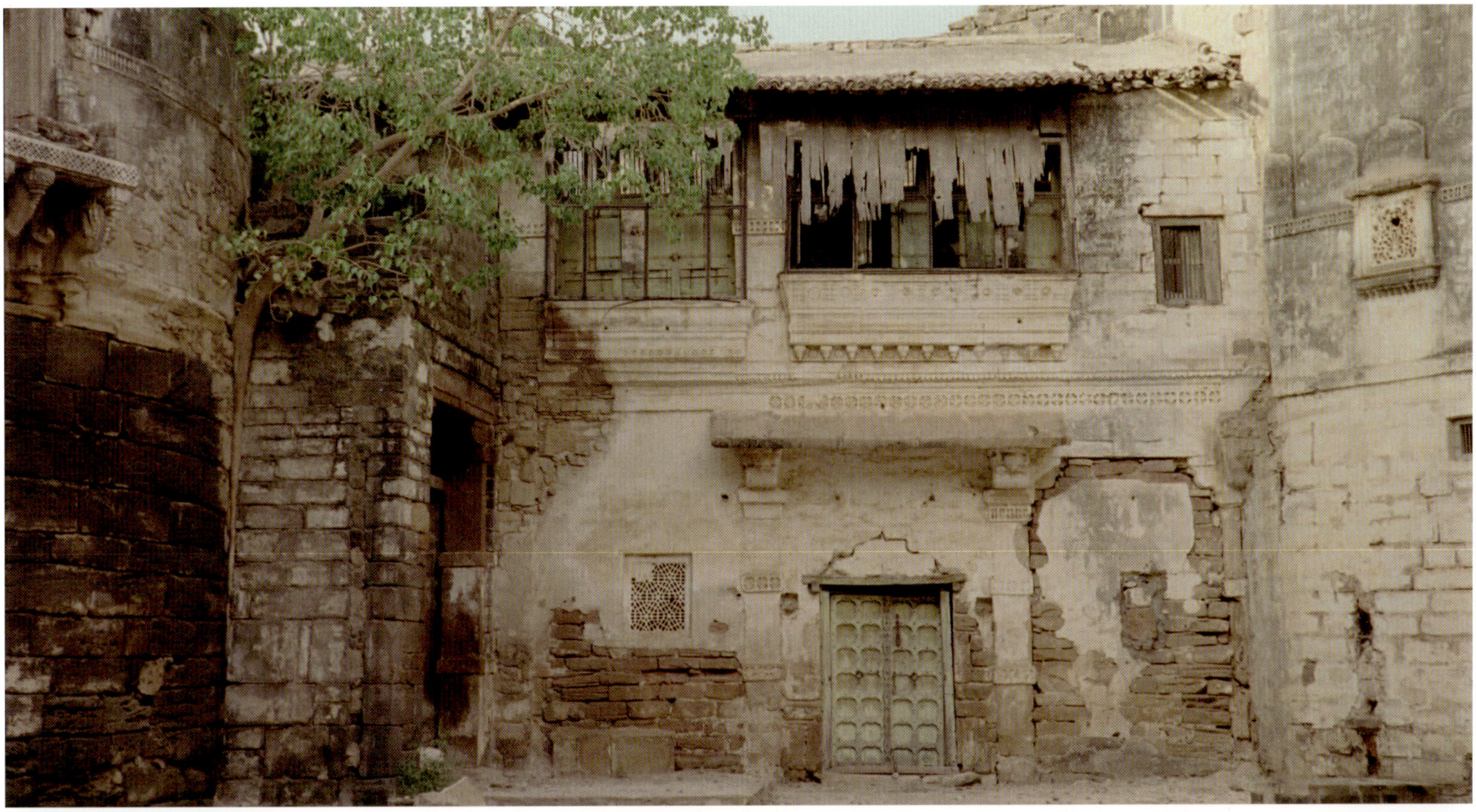

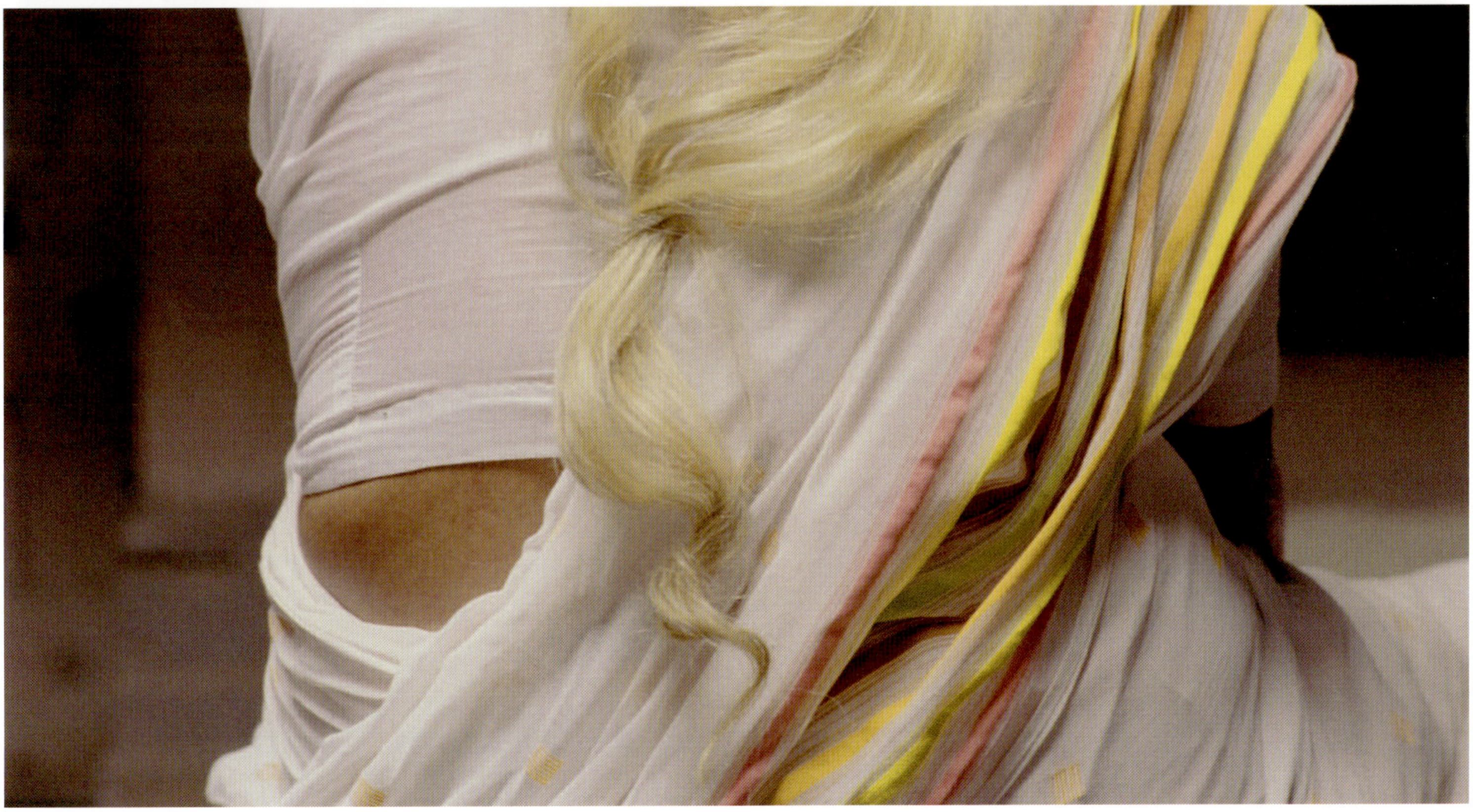

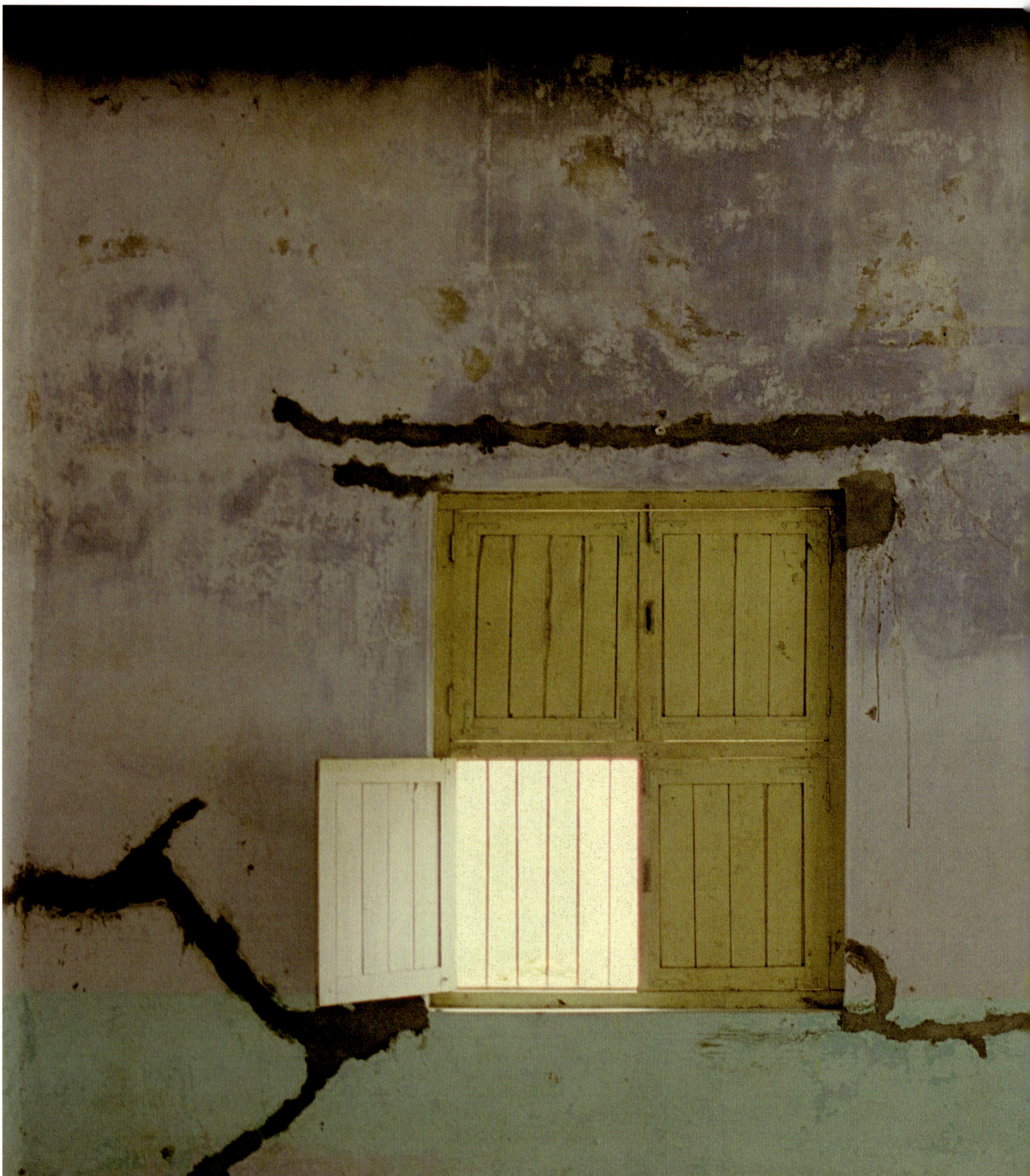

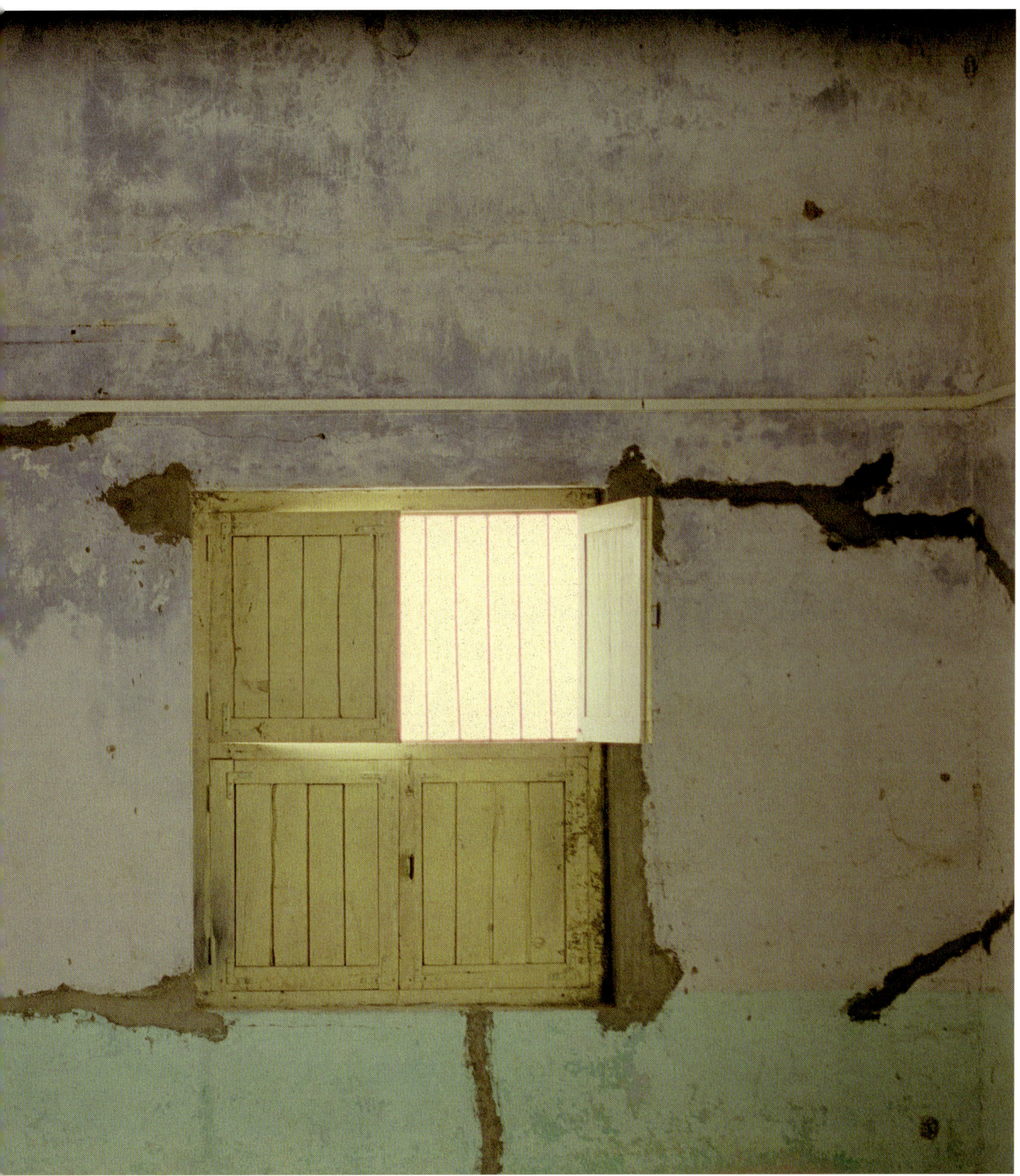

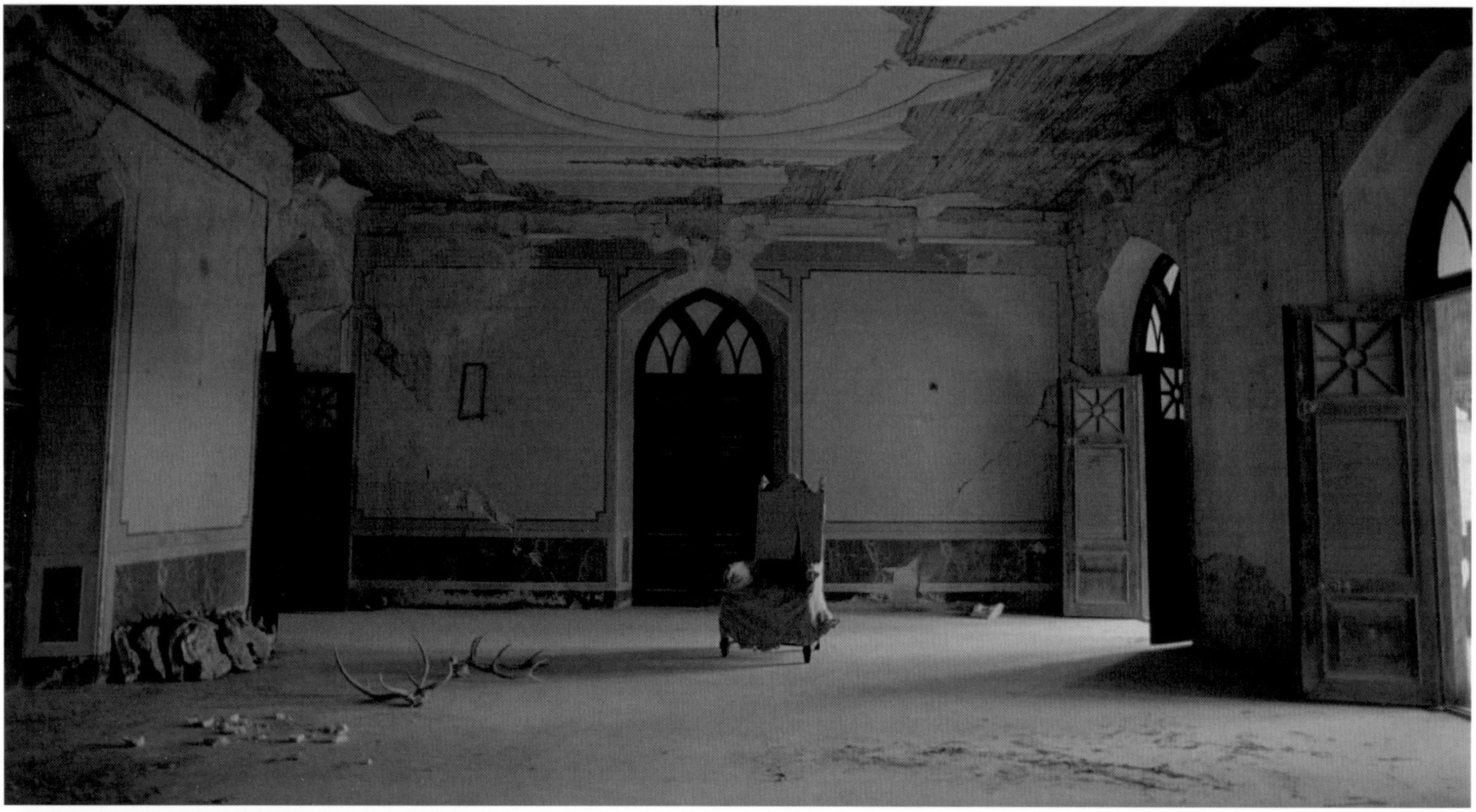

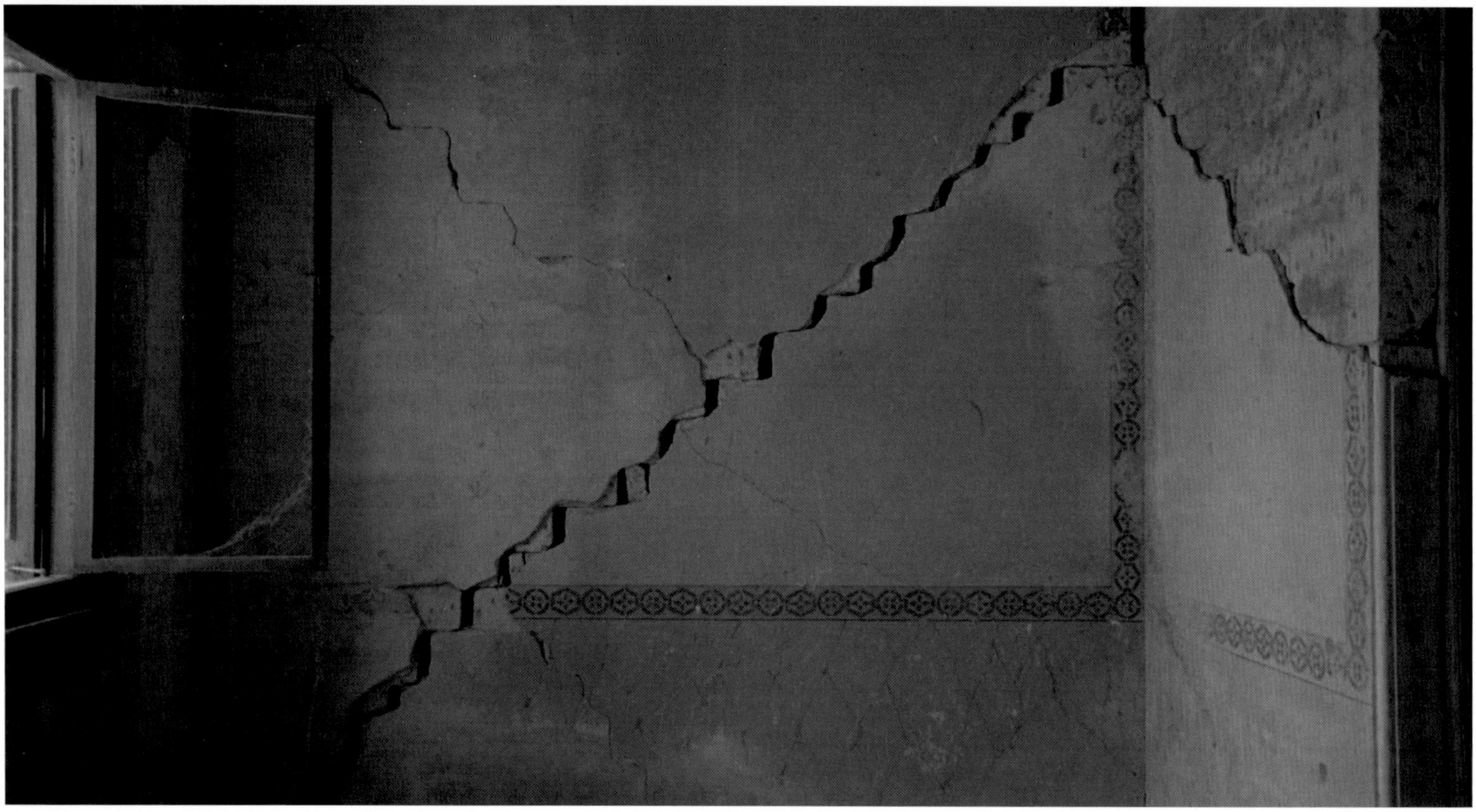

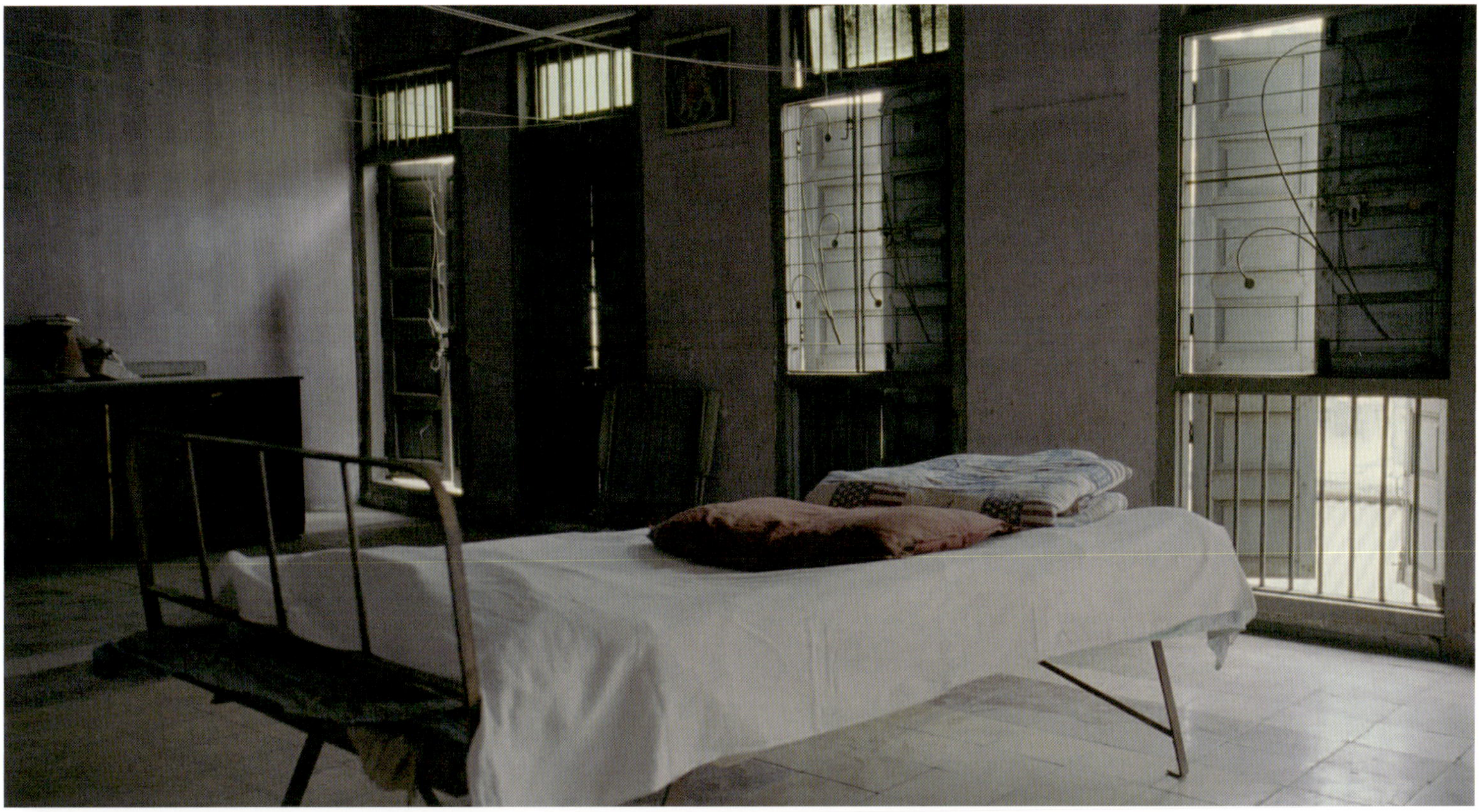

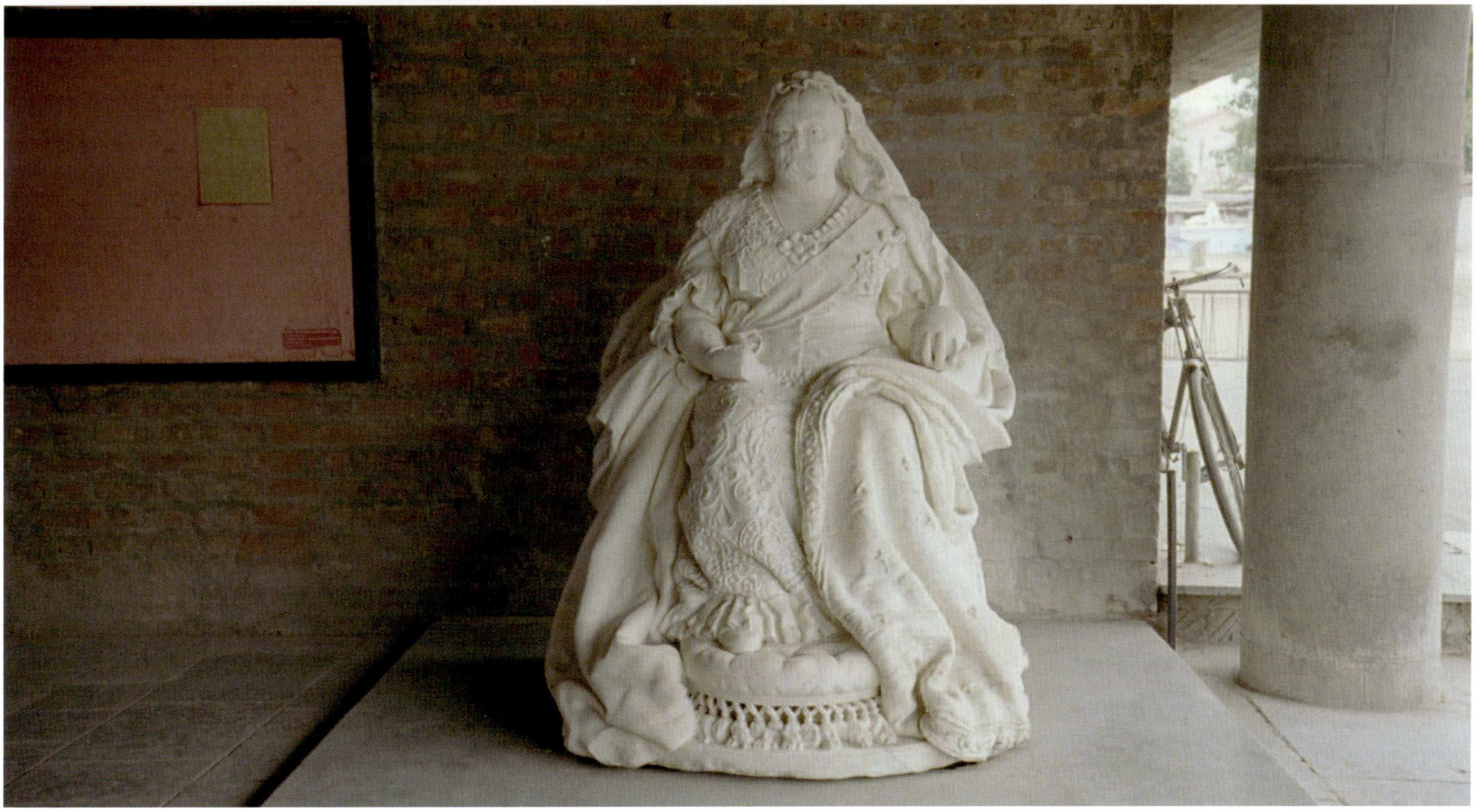

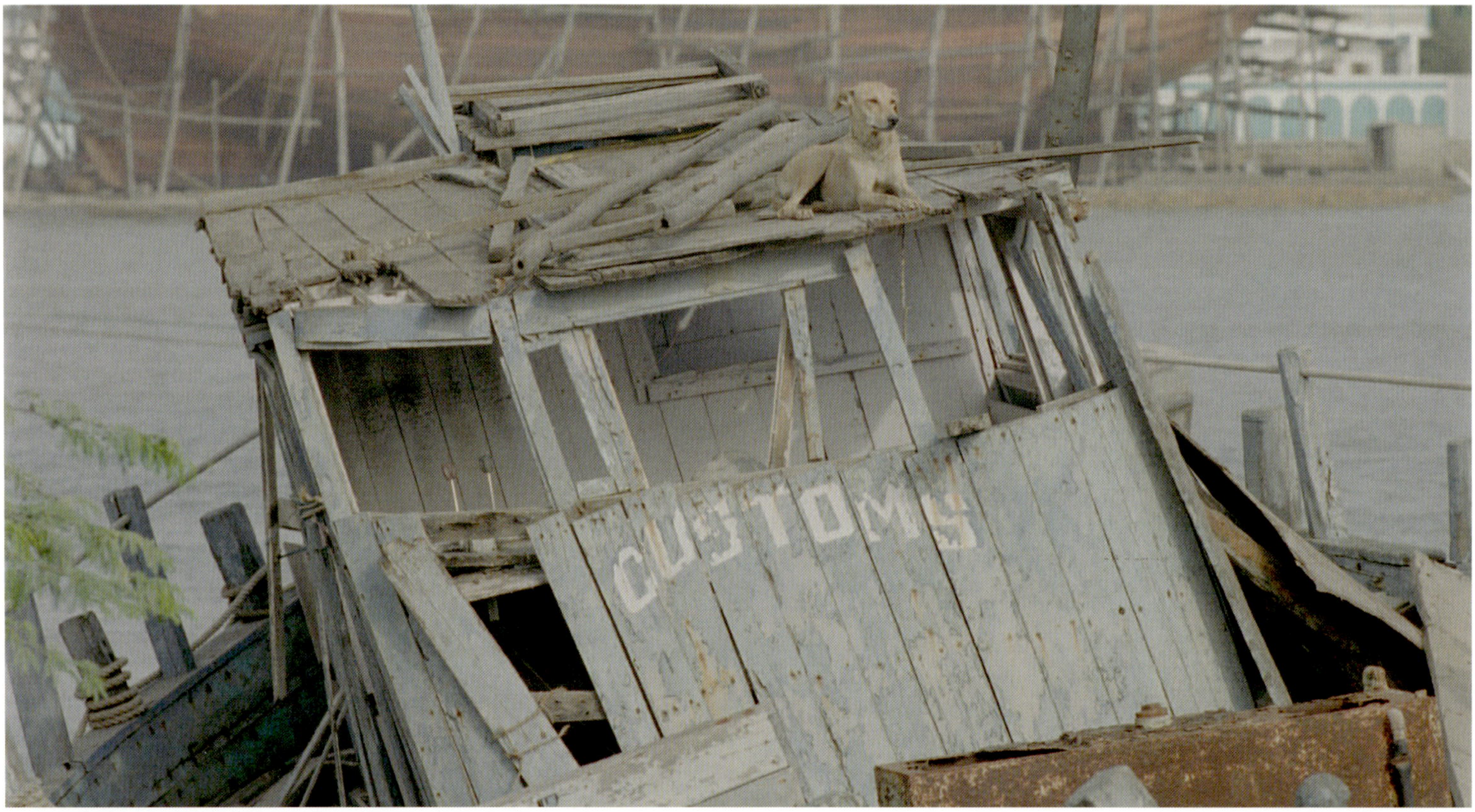

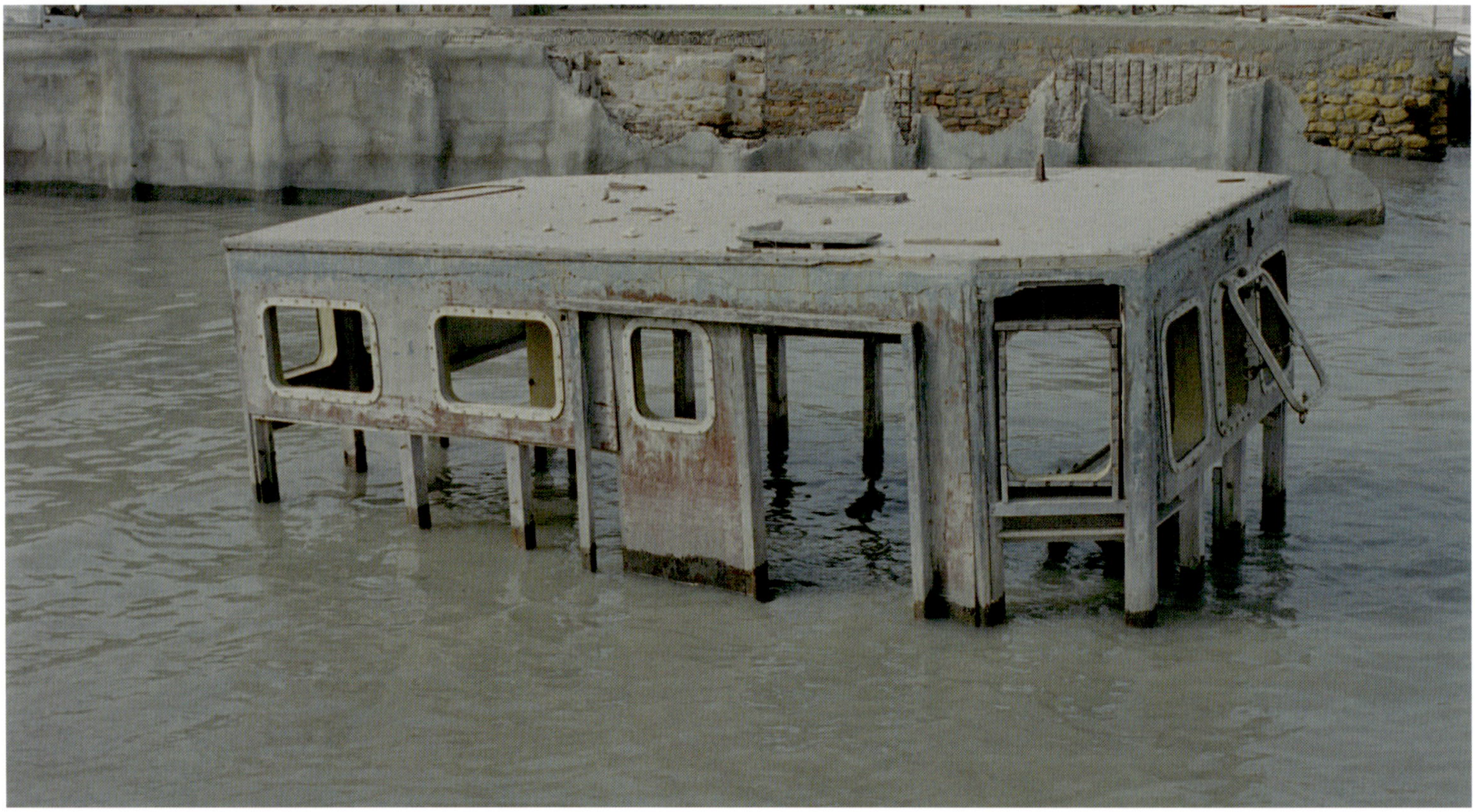

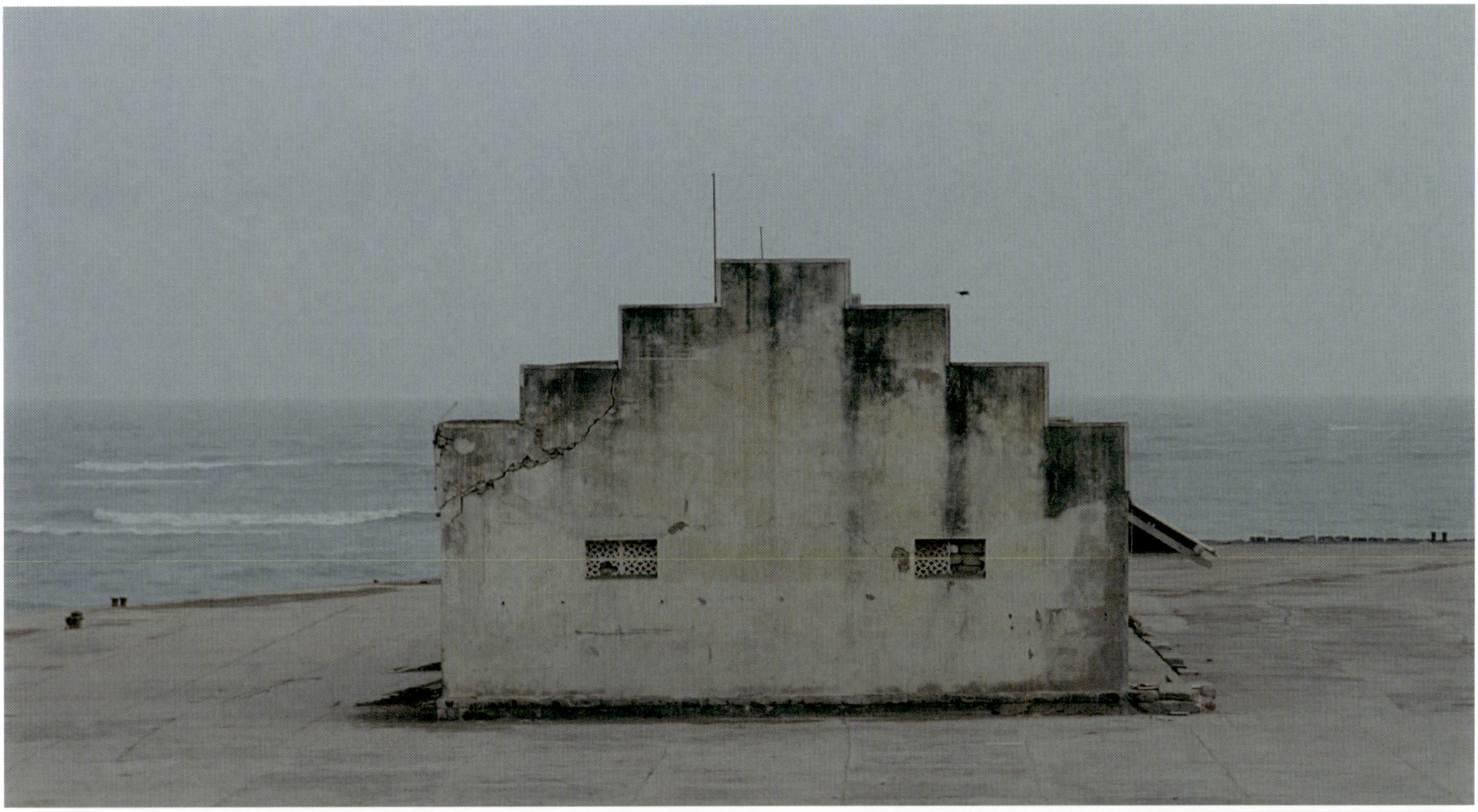

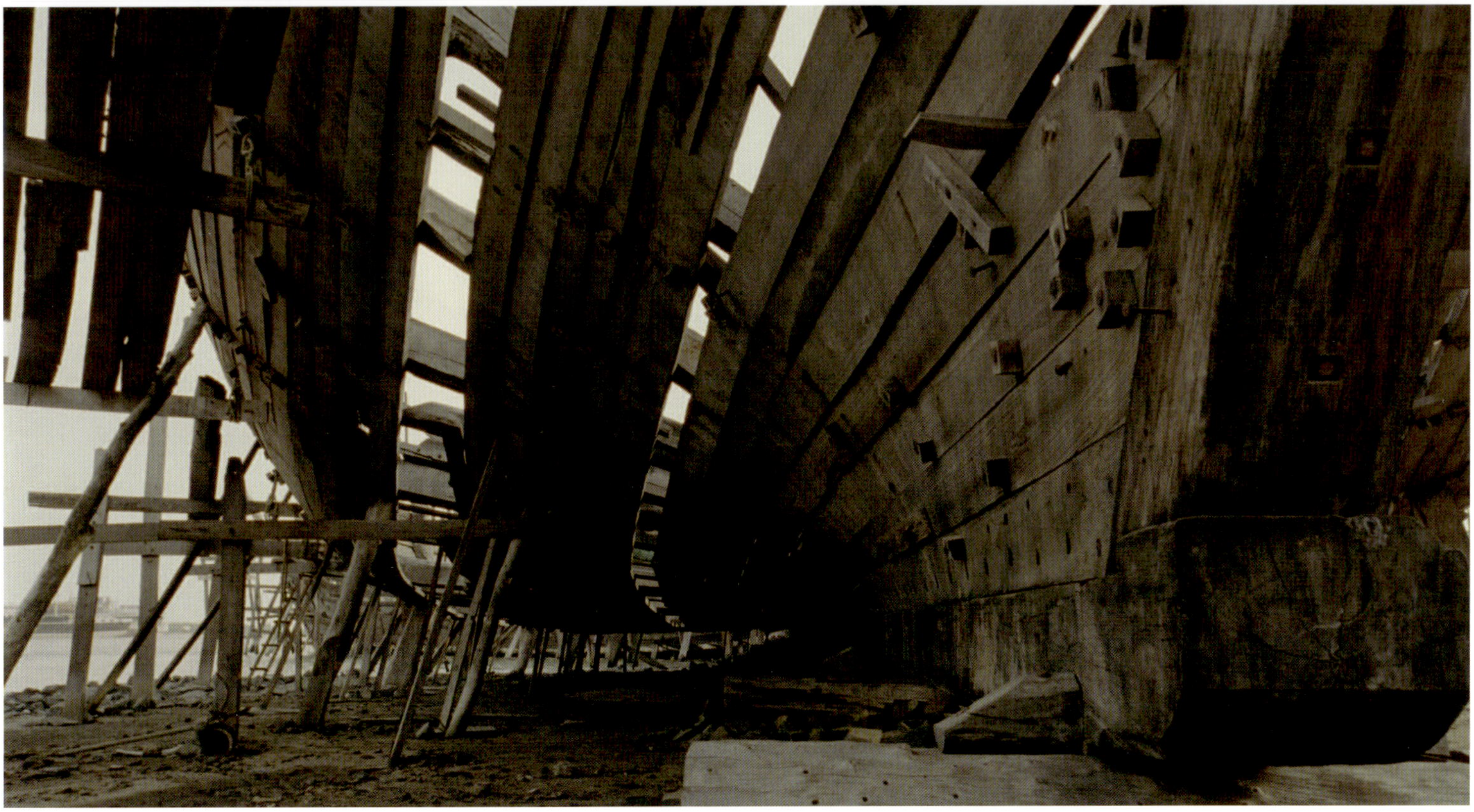

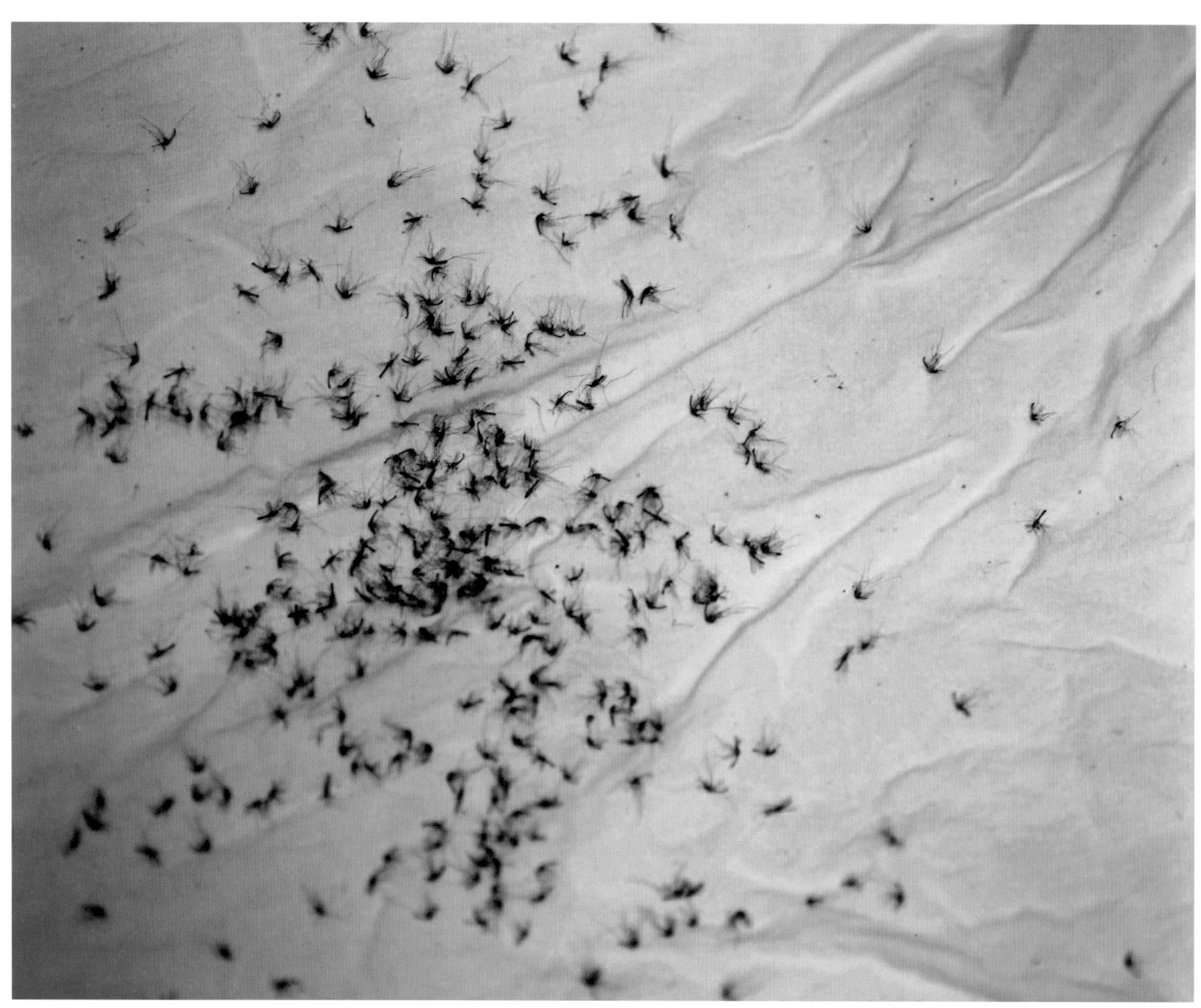

Encoding, 2000–2011

Red & Wet

This ongoing series of both black and white and colour photographs is rooted in research supported by Imperial College, Wellcome Trust London, the London School of Hygiene and Tropical Medicine, Artsadmin and Greater London Art, as well as the National Institute for Medical Research. Close-up shots of malarial mosquitoes bred under laboratory conditions in London are combined with images of hospital beds, mosquito nets and a malaria clinic in Africa. These simultaneously beautiful and disturbing images call up notions of fever, passion and love while also reflecting on common and often clichéd depictions of contemporary Africa.

Red & Wet, 2000–2011
Colour Eudura prints, 101.6 × 82.5 cm | 40 × 32½ in;
101.6 × 91.6 cm | 40 × 30 in; 101.6 × 102.1 cm | 40 × 40 ⅕ in;
fibre based print, 77 × 94 cm | 33 3/10 × 37 in

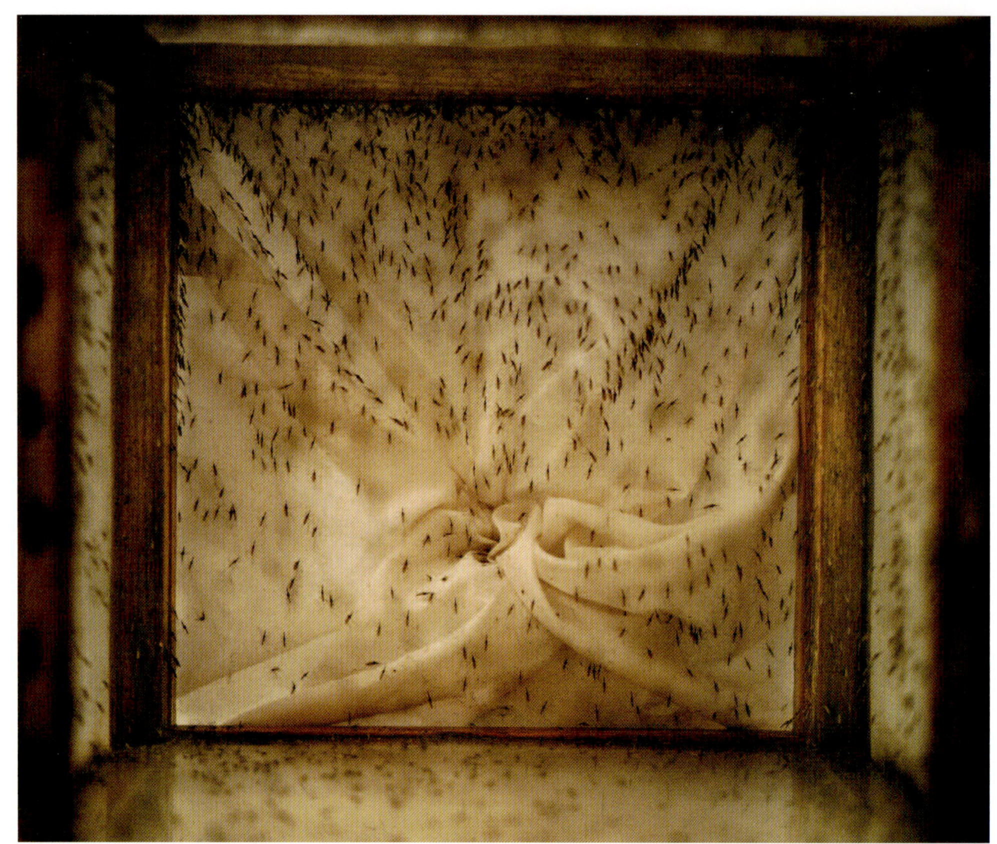

Tropical, 2000–2011

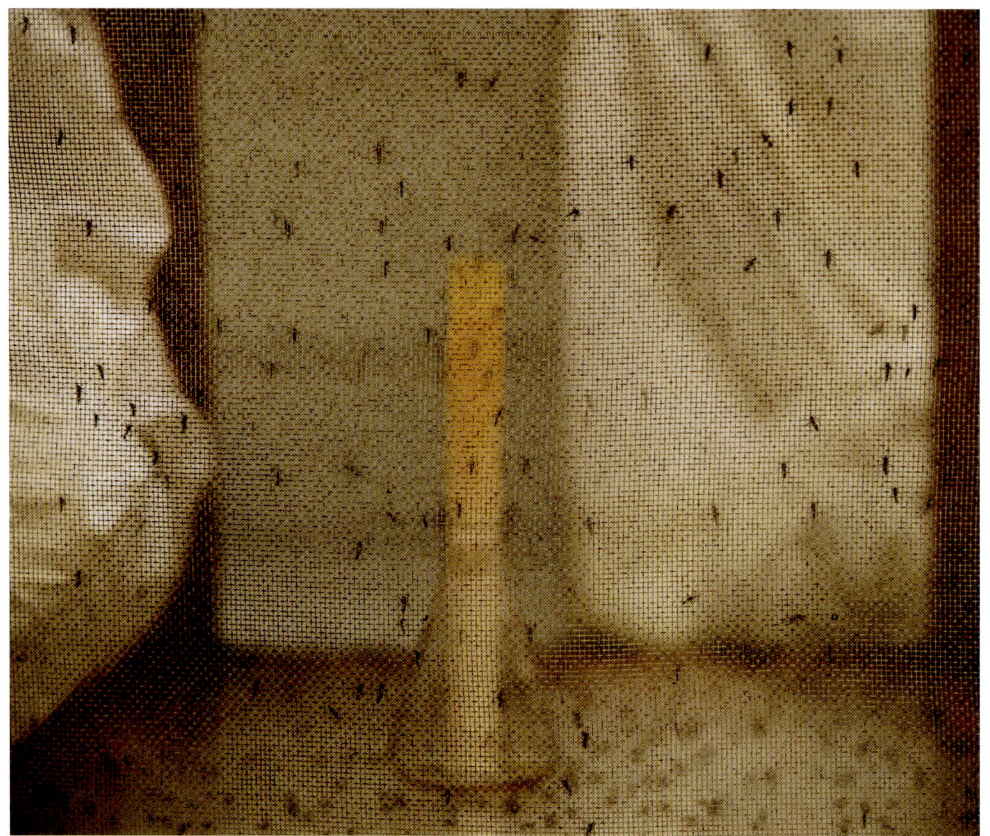

Enclosed, 2000–2011

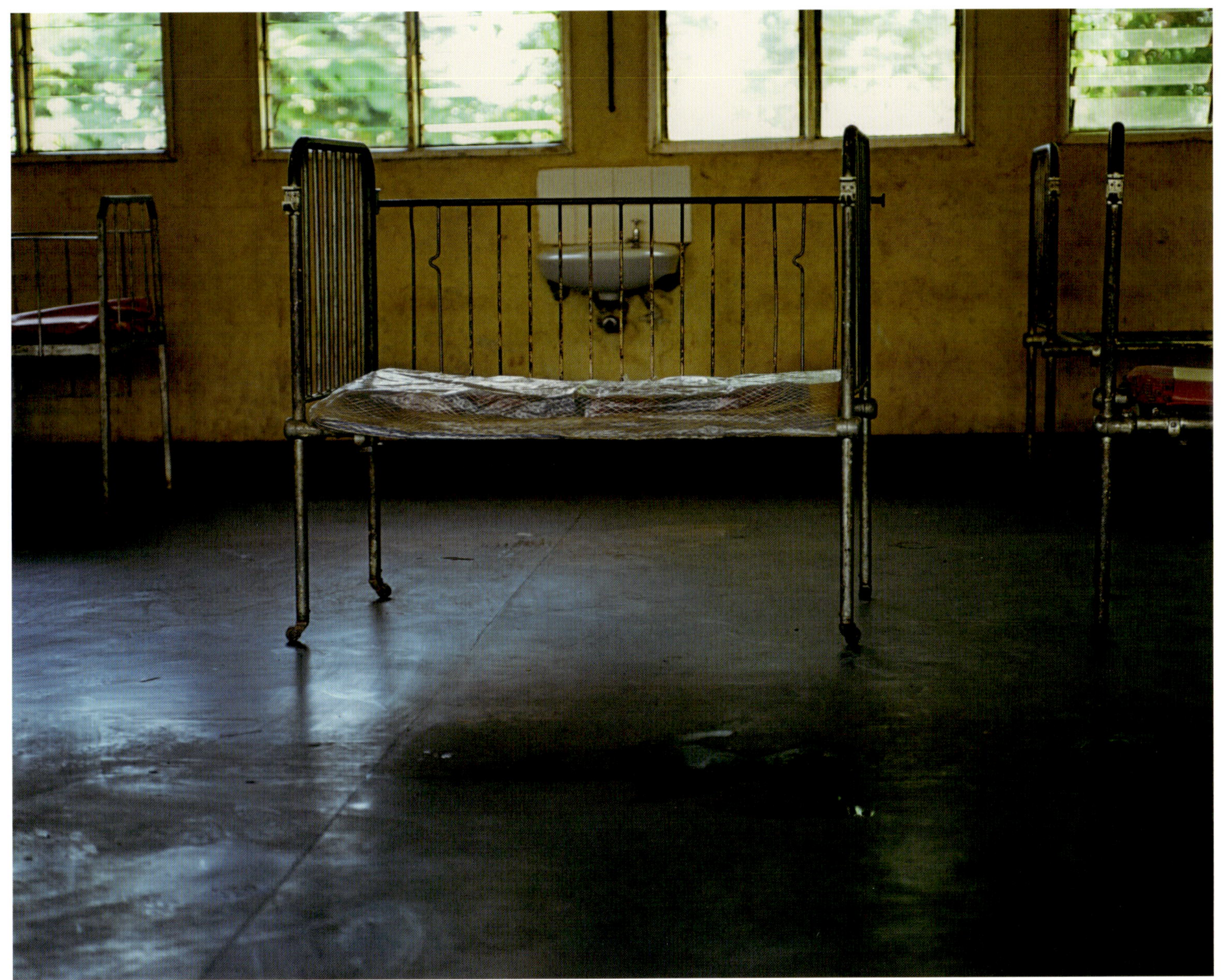

Fever, 2000–2011

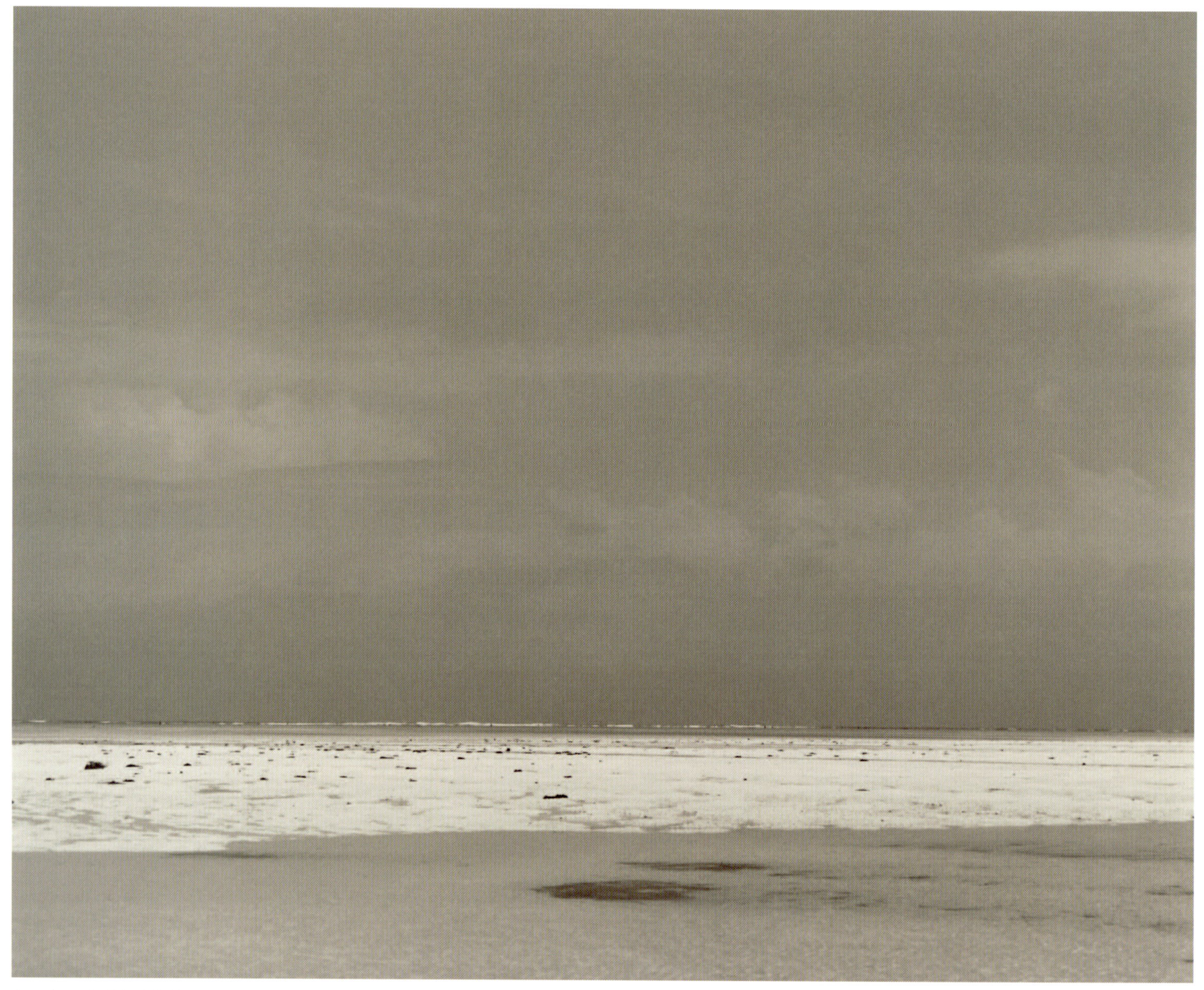

Jangbar, 1998–2011

Seascapes

These black and white seascape images were initially taken in Zanzibar in 1998 and preface both the *Love* series (1998–2007; p.87) and Bhimji's first film installation, *Out of Blue* (2002; p.77). Although printed and exhibited for the first time 13 years after they were taken, the seascapes mark a significant departure in Bhimji's way of working, reconnecting images from her more recent film installations with the more austere aesthetics of her earlier work. The artist has commented how these photographs for her evoke 'the end of the world. There is nothing to lean on. This space acts as a mirror to your mind. I want to travel to this space and watch it with my camera. Watch the days pass, watch the light, listen to the landscape. These spaces have an intense beauty yet are also imbued with a sense of uncertainty, disorientation and unfamiliarity. They transform the physical into the psychological.'

Seascapes, 1998–2011
Fibre based prints, 77 × 94 cm | 30 3⁄10 × 37 in

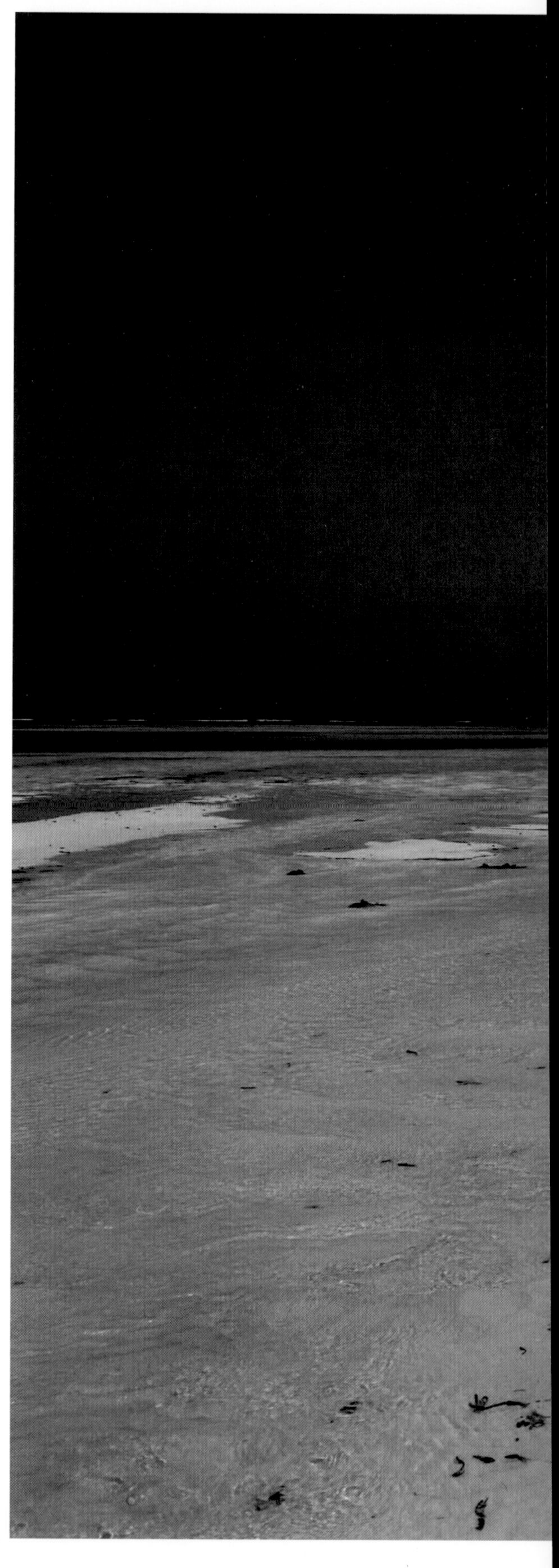

Revolution, 1998–2011

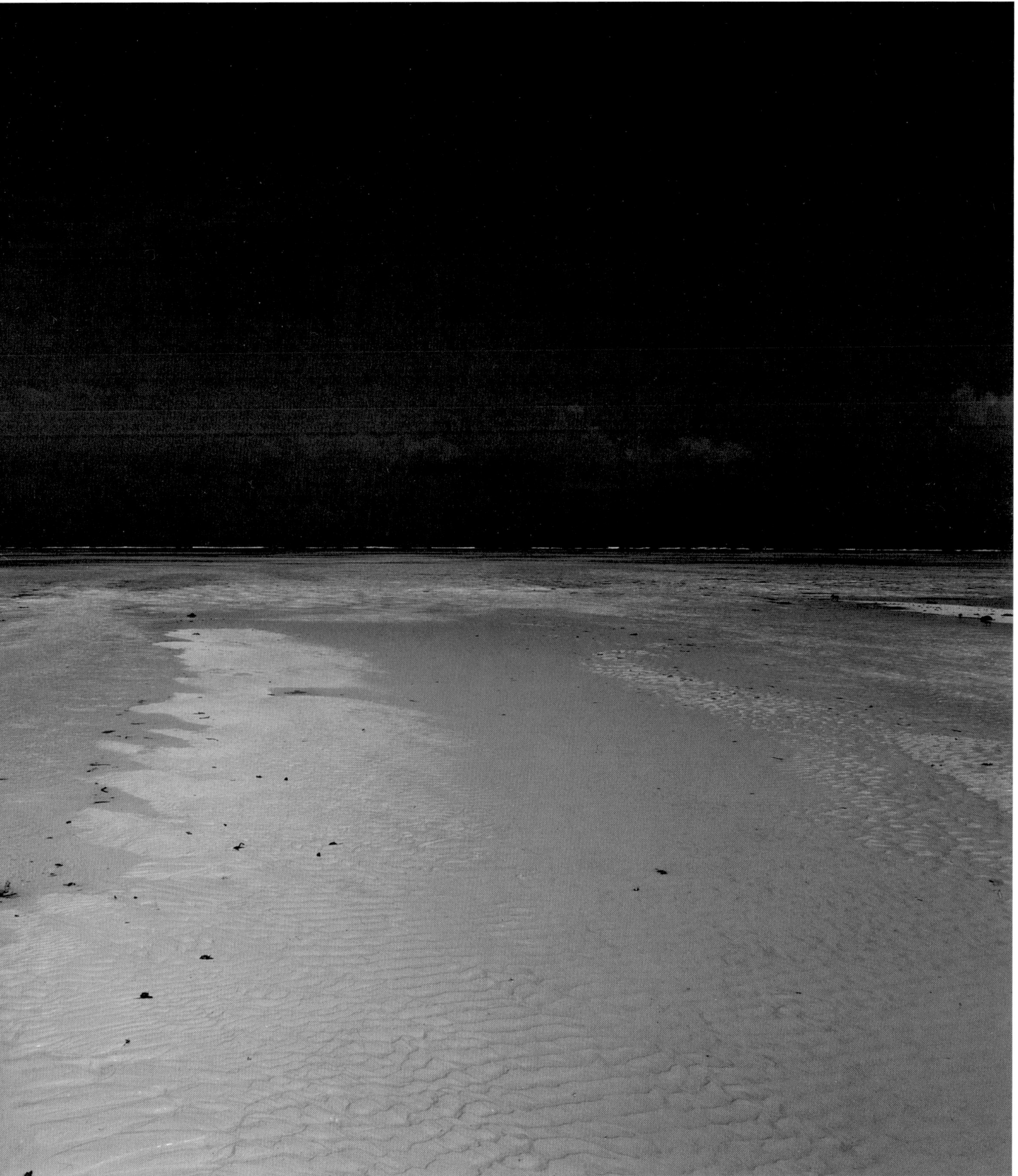

List of Works

Exhibited in *Zarina Bhimji* at Whitechapel Gallery and Kunstmuseum Bern

* indicates exhibited at Whitechapel Gallery only
** indicates exhibited at Kunstmuseum Bern only

She Loved to Breathe – Pure Silence, 1987
Installation consisting of eight hand-coloured gelatin-silver prints; text printed on muslin sandwiched between the photographs; latex gloves; plexi-glass; photocopied passports on the muslin; turmeric and chilli powder scattered on the floor
Each image 49.7 × 51 cm | 19⅕ × 20 in
Overall dimensions variable
Victoria & Albert Museum

Untitled, 1989
Polaroid photographs
Each 60 × 50 cm | 23⅗ × 19 7/10 in
Victoria & Albert Museum

Cleaning the Garden, 1998
A Black Indian Boy, 1998
Eighteenth-century newspaper text etched on mirror
61.2 × 51 cm | 24 × 20 in
Private Collection. Courtesy of Talwar Gallery, New York, New Delhi

Alcazar, 1998
Cibachrome photograph on aluminium
120 × 157.5 cm | 47⅕ × 62 in
Private Collection. Courtesy of Talwar Gallery, New York, New Delhi

Darkness oblivion, 1998
Cibachrome transparency lightbox
88 × 105 × 16 cm | 34⅘ × 41⅓ × 6⅓ in
Collection of the artist

Female government, 1998
Cibachrome photograph on aluminium
122.4 × 173.4 cm | 48⅕ × 68 3/10 in
Private Collection. Courtesy of Talwar Gallery, New York, New Delhi

Cleaning the Garden, 1998 (continued)
Friendly, 1998
Eighteenth-century newspaper text etched on mirror
61.2 × 51 cm | 24.1 × 20.1 in
Private Collection. Courtesy of Talwar Gallery, New York, New Delhi

Harsh pubic hair, 1998
Cibachrome transparency lightbox
88 × 105 × 16 cm | 34⅘ × 41⅓ × 6⅓ in
Private Collection. Courtesy of Talwar Gallery, New York, New Delhi

JAMAICA, 1998
Eighteenth-century newspaper text etched on mirror
61.2 × 51 cm | 24.1 × 20.1 in
Private Collection. Courtesy of Talwar Gallery, New York, New Delhi

Musâlimûn, 1998
Cibachrome transparency lightbox
88 × 105 × 16 cm | 34⅘ × 41⅓ × 6⅓ in
Private Collection. Courtesy of Talwar Gallery, New York, New Delhi

Strange domineering tenderness, 1998
Cibachrome transparency lightbox
88 × 105 × 16 cm | 34⅘ × 41⅓ × 6⅓ in
Purchased for Nottingham City Museums and Galleries, through the Contemporary Art Society Special Collection Scheme, with Lottery founding from Arts Council England 2001

Wallings, 1998
Cibachrome transparency lightbox
88 × 105 × 16 cm | 34⅘ × 41⅓ × 6⅓ in
Private Collection. Courtesy of Talwar Gallery, New York, New Delhi

WHEREAS a BLACK SERVANT BOY, 1998
Cibachrome photograph on aluminium
122.4 × 173.4 cm | 48⅕ × 68 3/10 in
Private Collection. Courtesy of Talwar Gallery, New York, New Delhi

Cleaning the Garden, 1998 (continued)
WHEREAS a BLACK SERVANT BOY, 1998
Eighteenth-century newspaper text etched on mirror
61.2 × 51 cm | 24.1 × 20.1 in
Private Collection. Courtesy of Talwar Gallery, New York, New Delhi

Untitled (A Sketch), 1999*
Three dresses made out of maps of the United Kingdom, East Africa and India
Framed: 93.5 × 182 cm | 36⅘ × 71⅗ in
Collection of the artist

Out of Blue, 2002
Single screen installation
Super 16 mm colour film, DVD transfer
24 min 25 sec
Collection of the artist

Love, 1998–2007
Grenade, 1998–2003
Transparency lightbox
130 × 170 × 12.5 cm | 51⅕ × 67 × 5 in
Collection of the artist

Howling Like Dogs, I Swallowed Solid Air, 1998–2003
Transparency lightbox
130 × 170 × 12.5 cm | 51⅕ × 67 × 5 in
Government Art Collection

Memories Were Trapped Inside the Asphalt, 1998–2003
Transparency lightbox
130 × 170 × 12.5 cm | 51⅕ × 67 × 5 in
Collection of the artist

Bapa Closed His Heart, It Was Over, 2001–06*
Ilfochrome Ciba classic print
127 × 160 cm | 50 × 63 in (framed)
Collection Kadist Art Foundation

Bullet Riddled, 2001–06*
Ilfochrome Ciba classic print
127 × 160 cm | 50 × 63 in (framed)
Collection of the artist

Love, 1998–2007 (continued)

Forgotten Us, 2001–06*
Ilfochrome Ciba classic print
127 × 160 cm | 50 × 63 in (framed)
Adam Prideaux

Frightened Goats, 2001–06*
Ilfochrome Ciba classic print
127 × 160 cm | 50 × 63 in (framed)
Courtesy Haunch of Venison, London

Indispensable Monument, 2001–06
Ilfochrome Ciba classic print
127 × 160 cm | 50 × 63 in (framed)
Collection of the artist

No Border Crossing, 2001–06
Ilfochrome Ciba classic print
127 × 160 cm | 50 × 63 in (framed)
Maysoune Ghobash

This Unhinged Her, 1998–2006
Ilfochrome Ciba classic print
127 × 160 cm | 50 × 63 in (framed)
Collection of Mrs Shamina Talyarkhan

Your Sadness is Drunk, 2001–06
Ilfochrome Ciba classic print
127 × 160 cm | 50 × 63 in (framed)
Courtesy Paul van Esch & Partners, Art Advisory

Rado Watch, Such Western Precision, 2001–06
Ilfochrome Ciba classic print
127 × 160 cm | 50 × 63 in (framed)
Courtesy Buzzy Moitre, Collector

Echo, 2007*
Ilfochrome Ciba classic print
127 × 160 cm | 50 × 63 in (framed)
Courtesy Haunch of Venison, London

Illegal Sleep, 2007
Ilfochrome Ciba classic print
127 × 160 cm | 50 × 63 in (framed)
De Primi Fine Art SA, Lugano

Breathless Love, 2007
Ilfochrome Ciba classic print
127 × 160 cm | 50 × 63 in
Courtesy Haunch of Venison, London

Shadows and Disturbances, 2007
Ilfochrome Ciba classic print
127 × 160 cm | 50 × 63 in
Courtesy Haunch of Venison, London

Waiting, 2007 **
Single screen installation
35 mm colour film, HD transfer with Dolby 5.1 surround sound
7 min 45 sec
Collection of the artist

Selected preparatory storyboards, 2008, for *Yellow Patch*, 2011
Dimensions variable
4 × 6 in photographic prints joined together with tape
Collection of the artist

Yellow Patch, 2011
Single screen installation
35 mm colour film, HD transfer with Dolby 5.1 surround sound
29 min 43 sec
Collection of the artist
(Note: all *Yellow Patch* images in present volume are screen grabs)

Red & Wet, 2000–2011

Encoding, 2000–2011
Fibre based print
77 × 94 cm | 33 3/10 × 37 in
Collection of the artist

Tropical, 2000–2011
Colour Eudura print
101.6 × 102.1 cm | 40 × 40 1/5 in
Collection of the artist

Enclosed, 2000–2011
Colour Eudura print
101.6 × 91.6 cm | 40 × 30 in
Collection of the artist

Fever, 2000–2011
Colour Eudura print
101.6 × 82.5 cm | 40 × 32 1/2 in
Collection of the artist

Seascapes, 1998–2011*

Jangbar, 1998–2011
Fibre based print
77 × 94 cm | 30 3/10 × 37 in
Collection of the artist

Revolution, 1998–2011
Fibre based print
77 × 94 cm | 30 3/10 × 37 in
Collection of the artist

Biography

b. 1963, Mbarara, Uganda

Education

1987–89
Slade School of Fine Art, University College, London

1983–86
Goldsmiths College, University of London, London

Selected Solo Exhibitions

2012
Zarina Bhimji, Whitechapel Gallery, London, UK and Kunstmuseum Bern, Switzerland
Zarina Bhimji: Yellow Patch, The New Art Gallery Walsall, UK

2010
Who Knows Tomorrow, Hamburger Bahnhof, Berlin, Germany

2009
Zarina Bhimji: Out of Blue, Art Institute of Chicago, Chicago, IL, US

2007
Zarina Bhimji, Haunch of Venison, Zürich, Switzerland
Galerie Lumen Travo, Amsterdam, The Netherlands

2006
Zarina Bhimji, Haunch of Venison, London, UK

2004
Institute of International Visual Arts, London, UK

2003
Matrix, Wadsworth Athenium Museum of Art, Hartford, CT, US
Art Now, Tate Britain, London, UK

2001
Talwar Gallery, New York, US

1998
Cleaning the Garden, Harewood House, Terrace Gallery, Leeds, UK

1995
Kettle's Yard, University of Cambridge, Cambridge, UK

1992
I will always be here, Ikon Gallery, Birmingham and tour

Selected Group Exhibitions

2011
He disappeared into complete silence, De Hallen Museum, Haarlem, The Netherlands
ARS1: Africa in Kouvola, Kouvola, Finland
Götebourg International Biennal, Götebourg, Sweden

2010
29th Bienal de São Paulo, Pavilhã o Ciccillo Matarazzo, São Paulo, Brazil

2009
Capturing Time, Kadist Art Foundation, Paris

2008
Third Guangzhou Triennial, Guangdong Museum of Art and Times Museum, Guangzhou, China

2007
Turner Prize 2007, Tate Liverpool, Liverpool, UK

2006
How to Improve the World: 60 Years of British Art, Hayward Gallery, London, UK
Zones of Contact, Biennale of Sydney, Sydney, Australia
Snap Judgments: New Positions in Contemporary African Photography, ICP, New York, US

2005
50 Years of Documenta 1955–2005, Kassel, Germany
British Art Show 6, Baltic Centre for Contemporary Art, Gateshead & UK tour
Experiments with Truth, The Fabric Workshop and Museum, Philadelphia, US

2004
strangerthanfiction, Leeds City Art Gallery, UK
In Our Time, Works from the Moderna Museet Collection, Moderna Museet, Stockholm, Sweden

2003
Istanbul Biennale, Istanbul, Turkey
Fault Lines, Venice Biennale, Venice, Italy

2002
Documenta 11, Kassel, Germany

2001
The Short Century, Museum Villa Stuck Munich and tour to Berlin, Chicago and New York
East 2001, Norwich Gallery, UK

1997
No place (like home), Walker Arts Center, Minneapolis, US
Public Relations, Stadthaus Ulm, Germany
Life's Little Necessities, Johannesburg Biennale
The Quick and the Dead: Artists and Anatomy, Hayward Gallery, London, UK and tour

1996
In/Sight, Guggenheim Museum, New York, US

1994
Iniva inaguaration exhibition, Iniva, London, UK

1993
Antwerp '93, MuHKA Museum, Antwerp, Belgium

1990
Shocks to the System '90s Political Art, Arts Council Collection
Intimate Distance, The Photographers' Gallery, London, UK and tour

1989
Whitechapel Open, Whitechapel Art Gallery, London
Towards a Bigger Picture, Victoria & Albert Museum, London, UK and tour

1988
The Essential Black Art, Chisenhale Gallery, London, UK and tour

1987
Dislocation, Kettle's Yard, University of Cambridge, Cambridge, UK

1986
From Two Worlds, Whitechapel Art Gallery, London, UK and tour

Selected Collections

Kadist Art Foundation, Paris, France
Art Institute of Chicago, Chicago, IL, US
Tate, London, UK
Government Art Collection, UK
Moderna Museet, Stockholm, Sweden
Wadsworth Atheneum Museum of Art, Hartford, CT, US
Victoria & Albert Museum, London
Arts Council Collection, London

Bibliography

Solo Exhibition Catalogues

Joanna Marsh, *Zarina Bhimji: matrix 150,* Wadsworth Atheneum Museum of Art, Hartford, CT, 2003.

Katharine Stout, *Art Now: Zarina Bhimji,* Tate Britain, London, 2003.

Zarina Bhimji: With an introduction by Marina Warner, Kettle's Yard, University of Cambridge, Cambridge, 1995.

Zarina Bhimji: I will always be here, Ikon Gallery, Birmingham, 1991.

Selected Group Exhibition Catalogues

Agnaldo Farias, Moacir dos Anjos, Adrian Piper, *et al.*, *29th Bienal de São Paulo catalogue: there is always a cup of sea to sail in,* Fundacão Bienal de São Paulo, São Paulo, 2010.

Udo Kittelmann, Chika Okeke-Agulu and Britta Schmitz (eds), *Who knows tomorrow,* Walther König, Köln, 2010.

Johnson TZ Chang, Shiming Gao and Sarat Maharaj (eds) *Farewell to Post-colonialism: 3rd Guangzhou Triennial*, Guangdong Museum of Art, Guangzhou, 2008.

How to Improve the World, Hayward Gallery, London, 2006.

Zones of Contact, Biennale of Sydney, Sydney, 2006.

Okwui Enwezor, *Snap Judgments: New Positions in Contemporary African Photography,* Steidl and ICP, New York, 2006.

Eija-Liisa Ahtila, Joseph Beuys and Christian Boltanski, *50 Years of Documenta: 1955–2005*, Steidl and Documenta, Kassel, 2005.

Emma Mahony, Alex Farquharson and Andrea Schlieker, *British Art Show 6,* Hayward Publishing, London, 2005.

Michael L. Sand and Anne McNeill (eds), *Continental Drift: Europe Approaching the Millennium; 10 Photographic Commissions*, Prestel, Munich, 1998.

Okwui Enwezor *et. al.*, *In/sight: African Photographers, 1940 to the present*, Guggenheim Museum Publications, New York, 1998.

Douglas Fogle (ed), *No Place (Like Home)*, Walker Art Center, Minneapolis, MN, 1997.

Neal Ascherson, *Shocks to the System (Social and political issues in recent British art from the Arts Council Collection),* South Bank Centre, London, 1991.

Dislocations: Simone Alexander, Zarina Bhimji, Mona Hatoum, Ruth Lakofski, Derek Mawudoku, Peter Robinson and Veronica Ryan, Kettle's Yard Gallery, Cambridge, 1987.

Anthologies

New Art on View, Contemporary Art Society and Scala, London, 2006.

Gilane Tawadros and Sarah Campbell (eds), *Fault Lines: Contemporary African Art and Shifting Landscapes,* Iniva, London, 2003.

The Whitechapel Art Gallery Centenary Review: Artist Page, Whitechapel, London, 2001.

Surface: Contemporary Photographic Practice, Booth-Clibborn Editions; Corte Madera, CA: Distributed in USA by Gingko Press, c.1996.

Map, Iniva, London, 1996.

The 20th Century Art Book, Phaidon, London, 1996.

Illuminations Television – CDROM incorporating work from the Rencontres au Noir Project, 1995

Interviews, articles and reviews

Marie Woolf, 'Picture, picture, on the wall, is the art minister on the ball?', *Independent on Sunday*, 2007.

Charlotte Higgins, 'No miracles as show moves North, but beware of the bear', *The Guardian*, 19 October 2007.

Dani Admiss, 'Turner Prize relocates to the cultural capital of Europe. *Art Rabbit* takes a look at the works that won the artists nominations this year.', *Art Rabbit*, 2007.

Deborah Cherry, 'Words and Images in Zarina Bhimji's *She Loved to Breathe – Pure Silence* (1987)', *Simulacrum*, 2007.

'International Centre of Photography', *Frieze*, 2006.

Zarina Bhimji in Sydney, *Haunch of Venison Bulletin no. 8*, 2006.

Marcus Field, 'There's antlers in my pantry!', *ABC, The Independent on Sunday*, 2–8 October 2005.

TJ Demos, Review of 'Experiments with Truth (Fabric Workshop and Museum, Philadelphia)', *Artforum,* February 2005.

Maite Lores (interview), 'Out of Blue', *Contemporary Art*, Issue 49, 2003.

William Furlong, 'Documenta 11 2002', *Audio Arts Magazine*, vol.20, no.4.

Holland Cotter, 'Zarina Bhimji: *Cleaning the Garden*', *The New York Times*, 5 October 2001.

Yasmin Alibhai-Brown, 'Sacred beauty', *The Guardian,* 15 January 2000.

'Gifted', *The Guardian Weekend*, 2 October 1999.

Marina Warner, 'A chilling bedside manner', *The Independent,* 4 March 1996.

'Guest Choice', *The Daily Telegraph*, 18 February 1995.

Richard Cork, 'Galleries', *The Times*, 11 February 1995.

'Zarina Bhimji: Public Art Commission', Portfolio, *The Catalogue of Contemporary British Photography*, no.21, 1995.

Mark Haworth-Booth, 'Zarina Bhimji', *The British Journal of Photography,* 1994.

'Black Women Artists', *Spare Rib*, July 1992.

A. Willette, 'BBC Open University', 15 March 1991.

Paul Morley, 'Towards the bigger picture, Part 2: Photography', BBC2 Reportage, 1989.

Acknowledgements and Credits

My deepest appreciation to Professor Robert Sinden, Bergit Arends, Isabel de Vasconcellos, Professor Eleanor Riley, Thomas Egwang, Kevin Marsh, Dr. Antony Holder, NIMR, Artsadmin, Amrita Jhaveri, Shamina Talyarkhan, the team at Eidotech, Okwui Enwezor, Sarat Maharaj, Pinky Ghundale, Craig Pruess, Nina Kellgren, Edwin Metternich, Michael Riley, Rose from Forwood Farm, Candida Gertler, Nick Aikens, Arts Council England, Ann Demeester, Andrew Mclintock, Julie Lomax, Anne McNeill, Mark Sealy, Photo 98, Paul Brooks, Deepak Talwar, Joshua Bennett, Mark Haworth-Booth, MuKHA Antwerp, Iwona Blazwick, Achim Borchardt-Hume, Shamita Sharmacharja, all of the lenders and supporters of this exhibition catalogue, Paula Morison, Chris Aldgate, Kevin Storrar, Kathleen Bühler, Stephen Snoddy, Deborah Robinson, Karsten Schubert, Doro Globus, Louisa Green, TJ Demos, Ann Pitz, Wolfgang Himmelberg, Tom Hurly, Yukiko Otsuka, Esteban Mauchi, Michael Dyer, Herman Lelie, Stefania Bonelli, Stuart Ward, James Greenwall at Dubbs, Mark Darbyshire, Martine d'Anglejan-Chatillon, Laumont Photographics, Niru Ratnam, Richard Deal, The British Library and Sue MacDiarmid, for each of their support, commitment and interest. I would like to express my deepest gratitude to Manick Govinda, and also to Andrew Love for his love and continuous input.

Exhibition Acknowledgements

De Primi Fine Art SA, Lugano
Paul van Esch & Partners
Maysoune Ghobash
Government Art Collection
Haunch of Venison, London
Kadist Art Foundation, Paris
Buzzy Moitre
Nottingham City Museums and Galleries
Adam Prideaux
Talwar Gallery, New York, New Delhi
Shamina Talyarkhan
Victoria & Albert Museum
And those who wish to remain anonymous

With special thanks to Karima and Gaurav Burman, Amrita Jhaveri, Hashoo Foundation UK and The ACNE White Art T-Shirt Project

The Whitechapel Gallery thanks its supporters, whose generosity enables the Gallery to realise its pioneering programme.

Whitechapel Gallery Director's Circle

Cranford Collection, London; Dimitris Daskolopoulos; Maryam & Edward Eisler; Tania & Fares Fares; Noor Fares; Zaza & Philippe Jabre; Jack Kirkland; Yana & Stephen Peel; Catherine & Franck Petitgas; Maya & Ramzy Rasamny; Maria & Malek Sukkar and all those who wish to remain anonymous

Whitechapel Gallery Exhibition Patrons

Clarence Westbury Foundation; Haro & Bilge Cumbusyan; Carolyn Dailey; Sarah & Louis Elson; Peter & Maria Kellner; Maha Kutay; The Loveday Family; Mundus Imaginalis Collection; Pascale Revert & Peter Wheeler; Renee & Mark Rockefeller, Jonathan Tyler and those who wish to remain anonymous

Whitechapel Gallery Patrons

Charlotte & Alan Artus; Nasser Azam; John Ballington; Arianne Braillard & Francesco; Cincotta; Emanuel Bresin; Hugo Brown; Debbie Carslaw; Sadie Coles HQ; Swantje Conrad; Alastair Cookson & Vita Zaman; DunnettCraven Ltd; Donall Curtin; Milovan Farronato; Nicoletta Fiorucci; Eric & Louise Franck; Alan & Joanna Gemes; David & Susan Gilbert; Louise Hallett; Isabelle Hotimsky; Phillip Keir Cliff Ireton – Willett Kingston Smith; Amrita Jhaveri; Matt & Kate Jones; David Keltie; James & Clare Kirkman; Victor & Anne Lewis; Lisson Gallery; Joshua Mack; Keir McGuinness; Warren & Victoria Miro; Mary Moore; Dominic Morris & Sarah Kargan; Mummery + Schnelle; Angela Nikolakopoulou; Simon Oldfield Contemporary Art; Maureen Paley; Dominic Palfreyman; The Porter Foundation; Tim Rich; Alex Sainsbury & Elinor Jansz; Kaveh & Cora Sheibani; Karen Smith; Peter Soros; Bina & Philippe von Stauffenberg; Hugh & Catherine Stevenson; Tom Symes; Helen Thorpe (The Helen Randag Charitable Foundation); Christoph & Marion Trestler; Emily Tsingou & Henry Bond; Kevin Walters; Cathy Wills; Withers LLP – Daniel McClean; Richard Wolff; Anita & Poju Zabludowicz and all those who wish to remain anonymous

The American Friends of the Whitechapel Gallery

Bill & Alla Broeksmit; The Nightingale Code Foundation; Jolana & Petri Vainio; Marjorie G . Walker; Audrey Wallrock and Cecilia Wong

Whitechapel Gallery Associates

Bettina Bahlsen; Gerald Brawn; John & Tina Chandris; Salima Chebbah; Crane Kalman Gallery; Amanda Caroline Cronin & Mark Daeche; Jeff & Jennifer Eldredge; Philippa Found; Nicholas Fraser; Albert & Lyn Fuss; David Gill; Richard & Judith Greer; Karen Groos; David Killick Trust; Mark & Sophia Lewisohn; Laetitia Lina; George & Angie Loudon; Kate MacGarry; Carol Manheim, Biblion; Janet Martin; Penny Mason & Richard Sykes; Lord & Lady Myners; Goaldie Nagpal – Noble Savage Properties; John Newbigin; Chandrakant Patel; Camilla Paul; Jasmin Pelham; Catherine Pollard; Lauren Prakke; Paul & Charlotte Pritchard; Alice Rawsthorn; Jon Ridgway; Fozia Rizvi; David Ryder; Cherrill & Ian Scheer; Karsten Schubert; Stuart Shave Modern Art; Henrietta Shields; Liam & Jackie Strong; Jane de Swiet

The Whitechapel Gallery is grateful for the ongoing support of Members

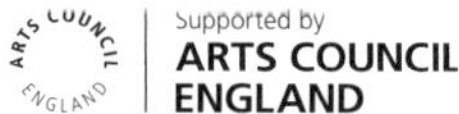

Whitechapel Gallery Staff

Director
Iwona Blazwick OBE

Managing Director
Stephen Crampton-Hayward

Verissa Akoto; Chris Aldgate; Sarah Auld; Marian Badekale; Sarah Barrett; Fatima Begum; Laurie Bird; Achim Borchardt-Hume; Poppy Bowers; Jussi Brightmore; Tara Brown; Emily Butler; Beth Chaplin; Emily Daw; Theo DeBoick; Emily Doran; Sue Evans; Tom Fleming; Michele Fletcher; Blanca Garay; Annette Graham; James Greene; Gary Haines; Clare Hawkins; Sophie Hayles; Rebecca Head; Daniel F. Herrmann; Quay Hoang; Charlotte Hogg; Annabel Johnson; Richard Johnson; James Knight; Patrick Lears; Selina Levinson; Daisy Mallabar; Zoe McLeod; Rachel Mapplebeck; Lucy May; Jo Melvin; Priyesh Mistry; Paula Morison; Rummana Naqvi; Maggie Nightingale; Victoria Norton; Kirsty Ogg; Rebecca Page; Dominic Peach; Faheza Peerboccus; Ilaria Peloso; Patricia Pisanelli; Chris Potts; Cookie Rameder; Megan Rumbelow; Robin Seddon; Shamita Sharmacharja; Nicola Sim; Maija Siren; Luke Smith; Marijke Steedman; Candy Stobbs; Jean Tormey; Sofia Victorino; Sarah Walsh; Monica Yam; Nayia Yiakoumaki; Andrea Ziemer

Kunstmuseum Bern Staff

Direktor/Director: Dr. Matthias Frehner
Kuratorin/Curator: Kathleen Bühler
Restauratoren/Restorers: Beatrice Ilg, Nathalie Bäschlin
Technische Leitung/Technical Coordinator:
René Wochner
Presse/Press: Ruth Gilgen, Brigit Bucher, Aya Christen
unterstützt von/supported by:
Stiftung GegenwART, Dr. h.c. Hansjörg Wyss
Credit Suisse, Partner des Kunstmuseums Bern

The New Art Gallery Walsall Staff

Director: Stephen Snoddy
Exhibitions: Deborah Robinson, Helen Jones, Hannah Anderson
Technical: Kevin Storrar, Mike Gallagher, Jeremy Hunt
Facilities: Rob Allen
Education: Zoe Renilson
Audience Development: Ioannis Ioannou
Collections: Jo Digger
Marketing: Chris Wilkinson
Operations: Mark Clancy, Linda Davies
Finance: Victoria Fletcher, Joanne Ball
Art Library and Archive: Cheryl Jones, Neil Lebeter
Gallery Assistants: Robert Conway, Leslie Curl, Faye Dudley, Michele Harris, Zaynul Hussain, Anita Jones, Julie Jones, David Jordan, Ramandeep Kaur, Paul McIntosh, Christine Sanders, Hayley Stephenson

Out of Blue credits

Commissioned by Documenta 11
Development: Ben Borthwick, Keith Griffiths, Seb Grant and Pinky Ghundale, Illuminations; Pre-Production: Sally Thomas, Maya Vision International

Invaluable support given by: Mr Igunduura and the staff at the Civil Aviation Authority of Uganda, The Republic of Uganda Prison Service, Mr Dhalia, The Hotel Equatorial Uganda and its staff, The staff at the Entebbe Military Airbase Uganda, The staff at the Ugandan Police Head-quarters Uganda, Fox Odoi-Oywelowo Uganda, Mr Mugyeni Uganda, Mr Tindifa Makerere University Uganda, Dr. Friedrich Meschede of DAAD Germany, Hajara Ndayidde at the Madrasa Resource Centre Uganda, Mumtaz Kassam Uganda, Talwar Gallery NY, Nick Fenton, Maggie Ellis and Gill Henderson of LFVDA London, Arts-admin London, Film Images London and Times Music India

Generously supported by: Documenta 11 Kassel Germany, LFVDA and London Arts London, Berliner Künstlerpro-gramm/DAAD Germany. Special thanks to: Sarat Maharaj, Okwui Enwezor, Michael Morris, Artangel London, The Paul Hamlyn Foundation, Manick Govinda, Deepak Talwar and Andrew Love

Sound: Adam Laschinger and Zarina Bhimji, Camera Assistant: Andrew Wiggins; Vocals: Begum Abida Parveen; Sound Design/Composer: Craig Pruess; Director of Photography: Adam Suschitzky; Editor: Sotira Kyriacou; Producer: Documenta 11 Kassel, Renée Padt and Zarina Bhimji; Director: Zarina Bhimji

Waiting credits

Producers: Michael Riley and Zarina Bhimji; Director of Photography: Nina Kellgren; 1st Assistant Camera: John Evans; Camera Grip: Kenneth Omutimba; Sound Recordists: Mark Kihara and Zarina Bhimji; Location Manager: Bernard Gathogo; Production Manager: Consolata Karani; Production Services Manager: Mario Zvan; Composer/Sound Designer: Craig Pruess; Editor: Sotira Kyruacou; Director: Zarina Bhimji. Thanks to: Margaret Matheson, Ross McKenzie, Gideon Koppel, Richard Fearon, Sara Hill and Blue Post Production, Paula Jalfon, Julian Ozzane, Karen Alexander, Angel Cobos, Benjamin Pelaez, Martin McGlone I-Lab UK

Neil Cuthbert, Mr. Robin Boyd-Moss, Robert Clarke, Zahid Dean, Mamdu Visram, Sidiq Ghalia, Hirji Shah, Aanal Chandaria, Stuart Ward, Herman & Stefania for long-standing friendship, Pilar Corrias for continuing dialogue and all at the Haunch of Venison in particular Jade, Harry and Graham, Tate Liverpool, Laurence Sillars, Sue MacDiarmid, and Andrew Love for his wonderful suggestions and understanding.

Yellow Patch credits

Development: Pinky Ghundale, Artangel, Doro Globus, Manick Govinda, Artsadmin and Andrew Love; invaluable support: Mrs Ashaben Sheth, Sanjay Udamale, Mr Gautam Dey, Aseem Bajaj, Shri V.R. Joglekar, Mr Rajan Adsul, Mr Dileep Chavan, Mr Suryakant Mane, Mr Digambar Koli, Shivjibhai Bhuda Fofindi, Rashida Anees, Nimish Patel Zaveri, Mrs Malika Amin, Mrs Krupa Amin, Marianne Callaghan, Maharao Shri Pragmalji of Kutch, all the staff at Pragmahal Palace, Mr Dilipsinhji, Mrs Rudrani Dilipsinhji, all the staff at Than Temple Kutch, Mr Nadir N. Damani, Mr Nikhil Vyas, Vijay Pandya, Vijay Ramchandani, Heritage Department of the Ahmedabad Municipal Corporation, Mrs Rashida Anees, Mr Promodbhai Jethai, Mrs Suhasben Shah, Mr Ramakantbhai Shroff, Jay Visva Deva, Rashmi Chandaria, Aanal Chandaria, Edward Simpson, Sadrubhai Hassam, Tejinder S Randhawa, Abudullah Rajwani, Rashmi Podder, Sandhini Poddar, Lekha Poddar, Amin Jaffer, Debashishji Nayak, Mahmad S Nathani, Amrita Jhaveri and Christopher Davidge, Shashi Sen, Meg Clark, Julius Sen, Ms Shernaz Italia, Herman Lelie, Stefania Bonelli, Rumi Verjee, Niraj Shah, Technicolor, Mr Anil Suri, Indian Ministry of External Affairs, Mr Salim Khoja, Mr Sadruddin Hudda, DCB Bank, Isaac Julien, Paula Jalfon, Finola Dwyer, Bennett McGhee, Eliza Mellor, Prasad Film Labs, Mrs Monika Kapil Mohta, Vijay Ramchandani, Indian High Commission London

Production Manager: Dinesh Shenoy assisted by Vivekanand Ahuja; Sound Recordists: Zarina Bhimji, assisted by K S Sivadas, Steve Felton; Camera: N. Ragiunathan, Babu, Santosh D. Zagade; Director of Photography: Nina Kellgren; Camera Assistant: Barnaby Crocker; Editor: Paul Carlin; Composing, Recording, Mixing: Craig Pruess; Sound Design: Craig Pruess, Zarina Bhimji; Colourist: Edwin Metternich; Post Producer: Andrew Mclintock; Online: Tim Greenwood; Vocals: Begum Abida Parveen, courtesy of Times Music India, Unyago by Bi Kidude, courtesy of RetroAfric; Executive Producer: Artsadmin; Producers: Manick Govinda, Ameenah Ayub Allen, Pinky Ghundale, Zarina Bhimji; Special thanks to Andrew Love; Director: Zarina Bhimji

Generously supported by Outset Contemporary Art Fund, Arts Council England, de Appel Arts Centre, The New Art Gallery Walsall, Framestore
Individual Donors: Shiraz Boghani, Salima Bhatia, Nazmin Kassam, Caroline Miller, Lupe Sanchez, Shashi Sen, Lew Hodges and Jaf Shah

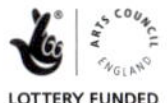

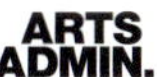

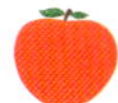
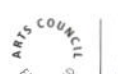

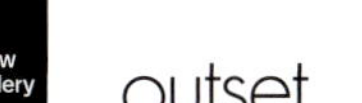

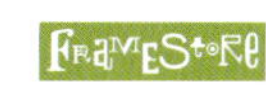

Published in 2012 by
Whitechapel Gallery
Kunstmuseum Bern
The New Art Gallery Walsall and
Ridinghouse

on the occasion of the exhibition

Zarina Bhimji
19 January–9 March 2012
Whitechapel Gallery
77–82 Whitechapel High Street
London E1 7QX
United Kingdom

1 June–2 September 2012
Kunstmuseum Bern
Hodlerstrasse 8–12
3000 Bern 7
Switzerland

Organised by Whitechapel Gallery, London
in collaboration with Kunstmuseum Bern

and

Zarina Bhimji: Yellow Patch
20 January–14 April 2012
The New Art Gallery Walsall
Gallery Square
Walsall
West Midlands WS2 8LG
United Kingdom

All rights reserved.
No part of this book may be reproduced or transmitted in any form or by any means, electronic or mechanical, including photocopying, recording or any other information storage or retrieval system, without prior permission in writing from the publisher.

British Library Cataloguing-in-Publication Data
A full catalogue record of this book is available from the British Library

ISBN 978 1 905464 51 7

Ridinghouse
5–8 Lower John Street
Golden Square
London W1F 9DR
United Kingdom
www.ridinghouse.co.uk

Distributed in the UK and Europe by
Cornerhouse
70 Oxford Street
Manchester M1 5NH
United Kingdom
www.cornerhouse.org

Distributed in the US by
RAM Publications
2525 Michigan Avenue Building A2
Santa Monica, CA, 90404
United States
www.rampub.com

For the book in this form © Ridinghouse and Whitechapel Gallery Ventures
All texts © the authors
Images © Zarina Bhimji and DACS, London, unless noted below:
© Mona Hatoum, A Western Front Video Production, Vancouver; Courtesy White Cube: p. 22
© Steve McQueen; courtesy Thomas Dane Gallery, London and Marian Goodman Gallery, New York, Paris: p. 23
Photo: Ralf Hoedt: p. 34
© Belvedere, Vienna; Österreichische Galerie im Belvedere, Vienna: p. 37
Photo: Matthew Hollow: p. 39
© Zarina Bhimji/Victoria & Albert Museum, London: pp. 54, 57

Edited by Achim Borchardt-Hume, Kathleen Bühler, Doro Globus, with additional support from Shamita Sharmacharja
Designed by Herman Lelie and Stefania Bonelli
Set in Perpetua and Frutiger Condensed
Repro by Dexter-Premedia, London
Printed by die Keure, Belgium

Whitechapel Gallery
Director: Iwona Blazwick OBE
Chief Curator: Achim Borchardt-Hume
Assistant Curator: Shamita Sharmacharja
Exhibitions Assistant: Paula Morison
Exhibitions Trainee: Priyesh Mistry
Installation: Chris Aldgate, Patrick Lears

Kunstmuseum Bern
Direktor/Director: Dr. Matthias Frehner
Kuratorin/Curator: Kathleen Bühler
Restauratoren/Restorers: Beatrice Ilg, Nathalie Bäschlin
Technische Leitung/technical co-ordinator: René Wochner
Presse/Press: Ruth Gilgen, Brigit Bucher, Aya Christen
Translation in German edition © Anne Pitz and Wolfgang Himmelberg

The New Art Gallery Walsall
Director: Stephen Snoddy
Exhibitions: Deborah Robinson, Helen Jones, Hannah Anderson
Technical: Kevin Storrar, Mike Gallagher, Jeremy Hunt

Ridinghouse
Director: Karsten Schubert
Publisher: Doro Globus
Publishing Assistant: Louisa Green
Copyeditor: Eileen Daly

This book was printed with funds from
The ACNE White Art T-Shirt Project

Whitechapel Gallery
Ridinghouse
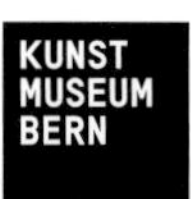

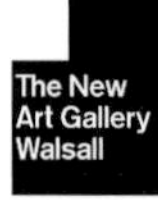

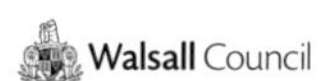